Commercial Competition
and National Security

Commercial Competition and National Security

*Comparing U.S. and German
Export Control Policies*

CLAUS HOFHANSEL

Westport, Connecticut
London

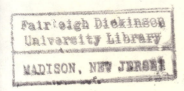
HF
1414.55
.U6
H64
1996

Library of Congress Cataloging-in-Publication Data

Hofhansel, Claus.
    Commercial competition and national security : comparing U.S. and
German export control policies / Claus Hofhansel.
        p.   cm.
    Includes bibliographical references and index.
    ISBN 0–275–95465–X (alk. paper)
        1. Export controls—United States.   2. Export controls—Germany.
I. Title.
    HF1414.55.U6H64   1996
    382′.64′0973—dc20   95–52996

British Library Cataloguing in Publication Data is available.

Library of Congress Catalog Card Number: 95–52996
ISBN: 0–275–95465–X

First published in 1996

Praeger Publishers, 88 Post Road West, Westport, CT 06881
An imprint of Greenwood Publishing Group, Inc.

Printed in the United States of America

The paper used in this book complies with the
Permanent Paper Standard issued by the National
Information Standards Organization (Z39.48–1984).

10 9 8 7 6 5 4 3 2 1

Contents

Preface

The everyday politics and administration of export controls is a fairly dry and technical affair. However, occasionally debates over export control policy arouse considerable passion, as when William Safire accused Germany of helping Libya acquire chemical weapons, or, as he put it, building "Auschwitz in the sand." During the Cold War the United States frequently clashed with its Western allies over the issue of East-West controls. In more blunt terms, as far as U.S. policy makers were concerned Western Europeans were living up to Lenin's famous statement about Western capitalists selling the rope with which they would be hanged later. On the other hand, in my conversations with German politicians, administrators, and representatives of the business community I frequently encountered considerable hostility and resentment over ill-considered or hypocritical U.S. policies. The Cold War has ended, and both U.S. and German policies have undergone considerable change. Yet, if one listens to some of the debates in the mid-1990s, there is considerable continuity in the arguments over arms and nuclear export policy.

As the title of this books implies, successful export control policies have to balance competing goals. This is one reason why export control policy sparked my interest. A study of export control policy can help to bridge the gap between international political economy and security studies. At the same time this book speaks to another division between subfields of political science, that between comparative politics and international relations (IR). Thus, this book is a comparative study of an IR issue.

The origins of this book go back farther than I care to admit. Essentially it began with a seminar paper for a political economy class taught by Jack Jacobsen. I am not sure whether he would agree with the direction my work has taken since then, but the book's discussion of institutions and the statist approach owes a considerable debt to Jack. Eventually I ended up writing a master's thesis on U.S. and German nuclear export policies and a dissertation on U.S. and German export control policies more generally. Jürg Steiner directed both of these projects, and he has been a continual source of support and encouragement throughout the lengthy process of getting this book published. I also greatly appreciated the comments of Gary Marks and Jack Donnelly.

The process of writing a book took much longer than it should have, and my father did not live long enough to see the completion of this project. In November 1993 I met Alex and since then she has heard and read more about export controls than she ever wanted.

Commercial Competition
and National Security

1

From Containment of Communism to Saddam Hussein: The International Politics of Export Controls

The purpose of this book is twofold. First, this book seeks to explain differences between U.S. and German export control policies. Second, it analyzes some of the dramatic changes in the international environment during the past few years in terms of their implications for U.S. and German export controls. The collapse of the Soviet Union, the dissolution of the Warsaw Pact, and the emergence of new security threats, such as ballistic missile and chemical weapons proliferation in the Third World, present new challenges for established policies. However, external shocks do not automatically result in changes in foreign economic policy. The U.S. and German governments may respond differently to similar pressures for policy change. In broad terms, this book argues that the following sets of variables can account for policy variations across countries and in the rate and extent of change in policies and institutions over time. Germany and the United States, first of all, differ in regard to their position in the international system and in their choice of economic strategies. Furthermore, the extent of domestic political support for strict export control policies varies between the two countries and over time. Finally, the German institutional framework for formulating and implementing export control policy provides better access for industry and presents different constraints and opportunities for policy innovation than its U.S. counterpart. The growing literature on foreign policy change generally follows three lines of inquiry: change in interests, ideas and values, and institutions. This book contributes to this debate with a particular emphasis on the role of institutions and norms.

An analysis of export control policy is not only significant in its own right but is also particularly well-suited to shed light on the broader foreign policy challenges that the United States and Germany face today. Export controls represent an attempt to restrict technology transfer. Typically, they have been imposed for national security reasons. On the other hand, exports secure jobs in the exporting economy, and technology transfer is important for assisting developing countries in protecting the natural environment. Furthermore, the export of telecommunications technology may play a useful role in transitions to democracy. Both Germany and the United States are looking for policies that promote military security, economic prosperity, a healthy natural environment, and the enlargement of democracy. An analysis of export control policy shows trade-offs among these goals but may also point out ways to minimize such trade-offs.

EXPORT CONTROLS IN A CHANGING INTERNATIONAL ENVIRONMENT

Export controls have served a variety of purposes. For example, in the early 1990s the United States restricted exports of crime control and detection equipment due to human rights concerns and placed very strict controls on trade with countries supporting terrorism, while crude petroleum and unprocessed western red cedar were subject to controls in order to ensure adequate domestic supply of these commodities.[1] This study will not concern itself with the full range of U.S. and German export controls but focus on controls directed against the former Soviet Union, Eastern Europe, and China, controls on the export of conventional weapons, and so-called proliferation controls, that is, restrictions on the spread of chemical and nuclear weapons and ballistic missile technology.[2] Both countries maintain national controls on arms and nuclear exports and they restrict high-technology trade with Soviet successor states, to varying degrees. Beyond that, however, the United States and Germany also participate in multilateral control efforts and export control regimes.

In the late 1940s the United States imposed a strategic embargo on trade with the Soviet Union. To ensure that its Western allies did not undermine U.S. trade policy toward the Soviet Union, the United States gained the cooperation of its Western European allies for multilateral export controls. CoCom, the Coordinating Committee for Multilateral Export Controls as it is now called, was created in 1949.[3] At the time of its dissolution in 1994 its members included all North Atlantic Treaty Organization (NATO) countries (with the exception of Iceland), Japan, and Australia. Physically, its headquarters were located in the annex to the U.S. embassy in Paris, which also underscores the dominant role of the United States in creating and maintaining the organization. CoCom compiled three lists of goods the export of which was restricted to proscribed countries, including the Soviet Union, Eastern Europe, and China. Two of these lists covered munitions and atomic energy, whereas the third and most important and controversial one was called the Industrial List (IL), which at the end of the Cold War was replaced with a much shorter "core list." Periodically, delegations from CoCom member countries met to review these lists to add or delete items. It was the responsibility of the individual member countries to incorporate these international CoCom lists into their national export control regulations. The extent to which national lists corresponded to current CoCom lists varied, however, and the United States, for example, typically controlled a wider range of commodities and technology than could be found on CoCom lists.

In its historical origins, CoCom was a product of the Cold War and the division of Europe into East and West. On November 9, 1989, the Berlin Wall did not "fall," but the opening of the Wall symbolized the end of the Cold War in Europe, and this called into question the legitimacy of institutions, such as CoCom, that had been built on Cold War assumptions. Since then, a number of authors put forward proposals for reforming CoCom. Among others, Rudolf suggested an expansion of CoCom functions to include controls on the spread of ballistic missile technology or restrictions on the international arms trade more generally.[4] A study by a National Academy of Sciences panel argued in favor of "shifting the focus of CoCom from an embargo on the export of listed items to proscribed countries to approval of items on a sharply reduced CoCom Industrial List, contingent on acceptable, verifiable end-use conditions approved by CoCom."[5] After the euphoria over the dramatic events of 1989 had died down, European politicians began voicing the fear that after military and political division, economic and social walls threatened the unity of the European continent divided between an impoverished East and the rich West. Rather than restricting technology transfer to Eastern Europe, the West should provide countries such as Poland and Hungary with the necessary high technology to build an up-to-date infrastructure. As Bertsch and Elliott-Gower pointed out, though, "[e]ven if COCOM fails to adapt to the post–cold war environment, it could simply drift off to the backwaters of international political affairs."[6] In 1992 the member countries recognized the new realities and at a high-level meeting agreed to create an informal forum to facilitate cooperation on export control issues between CoCom and CoCom's former targets, Russia and other former Soviet republics.[7] Also in 1992 Hungary was taken off the list of proscribed countries. At the end of 1993 CoCom members agreed to phase out CoCom but also to work toward the creation of a successor agreement on conventional weapons and dual-use technology. By early 1994, however, it had become apparent that the necessary negotiations would be difficult and unlikely to result in more than a partial success.[8] At the end of 1995 the most important political obstacles standing in the way of the CoCom successor organization were removed. Representatives of twenty-eight nations agreed on the basic principles of a new export control regime covering both dual-use goods and conventional weapons at a conference at the Dutch city of Wassenaar in December 1995. The group will have a larger membership than CoCom, including some former target states of CoCom, such as Hungary, Poland, the Czech Republic, and most importantly Russia. It is also clear, however, that the licensing/consultation procedures of the new regime will be looser than those of CoCom.[9]

As the security threat posed by the Soviet military power diminished, attention shifted to so-called "new threats," which refer primarily to the spread of advanced conventional arms technology and weapons of mass destruction among developing nations, such as Iraq.[10] At the level of international agreements and treaties, the most significant and relatively successful effort to counter this kind of threat has been the nuclear nonproliferation regime. A full discussion of this regime is beyond the scope of this book, rather we will focus on actions taken by nuclear suppliers to curb the spread of nuclear weapons technology and material through the use of export controls. In 1972 representatives from a number of nuclear supplier nations working together in the International Atomic Energy Agency's (IAEA) Zangger Committee agreed on a list of exports ("trigger list") for which the supplier states would require safeguards with the IAEA.[11] However, the Zangger Committee was only partially successful since the IAEA's Board of Governors did not approve the list as agency policy. Rather, in 1974 individual supplier countries notified the agency that they would require safeguards for items on the trigger list, but France, Belgium, Italy, and Switzerland did not participate.[12] A few years later, at the initiative of the Ford administration, a small group of seven nuclear supplier nations (Canada, France, West Germany, Japan, the United Kingdom, the United States, and the U.S.S.R.) began secret negotiations on minimum standards for nuclear trade.[13] The end result of these negotiations was a set of guidelines, known as the Nuclear Suppliers' Guidelines, which fifteen countries agreed to and which were published in 1978.[14] These guidelines specified when suppliers should require IAEA safeguards and end-use assurances and they called on suppliers to exercise restraint in exporting particularly sensitive technology. After 1978 the Nuclear Suppliers Group (NSG) did not meet until March 1991.[15] In April 1992 the NSG agreed to require export controls for a list of nuclear-related "dual-use" goods.[16] The Zangger Committee took up work again in the 1980s, and in 1984 and 1985 participating member governments sent letters to the Director

General that extended the trigger list for gas centrifuge enrichment and reprocessing technology.[17]

Nuclear nonproliferation as such is not a new issue, but what was new in the 1980s was that a number of developing countries began to acquire the technology for advanced delivery systems, or in more concrete terms, ballistic missiles. Israel, for example, is not only known to have nuclear weapons, but in 1988 it launched its first satellite. Besides the five declared nuclear weapons states, India is the only nation that openly tested a nuclear explosive device in 1974. Fifteen years later, "India startled the world in May of 1989 by launching a two-stage ballistic missile on a flight of 1,500 miles."[18] Iraq's nuclear and ballistic missile programs are not as advanced as either Israel's or India's, but in the war against Iran and in the most recent Persian Gulf war it launched a significant number of Scud missiles against its enemies, and it showed its ability to modify and extend the range of Soviet-supplied Scuds. To counter these trends, the United States initiated discussions with its major Western allies (Canada, France, Japan, West Germany, Italy, and the United Kingdom) to form a new export control agreement. The product of these negotiations was christened the Missile Technology Control Regime (MTCR) and was presented to the world on April 16, 1987. The MTCR has been credited with derailing a joint effort by Argentina , Iraq, and Egypt to develop the *Condor II* missile but it is generally regarded as too weak to stop ballistic missile proliferation.[19] In the past the MTCR only constituted an appendix to the nuclear nonproliferation regime because it only restricted the transfer of goods and technology for *nuclear-capable* missiles.[20] At their November 1991 meeting the member countries "agreed on the desirability of extending the scope of the regime to missiles capable of delivering all types of weapons of mass destruction."[21] In January 1993 the member countries revised the regime's export control guidelines by restricting "the transfer of missiles *intended* for the delivery of all weapons of mass destruction regardless of their range and payload."[22]

Although the MTCR was designed to prevent countries from acquiring nuclear-capable missiles, in the 1980s a number of developing countries made efforts to develop the poor man's bomb, chemical weapons. Iraq used such weapons extensively during the war with Iran, and one of the fears that fortunately did not materialize during the Persian Gulf war in 1991 was that Iraq conceivably could have launched missiles armed with chemical warheads against population centers in Israel. To stem such trends, initially nineteen countries led by Australia committed themselves to place export controls on an agreed list of precursor chemicals. Like the MTCR, the so-called Australia Group represents a fairly loose arrangement and lacks a permanent administrative infrastructure, such as the International Atomic Energy Agency for nuclear nonproliferation efforts or CoCom headquarters in Paris. However, the Australia Group can rely on a permanent secretariat in the Australian embassy in Paris. In January 1993 delegates of 130 countries signed the Chemical Weapons Convention (CWC) in Paris, which bans not only the use but also the production and possession of chemical weapons. Previously, the Australia Group had been regarded as only an interim arrangement pending the successful conclusion of the CWC negotiations. This became a controversial issue in the negotiations on the new convention with developing countries arguing in favor of an end to chemical export controls and the dissolution of the Australia Group.[23] Developing countries did not succeed with this demand since the Australia Group intends to continue its work.[24]

The end of the Cold War also generated renewed interest in restricting conventional arms transfers despite the failure of previous efforts, such as the Conventional Arms Transfer Talks of the 1970s. At this point, though, such attempts have had few practical results. The United Nations has instituted a register of conventional arms, and in December 1993 the United States called on other governments to ban the export of anti-personnel mines.[25] However, an arms transfer register is only a first step toward limiting such transfers, and at this point it is far from clear whether even the limited UN register will succeed.[26]

THE ROLE OF THE UNITED STATES AND GERMANY

The fate of export control regimes, such as the ones described above, depends on cooperation among key supplier states. Thus, it is important to understand what factors shape the policies of major exporters. If it is necessary to strengthen the nonproliferation regime and export controls on chemicals, there must be cooperation between Germany and the United States, the two states that for the past few years have alternated in the position of the world's largest exporting nation. Some degree of cooperation between Germany and the United States is not a sufficient but a necessary condition for the viability of any successor organization to CoCom.

As table 1 shows, in the 1980s Western Germany consistently was the largest Western exporter to the Soviet Union. German economic, cultural, and political ties to the Soviet Union/Russia and Eastern Europe have a long tradition, and this has important implications for future relations between Western and Eastern Europe. As Russia and Eastern European countries continue to undergo major changes, Germany will play a pivotal role in shaping the West's response to these changes both at the economic and political levels.

Table 1
Individual Country Shares of Total OECD Exports to the USSR

	1981 %	1982 %	1983 %	1984 %	1985 %	1986 %	1987 %	1988 %	1989 %	1990 %
West Germany	15	17	20	17	17	21	21	22	21	24
United States	11	11	9	15	12	6	7	11	15	11
Japan	15	17	13	11	13	15	13	13	11	9
France	8	7	10	9	9	7	8	8	6	6
United Kingdom	4	3	3	4	3	4	4	4	4	4
Italy	6	7	8	7	7	8	11	8	9	10
OECD Total	100	100	100	100	100	100	100	100	100	100

Source: OECD, *Monthly Statistics of Foreign Trade*, Series A.

Table 1 provides only an overall picture of the relative ranking of the Soviet Union's Western suppliers. In this book we are mainly interested in politically controversial areas of trade, and for East-West trade this primarily means technology exports. Technologically important exports often involve exports of machinery, such as highly sophisticated computer-controlled machine tools. Thus, table 2 presents data compiled by the Organization for Economic Co-operation and Development (OECD) on Western machinery and transport equipment exports (Standard International Trade Classification 7) to the Soviet Union. These figures confirm the prominent role that Germany played as a Western trading partner of the Soviet Union, whereas U.S. machinery exports to the Soviet Union were only of marginal significance. Notable also is the important role that Finland played in supplying machinery to the Soviet Union and the strong position of Japan.

Although the fortunes of East-West trade have fluctuated considerably over the past two decades, with healthy growth rates in the 1970s and contraction in the 1980s, civilian nuclear trade never lived up to its initial expectations. In 1976, for example, the U.S. Energy Research and Development Administration (ERDA) published a report on U.S. nuclear exports that included projections on the trade impact

Table 2
Individual Country Shares of Total OECD Machinery and Transport Equipment (SITC 7) Exports to the U.S.S.R.

	1982 %	1984 %	1986 %	1988 %	1990 %
West Germany	24	30	25	27	32
Japan	23	13	19	14	12
Finland	22	21	23	20	15
Italy	7	10	10	13	15
France	7	8	4	7	3
United States	4	2	2	2	3
OECD Total	100	100	100	100	100

Source: OECD, *Foreign Trade by Commodities*, Series C.

Table 3
Shares of Nuclear Reactor Export Market, 1965-1979

	1965-69 MW*	%	1970-74 MW	%	1975-79 MW	%
Canada	327	3.2	1229	3.8	1040	6.9
France	560	5.4	900	2.8	2744	18.2
West Germany	780	7.5	1612	5.0	2934	19.5
Sweden	-	-	1320	4.1	-	-
United States	8710	83.9	27060	84.3	8327	55.3
Total	10377	100.0	32121	100.0	15045	100.0

*megawatt.
Source: Westinghouse, *Nuclear Market Acceptance and Comparative Experience March 1, 1981* (Pittsburgh: Westinghouse), in Walker and Lönnroth, *Nuclear Power Struggles*, p. 34.

of the U.S. nuclear power exports until the year 2000. According to the ERDA forecast, nuclear exports should have accounted for between 1.8 and 2.0 percent of total U.S. exports in 1980 and between 2.4 and 2.7 percent in 1985. Actual market conditions turned out rather differently than anticipated, though. The ERDA estimates assumed a total demand among nonsupplier countries of 34,100 megawatt (MW) nuclear generating capacity for 1982–1984 alone.[27] In fact, no export orders materialized at all during those years. As shown in table 3, during the 1960s and early 1970s the United States clearly dominated the international market for nuclear reactors. In the mid to late 1970s, however, the U.S. nuclear industry confronted strong competition, particularly from West Germany and France. But even if the export market for nuclear reactors has virtually collapsed, some trade in nuclear materials and technology continues. For example, in 1987 West German authorities issued export licenses for nuclear goods worth 2.7 billion deutsche mark.[28]

One area in which German industry has not challenged the dominant position of the United States is the international arms trade. As illustrated in table 4, Germany has emerged as a significant arms exporter, but German figures pale in comparison to their U.S. counterparts. However, data on arms exports do not constitute the most reliable set of international trade statistics.[29] In fact, Michael Brzoska argued that data by the U.S. Arms Control and Disarmament Agency do not adequately cover German arms transfers.[30]

Even if available statistics understate German arms exports, they clearly do not approach the level of U.S. arms transfers. Thus, German cooperation may not be essential for efforts to restrict conventional arms transfers, but the situation looks rather different in the area of chemical weapons. As table 5 shows, Germany is the largest Western exporter of chemicals, followed by the United States. The chemical industry forms one of the pillars of German industry, and although Germany does not possess or produce chemical weapons itself, much of the technology needed for a chemical weapons program is dual-use technology with legitimate civilian and potential military applications.

Beyond their economic significance, Germany and the United States have been at the center of several heated international disputes over export control policy. After West Germany and Brazil had reached a wide ranging nuclear cooperation agreement in 1975, a *New York Times* editorial entitled "Nuclear Madness" denounced the deal as a "reckless move that could set off a nuclear arms race in Latin America, trigger the nuclear arming of a half-dozen nations elsewhere and endanger the security of the United States and the world as a whole."[31] In broader terms, this clash involved a conflict over appropriate standards in nuclear trade. Reflecting on transatlantic tensions during the Carter years, Pierre Lellouche argued that "[o]ne of the most striking paradoxes of the nonproliferation controversy . . . is that while the target of proliferation concerns was clearly centered on a series of un-

Table 4
Arms Exports by Major Suppliers

	World	USSR/ Russia	USA	France	UK	Italy	FRG	Dev. World
1981								
Value*	44610	17800	8600	4200	2800	1400	1600	3275
Market Share**	100.0	39.9	19.3	9.4	6.3	3.1	3.6	7.3
1982								
Value*	49270	18900	9300	3800	3300	1100	1000	6355
Market Share**	100.0	38.4	18.9	7.7	6.7	2.2	2.0	12.9
1983								
Value*	49290	19400	10700	4100	1900	1300	2100	4575
Market Share**	100.0	39.4	21.7	8.3	3.9	2.6	4.3	9.3
1984								
Value*	56450	19400	10800	5900	2100	1400	3000	7730
Market Share**	100.0	34.4	19.1	10.5	3.7	2.5	5.3	13.7
1985								
Value*	50360	17300	10800	7100	1600	1300	1400	4540
Market Share**	100.0	34.4	21.5	14.1	3.2	2.6	2.8	9.0
1986								
Value*	51280	21500	9400	4400	3700	825	1300	4320
Market Share**	100.0	41.9	18.3	8.6	7.2	1.6	2.5	8.4
1987								
Value*	60210	23100	14000	2900	5100	725	1500	6165
Market Share**	100.0	38.4	23.3	4.8	8.5	1.2	2.5	10.2
1988								
Value*	56550	22600	11100	2000	4800	490	1500	7795
Market Share**	100.0	40.0	19.6	3.5	8.5	0.9	2.7	13.8
1989								
Value*	51040	19800	10800	2300	4900	270	1300	5350
Market Share**	100.0	38.8	21.2	4.5	9.6	0.5	2.6	10.5
1991***								
Value*	30270	6600	10800	1600	4700	300	2400	2640
Market Share**	100.0	21.8	35.7	5.3	15.5	1.0	7.9	8.7
1993***								
Value*	21960	2600	10300	675	4300	400	1100	1755
Market Share**	100.0	11.8	46.9	3.1	19.3	1.8	5.0	8.0

*Values in million current U.S. dollars.
** Market shares computed by the author.
***1991 and 1993 data include unified German rather than West German data.

Source: ACDA, *World Military Expenditures and Arms Transfers 1993–1994* (Washington, D.C.: Government Printing Office, 1995), table II, and previous editions.

stable Third World countries, the main battle was fought between allied Western nations of Europe and America. . . . From a European standpoint, the nonproliferation debate of the 1970s constitutes the latest episode in a Euro-American rivalry that has lasted some forty years."[32]

Table 5
Worldwide Exports of Chemicals and Related Products (SITC 5) by Selected OECD Member Countries in 1991

	Value in million U.S. dollars	percentage (%)
Germany	51317.110	20
United States	42965.036	16
Japan	17396.203	7
France	28838.755	11
United Kingdom	24352.455	9
Netherlands	21541.527	8
OECD Total	262239.907	100

Source: OECD, *Foreign Trade by Commodities*, Series C.

In the early 1980s the Reagan administration fought a running battle with its Western European allies over East-West trade that reached a turning point with the controversy over the Siberian natural gas pipeline in 1982. U.S. officials and their political supporters argued that the Western Europeans, and the Germans in particular, were subsidizing the West's most formidable enemy, or, to use the well-known cliché, the Germans were selling the Soviets the rope with which they would be hanged later. Some German observers, however, saw a more sinister side to strict U.S. controls on high-technology exports and feared that the U.S. used export controls not only to maintain technological superiority over the Soviet Union but to gain a competitive edge against its Western allies and commercial rivals. The German East-West trade specialist Hanns-Dieter Jacobsen argued that

the intra-Western conflict over the correct East-West trade strategy long ago developed into a conflict among the industrialized nations over the best starting positions for their own future economic development and over the positions in the world markets within which advanced technology will play a central role.[33]

In light of recent developments one can find a great number of pieces of evidence for the thesis that the complex net of national security control mechanisms for the transfer of high technology abroad also serves the purposes of guaranteeing the technological preeminence of the USA, of improving the international competitiveness in the different high-technology sectors, and finally of ensuring the leading role of the USA in the international system in the future as well.[34]

Tighter control mechanisms have (for America) the desirable side effect of hampering the access of other Western countries to American high technology and/or making this access contingent on good behavior in security terms.[35]

More recently, the German government faced strong international criticism for the involvement of German companies in supplying Iraq and Libya with chemical weapons. After the news had broken that a West German company had been involved in building a chemical weapons plant in Libya, William Safire spoke of "Auschwitz in the sand."[36] Gary Milhollin wrote that "[i]t should come as no surprise that a West German company has been accused of helping Libya to build a plant to produce poison gas. If true, this is only the latest in a long line of irresponsible West German exports."[37]

Largely as a result of these recent scandals, German export control policy has been in a state of flux for the past few years. There was complete consensus in Germany that East-West controls needed to be relaxed, but at the same time Germany began to tighten controls directed against countries in the Middle East and other volatile regions. From December 1987 until February 1991 the foreign trade decree (*Ausssenwirtschaftsverordnung*) was amended fourteen times. Since 1989 the German *Bundestag* has passed two major revisions of the foreign trade act (*Aussenwirtschaftsgesetz*) and related legislation although both legislative packages encountered opposition in the second chamber, the *Bundesrat*. In February 1994 the federal government introduced yet another bill to amend the foreign trade act.[38] Beyond that, the German government decided first to reorganize the export licensing agency, the *Bundesamt für Wirtschaft*, and to more than triple the personnel level of its export control division. In a second step, the government created a new agency, the *Bundesausfuhramt*, with exclusive responsibility for export licensing. Potentially even more significant are the continued efforts by the European Community/European Union (EU) to fully integrate the economies of member countries. However, even after the 1992 deadline for establishing a single market, national export control laws have not been fully replaced by European Community law. Member country governments have been working on common policies in this area for a number of years. So far, considerable progress has been made in regard to export controls for dual-use goods, but it has been far more difficult to reach agreement on a common arms export policy. The key legal obstacle to a common EU arms export policy is article 223 of the treaty establishing the European Economic Community (EEC). It essentially says that the provisions of the treaty do not apply to trade in armaments. To the extent that the EU has agreed on common export control policies, this "harmonization" remains partial and leaves room for the continuation of a variety of separate national standards.

Furthermore, any common EU policy will in all likelihood be less strict than current German policies.³⁹ More specifically, in December 1994 the EU adopted a common export control list for dual-use goods, but even after European standards went into effect Germany continued to maintain tougher rules than other EU countries for arms-related exports to certain proscribed destinations.⁴⁰

The tightening of German export control laws also changed German interests in multilateral export control agreements, including a common European policy in this area. During the 1970s and 1980s West Germany frequently found itself on the defensive when it resisted calls for stricter controls, such as in the struggle over the adoption of full-scope safeguards for nuclear exports. Now, however, German controls are more restrictive than those of many of its European trading partners, and German industry has become concerned about losing export contracts to competitors with less onerous controls. Thus, since 1990/91 it has been the German government that has pushed for stricter controls in Europe.

In the United States, established export control practices have come under pressure for change as well, although the situation in the United States presents a more contradictory picture than the politics of export controls in Germany. On June 6, 1990, the House of Representatives passed a bill to reauthorize the Export Administration Act of 1979. The major thrust of the bill was to ease restrictions on technology exports to the Soviet Union and Eastern Europe, to limit bureaucratic infighting over export controls, and to strengthen the authority of the Department of Commerce at the expense of the Pentagon and the State Department.⁴¹ The House called its bill an "Export Facilitation Act." Hard-liners on U.S.-Soviet relations did not agree with its emphasis, however, and Frank Gaffney, Jr., of the Center for Security Policy called the bill the "Soviet Military Relief Act of 1990."⁴² In November 1990 President Bush pocket vetoed the bill because it contained a provision that would have forced the executive to impose sanctions against "companies and governments that contribute to the spread of chemical and biological weapons."⁴³ In October 1991 the House passed another export control bill, which the Bush administration at the time did not favor either because it would have liberalized telecommunications exports to the Soviet Union. On January 22, 1992, the Senate passed its version, but the conference committee did not finish work on a compromise bill until October 5, 1992. The following day, just before the House was about to adjourn, three Republican members of the House blocked final passage by threatening to tie the chamber up in a series of procedural votes. The three Republicans objected to provisions that would have enhanced the role of the Commerce Department and weakened the authority of the Pentagon in export licensing decisions.⁴⁴ Nevertheless, the United

States has moved to ease restrictions on East-West trade, but at the same time it put more emphasis on controls in other areas, and the war with Iraq played an important role in these contradictory developments. Under President Bush this reorientation of U.S. export control policy toward nonproliferation controls primarily took the form of a set of regulations known as the Enhanced Proliferation Control Initiative (EPCI).

On September 27, 1993, President Clinton announced the principles of his administration's nonproliferation and export control policies in a speech at the United Nations. In a fact sheet released by the White House that day the administration stated:

We will streamline the implementation of U.S. nonproliferation export controls. Our system must be more responsive and efficient, and not inhibit legitimate exports that play a key role in American economic strength while preventing exports that would make a material contribution to the proliferation of weapons of mass destruction and the missiles that deliver them.[45]

This statement expresses a concern for both nonproliferation efforts and economic competitiveness. In an ideal world all good things go together, but in the real world of scarcity trade-offs need to be made. Thus, the Clinton administration is being pushed in different directions, but on balance this administration has put a higher priority on opening markets for U.S. exporters than on denying dual-use technology to potential proliferators. Nevertheless, when the Clinton administration introduced its version of a bill to reauthorize the Export Administration Act (EAA) in February 1994, the bill was criticized by industry for not going far enough in the direction of decontrol, whereas nonproliferation hawks called the bill a "Christmas tree for exporters, with presents beyond their wildest dreams."[46] In Congress, the House Foreign Affairs Committee approved a bill emphasizing decontrol, whereas the Armed Services Committee favored a stricter bill. In July 1994 the chairmen of the two committees attempted to work out a compromise version but failed.[47] At the end of September the House Foreign Affairs Committee acknowledged failure by voting in favor of a one-year extension of the EAA without any major overhaul.[48]

EXPLAINING EXPORT CONTROL POLICY

State Interests and External Constraints

What can explain persistent differences between U.S. and German export control policies and recent changes in these policies? This book argues that these differences are rooted, first of all, in the different positions the two countries occupied in the international system. The German and U.S. positions in the international state system differed after World War II because of the discrepancy between the hegemonic alliance leader the United States and the defeated half-nation Germany, which regained only a modicum of sovereignty in 1955 and throughout the entire Cold War period depended on American protection for its security. Following this line of argument, we would also expect major policy changes to broadly reflect changes in the distribution of power.

To apply such reasoning to the policy areas at issue in this book, the Federal Republic of Germany forswore the acquisition of nuclear weapons in 1954 when it was still subject to occupation rule. When Adenauer made this commitment he clearly did not have much choice, but he regarded this obligation as conditional and subject to change if a different international environment warranted change. By the 1960s West Germany had begun to emerge as an independent actor on the international scene and it resisted American pressure to sign the Nuclear Non-Proliferation Treaty (NPT) until it, in concert with other nonnuclear powers, had extracted concessions in the treaty text from the United States and the Soviet Union.

In the 1970s the "economic giant but political dwarf" West Germany, to use Helmut Schmidt's terminology, challenged the U.S. position in international nuclear markets. From a technological and economic perspective, it is important to recognize that until the 1970s at least, nuclear technology possessed the aura of technological progress. As Walker and Lönnroth argue, Europeans perceived American leadership in nuclear technology in the 1960s as part of a more general technological threat and thus "the symbolic value of nuclear technology imbued the attempts to counter U.S. supremacy with nationalistic intensity."[49] In the 1970s European producers of power-generating equipment regarded nuclear technology and nuclear exports not only as important because of the direct benefits, which such exports produced, but also as part of a wider struggle not only with U.S. competitors but also Japanese companies, which had started to make considerable inroads into the world market for conventional power equipment.[50] Furthermore, when the different suppliers installed their production capacities, the West Germans included a higher margin of spare capacity for exports than their U.S. competitors. The extra capacity for nuclear exports reflected the degree to which manufacturers had depended on export sales in conventional markets, and this was higher in Germany than in the United States.[51] Furthermore, smaller nuclear suppliers, such as West Germany, hoped to achieve economies of scale through exports to be able to compete with American suppliers with their large domestic market.[52]

Politically, the United States and West Germany developed two conceptually different approaches to nuclear export policy. The United States sought to deny sensitive technology to proliferation-risk countries in the Third World. West Germany countered this approach with a policy of cooperation. A recurring theme in West German nuclear policy statements in the 1970s was that any attempts to strengthen the nonproliferation regime had to be based on the participation of as many countries as possible, including countries of the Third World. Attempts by a single country or a small group of nations, such as the United States or a nuclear exporter cartel, to unilaterally change the rules of the game would prove to be counterproductive. Any nonproliferation agreements had to be "multinational, non-discriminatory and universally binding."[53] West Germany denied that there was any inherent conflict between nuclear exports and nonproliferation. Instead, nuclear exports, even to countries that had not signed the NPT, could in the long run advance nonproliferation goals more than shortsighted technology denials because export contracts and nuclear cooperation between supplier and customer countries helped to integrate the recipients of nuclear technology into the existing international safeguards system to control the spread of nuclear weapons.

In 1990 the two Germanys reaffirmed their commitment to a nonnuclear status in the so-called "two-plus-four treaty," but one could argue that this was one last concession the two Germanys had to make to regain full sovereignty, which finally occurred in 1991 after the Soviet Union had ratified the treaty. Following a neorealist analysis, we would expect the newly sovereign Germany to begin to play its role as a great power and eventually this should lead to the German acquisition of nuclear weapons.

In the area of East-West trade, the United States as the leader of the Western alliance bore not only a disproportionate share of NATO's defense burden, but the United States played a leadership role in regulating East-West commerce as well. In practice this meant that U.S. national security export controls were stricter than those of its Western European allies. To use more abstract language, the United States acted as a benevolent hegemon and provided public goods (security), whereas West Germany was a free rider. However, we also see the impact of changes in the distribution of power. In 1962/63, during the first pipeline embargo, West Germany bowed to American pressure against the export of large diameter pipes to the Soviet Union. By 1982, though, the United States had experienced a relative decline, whereas Germany's stature had grown, and in this case the Federal Republic defied the Reagan administration's pipeline sanctions. In the 1960s the United States was able to compensate its Western European allies for trade opportunities forgone with the Soviet Union, but in 1982 American offers of increased American coal shipments to substitute for Soviet natural gas were not realistic.

In regard to arms exports, Albrecht argues that "[i]t . . . makes little sense to study the flow of arms out of the Federal Republic [of Germany] in the context of diplomatic aims."[54] According to him, this is so because "[i]n contrast to the global calculus of the superpowers, the European nations are regional powers with limited foreign policy objectives."[55] Parallel to the case of nuclear exports, this line of argument has an economic and technological base. European arms manufacturers with their small domestic markets needed exports more than the U.S. defense industry to achieve the economies of scale necessary to maintain an independent defense industry. Although this is an oversimplification, because it underestimates both the economic significance of arms exports for the United States and instances where Germany has used arms transfers as political instruments, on balance German arms transfer policy is more commercially oriented than that of the United States.

State Strategies and their Normative Basis

Rather than emphasizing differences in the distribution of power, an alternative explanation focuses on differences in state strategies. In contrast to the United States, (West) Germany after the war began pursuing a trading state strategy.[56] In the post–World War II period West German policy makers repeatedly made attempts to learn lessons from recent German history to prevent the Bonn republic from becoming another Weimar. The basic thrust of West German foreign economic policy can be seen in the title of a book by West Germany's famous economics minister of the 1950s, Ludwig Erhard: *Germany's Return to the World Market.* On the first page of the preface Erhard contrasts his world-market orientation, or trading state strategy to use Rosecrance's terminology, to nationalist strategies that restricted free trade and strove for autarky.[57] He clearly was referring to Nazi foreign trade policy.

To apply these broad arguments to export control policy, export controls must address a tension between potentially conflicting goals. On the one hand, increased exports contribute to the economic well-being of the exporting nation. On the other hand, sometimes controls are necessary to safeguard national security and to prevent Pakistan from acquiring the bomb and Libya from stockpiling chemical weapons, for example. As a trading state, Germany has resolved this trade-off differently than the United States, at times with scandalous consequences. As Ellen Frost and Angela Stent have pointed out in regard to East-West trade, "[t]he American concept of security is overwhelmingly military in nature, whereas that espoused by the Europeans is as economic as it is military."[58] With the end of the Cold War, however, this has changed as shown by the Clinton administration's emphasis on economic security. Thus, in 1994 a Commerce Department official justified a change in export control policy for satellite technology by arguing that

This is a new era. We believe national security and economic security are intertwined In order to have national security, you have to have vibrant and competitive industries that are allowed to do what they do best.[59]

More broadly, the Clinton administration has been more receptive than previous administrations to the concept of "common security" or, as it is also called, "cooperative security." A major study by the Brookings Institution argued that cooperative security goes beyond more traditional and narrow conceptions of national security that define national security simply in terms of military security. Cooperative security emphasizes reassurance rather than deterrence. According to its proponents, the use of military force should be contemplated only as a last resort and only if it is legitimated by a multilateral body, such as the UN Security Council.[60] The authors of the Brookings study included Secretary of Defense William Perry and the Assistant Secretary for Nuclear Security and Counterproliferation Ashton Carter. Although it is doubtful whether the Clinton administration is really fully committed to multilateralism, the adoption of the rhetoric and some of the substance of the concept of cooperative security implies a partial convergence of U.S. and German thinking on national security.[61]

Either neorealist arguments about power differentials or a focus on state strategies provide a useful first cut for explaining differences between U.S. and German export control policies, but they leave out important pieces of the puzzle. The choice of state strategies does not simply reflect systemic constraints or interests but is also influenced by the normative context within which decision makers operate and the values decision makers themselves hold and project.[62]

Thus, Germany's choice of a trading state strategy, the emphasis on multilateral institutions in German foreign policy, and restrictions on arms exports and the use of German armed forces in part represent a moral response to German militarism and the Nazi experience. Although Germany has benefitted materially from its choice of a trading state strategy, this choice also contained a normative component. In more specific terms, "the collapse of the Weimar Republic and the structure and practice of National Socialism . . . initiated a process of learning which resulted in the discovery or rediscovery of political and economic liberalism," emphasizing market forces rather than state intervention.[63] To apply this to foreign trade policy, during the parliamentary debate on the West German foreign trade act of 1961 deputy Margulies of the liberal Free Democratic party criticized the government bill for restricting the freedom of exporters too much, and economic freedom was what distinguished the West German political system from communism.[64] Nevertheless, the West German government curtailed the freedom of German exporters through the formulation of a new restrictive arms transfer policy at the end of the 1960s and early 1970s after an intense domestic debate. If German policy had reflected primarily external constraints, we would not have expected West Germany to restrict its arms transfers in the early 1970s when West Germany gained international stature and diplomatic leeway but in the 1950s or early 1960s when German foreign policy operated under much tighter constraints.

Besides the adoption of state strategies, we also need to address their evolution. Peter Katzenstein suggested in a study of German and Japanese internal security policies that changes in international structures, such as the end of the Cold War, do not necessarily lead to corresponding changes in policy or state strategies because decision makers may continue to follow norms that provide roadmaps in times of uncertainty.[65] On the other hand, norms and values are subject to change as well. Once norms that support particular strategies erode, this will create pressures for a shift in strategies. To answer the question of whether such an erosion process has taken place, we need to analyze the broader policy debates, including not only formal position papers but also the output of think tanks and the editorial pages of leading magazines and newspapers.

Nevertheless, some values are more resistant to change and erode more slowly than others. This, of course, raises the question of what factors have an impact on resistance to change. Here psychology tells us that beliefs that are central to a decision maker's belief system are less likely to change than those that are peripheral. Furthermore, belief systems that are internally consistent are less vulnerable to challenges than inconsistent ones.[66] Besides cognitive factors, some ideas have been more firmly institutionalized than others which again inhibits change.[67] Furthermore, even if established ideas have been discredited, this only creates a window of opportunity for a policy change or a shift in state strategies. Major policy shifts depend on the supply of new ideas, which can provide the intellectual and political underpinnings for change. If such ideas are not available or lack widespread appeal, far-reaching change will not occur.[68] New ideas may originate domestically, but they may also be transmitted through what Risse-Kappen calls "transnational networks." Such networks form when different national intellectual communities "sharing political values and policy concepts" regularly exchange their views on a common set of policy issues.[69] An example is the interactions and exchanges among the American arms control community, European peace researchers, European Social Democratic parties, and Soviet scientists and policy analysts in the 1980s.

The transnational diffusion or transmittal of new ideas requires carriers. We may expect those actors who are tied into transnational networks to introduce new ideas more readily than actors who are either on the periphery or outside of transnational networks. New ideas do not necessarily and automatically have an impact on policy, however. What matters in this regard is the institutional setting within which policy is made. If, and only if, the institutional setting provides access to policy entrepreneurs promoting new ideas, policies may change in response to these ideas.[70] Easy access is not enough, though, to achieve lasting and comprehensive policy change. As Risse-Kappen and others have pointed out, the fragmented American political system is quite open to new ideas, but this same fragmentation makes it very difficult to achieve broad policy change and to faithfully implement new initiatives.

In regard to Germany, it is quite conceivable for German armed forces to (reluctantly) participate in a wide range of military missions outside of the traditional NATO area in the foreseeable future. However, the German commitment to multilateralism is stronger than the still powerful aversion to the use of military force. Thus, the erosion of traditional West German norms has resulted in fewer restrictions on the use of force, but only within a multilateral context.[71] One way to explain the strong commitment of German policy makers to multilateralism is to show that this commitment stems from "a conception of belonging to and participating in an international Grotian community."[72] The use of force is compatible with such a view as long as the use of force is sanctioned by the international community. Traditional great power politics, on the other hand, would violate these norms, and this study argues that Germany is unlikely to seek traditional great power status.

Furthermore, even before the 1994 ruling of the German constitutional court many analysts considered the constitutional arguments against out-of-area operations as fairly weak.[73] On the other hand, the German constitution is quite explicit in its support of international law and supranational institutions. Article 24 of the Basic Law states in its first section that the federal government may transfer sovereign rights to supranational institutions, whereas the second section addresses the possibility of securing peace through a system of collective security, which may again involve a transfer of sovereign rights.   Article 25 specifies that the general principles of international law take precedence over regular German laws.

More specifically in regard to export control policy, German policy remained fairly stable throughout the 1970s and much of the 1980s. However, a closer look shows that in the 1980s the German foreign office began to develop the conceptual basis for a new German nonproliferation policy.[74] These efforts did not have a major impact on export controls until 1989 because the economics ministry dominated the decision process in that area, and the economics ministry clung to the old policies of the 1970s. It is no accident that the foreign office was more receptive to new developments in the international debates on nonproliferation issues than the more domestically oriented economics ministry.

For the United States the erosion and collapse of normative expectations from the Cold War period has led to a somewhat more commercially oriented export control policy. But this was not such a dramatic shift because the tension between a strong military security orientation and commercialism has been present in U.S. policy for a long time.   This also means that the pendulum may swing in the other direction again. On the other hand, the United States is less likely to embrace a multilateralism that gives international organizations, such as the United Nations, broad independent powers, despite the leading role the United States had played in the creation of various multilateral institutions after 1945 and the few steps in that direction by the Clinton administration.[75]   As Janne Nolan noted, "the attachment to unilateral action is a powerful political undercurrent."[76] Multilateralism is a defining issue for ideological divisions in American foreign policy.[77] Recent examples outside the area of export control policy include the aversion to having U.S. troops serve under foreign commanders and opposition to the new World Trade Organization because it allegedly undermines U.S. sovereignty.

Domestic Support for Export Controls

An alternative approach to explaining foreign economic policy starts from the premise that policies require political support. Following Gourevitch, such an analysis would emphasize societal actors (business and labor, for example) and their "preferences . . . as shaped by their situation in the international economy and the domestic economy."[78] The impact of societal actors on policy may be mediated by associations, such as political parties and interest groups, which have their own perceptions and preferences. For the purposes of this book, this means considering the social context of export control policies. Does the business community aggressively support a loosening of export controls? What is the position of labor? Which interest groups are active in this area? How well are they organized, and how do they compare in terms of resources they can mobilize?

A comparison of the domestic politics of U.S. and German export control policies shows that in the United States policy disputes primarily involve different executive branch agencies and Congress, which has attempted to restrict executive discretion on nuclear exports, arms sales, the imposition of foreign policy export controls and a host of other issues. A variety of interest groups have become actively involved in the policy-making process with the pro-Israel lobby seeking to block arms sales to Saudi Arabia and business interests pushing for an elimination of export controls on telecommunications equipment to Eastern Europe, to give only a couple of examples. In Germany export control policy rarely made the headlines until the late 1980s. The policy community essentially consisted of lower and mid-level officials in the economics ministry, industry as the primary client of these policies, and on occasion officials in the foreign office. When export control policy did become controversial, such as in the late 1980s, political parties articulated the major policy alternatives.

Neorealist analysts who argue that systemic pressures will eventually result in a reconsideration of Germany's nonnuclear status pay insufficient attention to the fact that there is very little domestic support for German nuclear weapons.[79] In the 1960s the German signature of the NPT was quite controversial, but now German nonproliferation policies enjoy broad support. Should a future German government decide to acquire nuclear weapons it would not only face negative repercussions abroad but it would also have to overcome considerable, if not insurmountable, domestic opposition. In the area of arms exports, German export restrictions are not uniformly tight, or loose as many critics of German policy would argue, but vary by type of weapon. There are fewer restrictions on the export of naval vessels than on tanks, for example, and an explanation of this difference has to include domestic factors.

The United States has played a leading role in the creation of all existing export control regimes. Yet, at other times the United States for domestic reasons neglected its leadership responsibilities and in effect undermined the effectiveness of the very regimes it had helped to establish. Examples include U.S. CoCom policies in the 1970s and Nixon administration policies on enrichment services that diminished U.S. credibility as a reliable nuclear supplier.

Institutions and the State

Finally, as touched on already, institutions make a difference as well.[80] Institutional or state-centric analyses generally follow one of two lines of argument. First, some authors conceive of the state as an actor seeking to achieve distinct goals and objectives that cannot be reduced to mere expressions of societal interests.[81] States differ in their capacity to implement their goals or, as Nordlinger puts it, their ability to translate their "own preferences into authoritative actions."[82] This capacity or strength of a state depends on its structure.

It is possible to reduce the state structure argument to two core elements: state centralization and policy networks.[83] The concept of state centralization itself consists of several dimensions: "The executive dominates the legislature; within the executive, interagency relations are coordinated, and their differences minimized. Second, overlapping authority among government agencies may be minimized. Agencies enjoy unchallenged jurisdiction over distinct policy arenas."[84] The rationale underlying this argument is that the executive constitutes the center of the state and pursues broad long-term objectives, or what Krasner calls the national interest.[85]

Legislatures, on the other hand, are more responsive to parochial constituencies and are more accessible to so-called "special interests." Furthermore, the state is an actor and not just a loose collection of bureaucracies that requires a certain degree of cohesiveness. Thus, in a centralized state lines of authority are clearly drawn, and interagency conflict over turf is minimized. Applied to export control policy, a centralized state will be better equipped to formulate a coherent policy and to implement controls than a fragmented state.

The notion of policy networks refers to structures that provide links between state and societal actors. According to Peter Katzenstein who developed this concept, in the United States "[g]overnment-business relations tend to be distant and adversarial rather than integrated and cooperative."[86] This leads to a situation where "[t]he autonomous ability of the American state to formulate many of its objectives is thus small, its ability to implement policy, brittle."[87] Germany, on the other hand, exhibits a large variety of "parapublic" institutions linking state and society, and thus blurring the distinction between the two.[88] The consequences of such a pattern for the strength of the German state are ambiguous, however:

It is implausible to view the West German state as an actor that imposes its will on society. . . . But because it has drawn so many "private" actors into its political orbit, it is at the same time strong. . . . History has endowed West Germany with a generous dose of state tradition; and international politics has rendered traditional pillars of state power, such as the military, largely irrelevant. As a result, the power of the West German state has not been broken but transformed.[89]

If this characterization of differences between U.S. and German policy networks holds up in the area of export controls, we would expect to find relatively smooth cooperation between industry and the state in Germany. We would also expect, however, that the German state lacks the ability simply to impose its policies against the opposition of industry. In the United States, on the other hand, conflict between industry and export control authorities should be more frequent.

One could argue, of course, that it was precisely such a cozy relationship between exporters and German export control agencies that made the Rabta and Iraq scandals possible. Yet, a German diplomat with responsibility for nonproliferation issues emphasized in a recent publication that the tightening of German export control laws after 1989 took place in agreement with German industry, which had become concerned about its image as "merchants of death."[90] In the United States, on the other hand, throughout the 1980s one of the persistent complaints by business representatives was their lack of access. For example, in contrast to the situation in Germany, U.S. exporters could not sue if the Commerce Department had denied export license requests. Besides differences in the "policy networks" linking state and society, the U.S. and German states differ in their internal structures. This book does not support some of the early claims of the statist literature on the impact of state centralization on state autonomy or state capacity, but the extreme fragmentation of the American state with its multiple veto points does make it difficult to achieve broad and comprehensive policy change.[91]

Instead of conceiving of the state as an actor, a second approach conceptualizes "the state primarily as an organizational structure, or set of laws and institutional arrangements shaped by previous events."[92] One of the most important claims put forward by proponents of this approach concerns its conceptualization of institutional change. More specifically, authors such as Stephen Skowronek criticize functionalist arguments and point to the "inadequacy of approaching state building as the natural and adaptive reaction of governments to changing conditions."[93] Institutional change does not occur gradually and in response to changing environmental conditions, rather change tends to take place infrequently but rapidly, often in connection with major crises, such as international wars.[94] Methodologically, this leads to an emphasis on historically grounded research.[95] Concerning export control policy, this means that we should pay particular attention to the formation of the institutional framework for export controls in the Cold War period.[96] This proved to be a watershed not only in American foreign policy, but the immediate postwar period led to an even more dramatic restructuring of German political and economic institutions. Although many of the conditions under which United States export control institutions were first established no longer exist, institutions, once established, tend to endure and constrain future policy choices.[97]

The Cold War ended with the revolutionary events in Eastern Europe in 1989 and the subsequent collapse of the Warsaw Pact, but Congress and the executive branch have been unable to agree on a successor to the Export Administration Act of 1979, despite several attempts to bring this centerpiece of U.S. export control legislation in line with the realities of post–Cold War politics. In November 1993 the House of Representatives finally passed a bill deleting references to the Soviet Union and Communism scattered throughout numerous statutes. However, this bill did not touch the Jackson-Vanik amendment.[98] In Germany, on the other hand, once a series of scandals had forced export controls to the top of the political agenda, the German parliamentary system presented fewer obstacles to a comprehensive reform of export control policy although the German version of "divided government" due to German federalism and coalition politics caused some delay.[99]

Links Between Different Levels of Analysis

To some extent, arguments about distributions of power, state strategies, domestic politics, and institutional analysis represent competing explanations of foreign economic policy. They can also complement each other, though, which raises one of the largest issues in international relations theory, the relationship between second and third image explanations.[100] In fact, some of the most interesting work in the discipline currently addresses the various links between domestic politics and international negotiations.[101]

Throughout the Cold War period and beyond the United States has tried to influence the export control policies of its allies. At times these efforts were crowned with success, at other times they failed. One possible explanation is that over time the ability of the United States to compensate its allies for foregone trade opportunities or to punish its allies for noncompliance decreased. In other words, what matters is the distribution of power. This is essentially how Jentleson explains the history of disputes within the Western alliance on East-West energy trade. He argues that "the imbroglio over the 1982 natural gas trade sanctions was far more severe and had an outcome far less favorable to American policy than the dispute over the 1962 oil trade sanctions because *the sources of conflict had increased while the American resources of leverage had decreased.*"[102]   However, the United States also put pressure on West Germany to change its nuclear export control policies both in the 1970s and the late 1980s. U.S. pressure failed in the 1970s but proved successful in the late 1980s when arguably the United States had experienced a relative decline in power.

Putnam's concept of "reverberation" is helpful in explaining this pattern. Reverberation occurs when international pressure changes domestic politics by either bringing the policy preferences of domestic actors closer in line with the preferences of the foreign negotiator exerting pressure (positive reverberation) or by producing a domestic backlash (negative reverberation).[103]   Schoppa has extended Putnam's model by arguing that the chances for pressure to succeed increase when foreign pressure leads to an expansion of participation. Participation may increase if closed decision processes open to the participation of other elite actors, such as previously excluded government agencies, or if the mass public becomes involved. Furthermore, "[p]articipation expansion is likely to work best when involvement in decision making (before the initiation of foreign pressure) is limited and when latent support for foreign demands exists outside the privileged elite."[104]

To apply this to German-American interactions on nuclear export controls, in the 1970s the Carter administration severely criticized West German policies, but U.S. pressure for the most part failed. At that time official West German policies enjoyed broad domestic support, including all relevant government agencies and significant political parties. In the 1980s this domestic consensus broke down. Within the executive branch the foreign office began to push for a change in policies but the foreign office's efforts were frustrated due to the entrenched position of the economics ministry which dominated the decision process. Starting in 1986 the Reagan administration began to supply German decision makers with intelligence information on the Rabta chemical weapons project. Yet, this pressure also yielded no results until early 1989 when the Libya scandal dominated the headlines of both U.S. and German newspapers. After initially discounting the American reports, the German media severely criticized the government and the government faced embarrassing scrutiny by parliament. German foreign minister Genscher accused George Shultz of leaking this information to the press, but in his memoirs Shultz denied this.[105]

Reverberation also provides at least a partial explanation for the two pipeline cases. In the 1962/63 case the pipe embargo, which the United States had been pushing, generated considerable domestic opposition in West Germany, partly because the embargo imposed significant economic costs on West German steel companies. As the controversy escalated, however, the conflict was redefined as a test of loyalty to the United States, and on that basis the Adenauer government enforced the embargo.[106] In 1982, on the other hand, heavy-handed pressure by the Reagan administration resulted in negative reverberation and only reinforced the gunslinging cowboy image that Reagan had acquired at that time among parts of the European public.

These assessments applied primarily to the past, which raises the important but thorny question of whether they are still valid for U.S. and German policies in the early 1990s.[107] After unification a wide-ranging debate began in Germany on the need to reorient German foreign policy. Hanns Maull coined the term "civilian power" and argued that the German emphasis on multilateral diplomacy and integration in supranational institutions represented the wave of the future and could exercise a "civilizing" influence on world politics.[108] Others, such as Gregor Schöllgen and particularly Arnulf Baring, would regard such claims as pure hubris.[109] Rather, Germany needed to rediscover that international politics is primarily about power, but after the disastrous experience of the first half of the century the newly united Germany of the 1990s had to learn to use its enhanced power responsibly. Furthermore, the united Germany, in contrast to the old West Germany, again found itself in the center of Europe, the famous *Mittellage*. Among German decision makers Klaus Naumann, Germany's highest-ranking soldier, agrees with the need to learn how to use power responsibly. He also argues, though, that Germany should avoid anything that smacks of the old *Mittellage*, rather Germany should remain firmly anchored in the Atlantic alliance and the Western community of values.[110] In terms of actual policy, so far German foreign economic policy has shown a fairly high degree of continuity and "[d]espite the seismic changes on the domestic scene since November 1989, the politico-economic coalition underpinning export-led growth remained intact in a united Germany."[111] On the military side, Germany has faced a drastically changed security environment. Furthermore, the German *Bundeswehr* had to cope with incorporating remnants of the old East German armed forces, face drastic reductions in its own forces and deal with an agonizing debate over out-of-area missions. On balance, German elites have recognized that the country has to take on "new responsibilities" in its foreign policy, but "Germany also maintains a strong preference for economic, political, and diplomatic instruments, arms control, and dispute settlement as the preferred means of security policy. This preference contrasts sharply with a reluctance . . . to consider military means as a legitimate instrument of foreign policy."[112] All of this is compatible with the continued pursuit of a trading state strategy. For the United States the key question is whether it will continue to play a leadership role on export control issues. As of late 1995 it appears that U.S. policies will be inconsistent and combine lofty rhetoric with a limited willingness to commit substantial resources to such issues.

CASES

In this book I devote three chapters to an institutional comparison of U.S. and German export controls and to an analysis of international and domestic constraints on U.S. and German policies. At a lower level of aggregation I will also analyze the political decision-making process in six specific cases. These cases involve

1. the export of a German nuclear plant to Argentina;

2. the export of a U.S. nuclear power plant to the Philippines;

3. the proposed but never implemented sale of German *Leopard* II tanks to Saudi Arabia;

4. the sale of Airborne Warning and Control System (AWACS) planes and combat aircraft by the United States to Saudi Arabia;

5. West German decision making in the negotiations with the Soviet Union over the Yamal (Urengoj) natural gas pipeline deal; and

6. the attempt of the Reagan administration to block the Yamal (Urengoj) pipeline deal through the revocation of export licenses for pipe layers and rotors for gas turbine compressor stations to be used in the construction of the pipeline.

In the American cases we would expect the decision-making process to be relatively open, and opponents of executive decisions should find it relatively easy to challenge those decisions through Congress or the use of lawsuits. To the extent that these cases generated political conflict, different executive departments, individual members of Congress and interest groups should represent the conflicting positions. For the German cases, on the other hand, we would anticipate a more closed decision process, a greater emphasis on consensus, and the prominence of political parties in any conflicts.

The primary criterion I used for selecting these cases was "comparability" in the sense of Lijphart's discussion of the comparative method.[113] In other words, within the three issue areas I looked for cases that had important characteristics in common. This is the reason why I selected two arms export cases with the same recipient government, Saudi Arabia. One specific consideration that went into the selection of the cases was comparability across time. The debates within the United States and Germany over arms and nuclear export policy are part of a larger international debate. To take the example of nuclear exports, one crucial event in that issue area was the explosion of a nuclear device by India in 1974. This event significantly changed the international climate in nuclear trade. Thus, it would not make much sense to compare the first German reactor export to Argentina in 1968 with the export of a Westinghouse reactor to the Philippines in 1980. Therefore, I selected the second export of a German nuclear plant to Argentina in 1980. The arms export and East-West trade cases are set in the early 1980s. Although these cases all describe events in the late 1970s or early 1980s, the issues they raise are of more than just historical interest. The Westinghouse reactor export to the Philippines, for example, led to a debate on whether or not the U.S. government should consider environmental concerns in its export credit and licensing decisions. In 1994 Westinghouse became embroiled in a similar controversy over nuclear exports to the Czech Republic.[114]

Another consideration was to select cases that are similar in their economic significance. One of the most interesting set of nuclear export cases in the United States was the controversy over fuel shipments to the Tarapur nuclear power station in India. However, since I had decided to select a German reactor export case, using the well-documented Tarapur case would have presented a problem. Nuclear power plant exports involve billion dollar contracts, whereas nuclear fuel shipments consist of relatively small sums. Therefore, I decided to take two reactor cases. The proposed sale of several hundred German tanks to Saudi Arabia was roughly comparable in economic terms to the sale of U.S. fighter jets and AWACS planes to the same recipient. The two East-West trade cases, however, differed on this dimension. The gas pipeline deal was much more significant for the German economy than the export of pipe layers and rotors was for the United States.

A final consideration that influenced the selection of cases was to compare cases that belong to the same type of decision. Both the nuclear and the East-West trade cases involve licensing decisions. Although I paid attention to time, economic significance, and type of decision, I did not select typical cases. The Nuclear Regulatory Commission (NRC) granted an export license for the Philippine reactor in 1980. That year the NRC granted a total of 462 export licenses.[115] Together with actions taken on several export applications for nuclear fuel for the Tarapur nuclear plant in India, the Westinghouse export to the Philippines was the most significant licensing decision made in 1980. The Westinghouse export was atypical because it involved the export of a complete nuclear plant and because it received far more attention and was far more controversial than the other licensing decisions. What I was interested in was not "typical" cases but cases that were well suited to show the tensions resulting from conflicting goals of the actors involved.

It also would have been desirable to have two U.S. and German cases in which the nonproliferation issue was salient to the same extent. However, there are problems in coming up with such cases. First of all, the drought in the international market for nuclear power plants has meant that there are few exports to choose from. Second, for this kind of case study only well-documented cases are useful. This was one advantage of the exports to Argentina and the Philippines. The list of countries that posed the most risks in terms of proliferation included Argentina, Brazil, India, Iran, Iraq, Israel, Libya, Pakistan, and South Africa. Germany has exported power plants to Argentina, Brazil, and Iran. The United States exported nuclear plants to Brazil and India, but these exports were negotiated before the watershed of 1974, the explosion of a nuclear device by India. Other relevant U.S. nuclear power plant exports include sales to South Korea and Taiwan. These countries were not regarded as high proliferation risks, though, and their close economic, political, and security ties to the United States pose problems for a comparison with German nuclear exports.

In regard to the data collection for the case studies, I relied on a number of different sources. The primary sources of information for the nuclear export cases were government documents, newspaper articles, and nuclear industry journals. The U.S. case study was based to a large extent on documents that I obtained through the Public Documents Room of the Nuclear Regulatory Commission. It was more difficult to obtain information on the German case. In general, German government agencies tend to be more secretive than their U.S. counterparts. I was able to overcome this handicap to some extent by conducting interviews with German officials in the ministry for research and technology and the foreign office.

For the arms export cases I also relied heavily on government documents, newspaper and journal articles, and other secondary literature. For the German case in this area, I also wrote to seven members of the *Bundestag*, the German-Arab society, the German-Israeli society, the German trade union federation, and other organizations for information on German arms exports. I received replies from most of the people whom I had contacted. Concerning the pipeline controversy, I was fortunate since the conflict is very well documented. On the German side, a number of excellent secondary sources are available. In addition to that, I conducted several interviews with government officials and representatives of the

German business community during the fall of 1986 and the summers of 1990 and 1995.

CONCLUSION

The present system of international export controls originated in the Cold War period. Although the Cold War has now ended, export controls will persist, even if some of their targets have changed. This study fills important gaps in the literature on export controls. There is a body of literature that deals with various aspects of restrictions on East-West technology transfer, arms exports, and nuclear nonproliferation efforts, but there also is a dearth of explicitly comparative studies. Some edited volumes include chapters on export control policies of various other countries besides the United States, but many of these studies suffer from the weaknesses of edited volumes, such as the lack of a common theoretical framework and of a clearly defined focus. My book helps to remedy this problem. Furthermore, my work fills some of the gaps in the literature on German export controls, since my book discusses German policies in greater depth than chapters in edited volumes. Given the fact that Germany and the United States have been the world's largest exporters, an understanding of German and U.S. practices is critical for any efforts to control the flow of sensitive goods to customers with nuclear or chemical weapons ambitions or ballistic missile programs.

Another drawback of much of the existing literature on export controls is that it tends to be compartmentalized into different subcategories. Specialists on nuclear nonproliferation issues have written about nuclear export controls, other authors have focused on the arms trade or on East-West trade. Although each one of these three areas presents specific problems, which are unique to that area, these three areas of trade are related in that all three involve very sensitive security issues. This book compares the export control systems of two countries across the areas of trade in arms, nuclear technology, and with the former Soviet Union, in contrast to much of the literature, which focuses on one of these three issues and excludes the others.

But it is not only the policy literature that has been plagued by excessive fragmentation. The same can be said about the theoretical literature relevant to this study. For all too long the study of international relations has been rigidly divided into security studies and international political economy. A theoretically informed study of export control policy can make at least a small contribution to bridge this gap since export controls are an economic tool to address security problems, such as the spread of advanced weaponry. Along related lines, this book bridges the division between comparative politics and international relations by examining a foreign policy issue from a comparative perspective.

Recently, the study of foreign policy change has received a lot of attention, for obvious reasons. However, many discussions of change in German foreign policy, for example, are based on rather narrow assumptions. Some self-proclaimed neorealists who argue that Germany will sooner or later act like a great power again do not recognize that Germany faces a more complex set of choices than either great power status or the trading state/civilian power alternative. Furthermore, changes in interests do not automatically lead to changes in policy. Those who claim that Germany will not use military force again because of a set of post–World War II anti-militarist values that by now are deeply ingrained in German political culture, discount the possibility that values themselves change. In the literature on the role of ideas in policy change, one frequently finds the notion of a diffusion of ideas from one country (or national epistemic community) to another without a clear specification of why some ideas diffuse more easily than others and of how decision makers select certain ideas and discard others. All too often this shows only the problem of working with diffuse concepts. Over time, ideas become institutionalized. Parts of the institutionalist literature, though, treat the term institution simply as a fancy label for inertia. This book hopes to provide a more nuanced discussion of change in foreign policy.

Chapter 2 begins by taking a chronological perspective and examines changes and continuity in the statutory basis of U.S. and German export controls and in the institutions that implement these policies. Although U.S. export control policy has been characterized by a remarkable degree of continuity, in Germany major shifts occurred in 1961 and in the years following 1989. Chapter 2 then compares state institutions in Germany and the United States in regard to the degree of state centralization and the policy networks linking state and society. Differences in state centralization do not account for the observed policy differences. The blurring of the distinction between state and society in Germany contributed to the smooth cooperation between state and industry, in contrast to the more conflictual pattern in the United States.

The material in chapter 3 is based on the premise that state action depends on a state's position in the international system. Essentially, the chapter puts forward two arguments. First, after World War II the United States emerged as a hegemonic power and leader of the Western alliance in contrast to the defeated Germany. As part of its leadership role the United States had to impose tougher limits on its own exports to the Communist world than its (junior) partners in the alliance. Second, in the 1950s West Germany began pursuing what Rosecrance calls a trading state strategy, which resulted in a highly export-oriented economy. A large part of the chapter consists of a discussion of the economic significance of East-West trade, and of arms and nuclear exports for the two economies.

Chapter 4 focuses on the positions of various interest groups and, particularly in the case of Germany, political parties on the issue of export controls. The chapter also considers changes in the domestic politics of export controls during the past few years, including the controversy surrounding changes in German export control laws following the Libya affair of 1989 and congressional debates on the latest reauthorization of the Export Administration Act of 1979. The following two chapters describe and analyze the six arms and nuclear export and East-West trade case studies. The concluding chapter includes a summary of the findings of this book and a discussion of the future of export control policy as a nonproliferation tool.

NOTES

1. U.S. Department of Commerce, *Export Administration Annual Report 1992* (Washington, D.C.: Government Printing Office, 1993).

2. National Academy of Sciences, *Finding Common Ground: U.S. Export Controls in a Changed Global Environment* (Washington, D.C.: National Academy Press, 1991).

3. For an early history of CoCom see Gunnar Adler-Karlsson, *Western Economic Warfare 1947–1967: A Case Study in Foreign Economic Policy* (Stockholm: Almqvist & Wiksell, 1968). A more recent account has been provided by Michael Mastanduno, *Economic Containment: CoCom and the Politics of East-West Trade* (Ithaca: Cornell University Press, 1992).

4. Peter Rudolf, "Die Vereinigten Staaten und CoCom: Strukturen, Entwicklungen, Reformperspektiven," *Europa Archiv*, 40 (June 6, 1990): 367–368.

5. National Academy of Sciences, *Finding Common Ground*, p. 118.

6. Gary K. Bertsch and Steve Elliott-Gower, "U.S. COCOM Policy: From Paranoia to Perestroika?" in *After the Revolutions: East-West Trade and Technology Transfer in the 1990s*, eds. Gary K. Bertsch, Heinrich Vogel, and Jan Zielonka (Boulder: Westview Press, 1991), pp. 28–29.

7. Keith Bradsher, "Allies Ease Exports to Ex-Soviet Countries," *New York Times*, 3 June 1992, p. C9.

8. "Das Ende von Cocom hat jetzt begonnen," *Frankfurter Allgemeine Zeitung*, 3 January 1994, p. 9.

9. *Arms Control Today*, September 1995, pp. 31–33, December 1995/January 1996, p. 24.

10. Robert Inman, Joseph Nye, William Perry, and Roger Smith, eds., *New Threats: Responding to the Proliferation of Nuclear, Chemical and Delivery Capabilities in the Third World* (Lanham, Md.: Aspen Strategy Group and University Press of America, 1990).

11. Benjamin N. Schiff, *International Nuclear Technology Transfer: Dilemmas of Dissemination and Control* (London: Croom Helm, 1984), pp. 142–143; James F.

Keeley, "Containing the Blast: Some Problems of the Non-Proliferation Regime," in *Nuclear Exports and World Politics: Policy and Regime*, eds. Robert Boardman and James F. Keeley (New York: St. Martin's Press, 1983), p. 213.

12. Schiff, *International Nuclear Technology Transfer*, pp. 142–143.

13. William Walker and Måns Lönnroth, *Nuclear Power Struggles: Industrial Competition and Proliferation Control* (London: George Allen & Unwin, 1983), pp. 145–148.

14. In 1976 the fifteen members of the Nuclear Suppliers Group were Belgium, Canada, Czechoslovakia, France, German Democratic Republic, Federal Republic of Germany, Italy, Japan, Netherlands, Poland, Sweden, Switzerland, the United Kingdom, the United States, and the U.S.S.R. By early 1993 the group had expanded to include Australia, Austria, Bulgaria, Denmark, Finland, Greece, Hungary, Ireland, Luxembourg, Norway, Portugal, Romania, and Spain.

15. Zachary S. Davis, *Non-Proliferation Regimes: A Comparative Analysis of Policies to Control the Spread of Nuclear, Chemical and Biological Weapons and Missiles* (Washington, D.C.: Congressional Research Service, 1991), p. 10.

16. "Nuclear Suppliers Group Agrees On 'Dual-Use' Export Controls," *Arms Control Today*, April 1992, p. 19.

17. Davis, *Non-Proliferation Regimes*, p. 78.

18. Janne E. Nolan and Albert D. Wheelon, "Third World Ballistic Missiles," *Scientific American* 263 (August 1990): 38.

19. Kathleen Bailey, "Can Missile Proliferation Be Reversed," *Orbis* 35 (Winter 1991): 14; Inman et al., *New Threats*, p. 14.

20. Bailey, "Missile Proliferation," p. 10.

21. Jon Wolfsthal, "Israel Accepts MTCR Guidelines," *Arms Control Today*, November 1991, p. 20.

22. *Arms Control Today*, January/February 1993, p. 22.

23. Prakash Shah, "The Chemical Weapons Convention: A Third World Perspective," *Disarmament* 16 (1): 88–99.

24. James F. Leonard, "Rolling Back Chemical Proliferation," *Arms Control Today*, October 1992, p. 17.

25. "Makers of Anti-Personnel Mines Are Urged by U.S. to Ban Exports," *New York Times*, 16 December 1993, p. A14.

26. For a more detailed discussion see Ian Anthony, "Assessing the UN Register of Conventional Arms," *Survival* 35 (Winter 1993): 113–129.

27. U.S. Energy Research and Development Administration, *Final Environmental Statement: U.S. Nuclear Power Export Activities* (Washington, D.C.: Government Printing Office, 1976), table 4.3.

28. West Germany, Deutscher Bundestag, *Drucksache* 11/2120, p. 1.

29. Michael Brzoska, "Arms Transfer Data Sources," *Journal of Conflict Resolution* 26 (March 1982): 77–108.

30. Ibid., p. 99.

31. "Nuclear Madness," *New York Times*, 13 June 1975, p. 36.

32. Pierre Lellouche, "Breaking the Rules Without Quite Stopping the Bomb: European Views," in *Nuclear Proliferation: Breaking the Chain*, ed. George H. Quester (Madison: The University of Wisconsin Press, 1981), pp. 40–41.

33. Hanns-Dieter Jacobsen, "Die Osthandelspolitik des Westens: Konsens und Konflikt," *Aus Politik und Zeitgeschichte*, 2 February 1985, p. 31.

34. Hanns-Dieter Jacobsen, "Die amerikanischen Exportkontrollen als bündnispolitisches Problem," *Osteuropa-Wirtschaft* 31 (September 1986): 200.

35. Hanns-Dieter Jacobsen, "High Technology in US Foreign Trade Relations," *Aussenpolitik* 36 (1985): 414.

36. William Safire, "The German Problem," *New York Times*, 2 January 1989, p. 19.

37. Gary Milhollin, "Bonn's Proliferation Policy," *New York Times*, 4 January 1989, p. 1.

38. Germany, Deutscher Bundestag, *Drucksache* 12/6911.

39. Jürgen Nötzold and Hendrik Roodbeen, "The European Community and COCOM: The Exclusion of an Interested Party," in *After the Revolutions: East-West Trade and Technology Transfer in the 1990s*, eds. Gary K. Bertsch, Heinrich Vogel and Jan Zielonka (Boulder, Colo.: Westview Press, 1991); "EG-Initiative zur Regelung von Dual-Use Exporten," *Handelsblatt*, 23 January, 1992, p. 8; Wolfgang H. Reinicke, "Arms Sales Abroad: European Community Export Controls Beyond 1992," *Brookings Review* 10 (Summer 1992): 23; Harald Mueller, "The Export Controls Debate in the 'New' European Community," *Arms Control Today*, March 1993, pp. 10–14; "Kobra mit Loch," *Der Spiegel*, 3 May 1993, pp. 26–27; Bernd W. Kubbig and Harald Müller, *Nuklearexport und Aufrüstung: Neue Bedrohungen und Friedensperspektiven* (Frankfurt: Fischer Taschenbuch Verlag, 1993), pp. 124–140; Germany, *Verhandlungen des Deutschen Bundestages*, 12. Wahlperiode, Stenographische Berichte 12/202, pp. 17449–17465.

40. Council Regulation (EC) No 3381/94 (OJ No L 367, 19.12. 1994); "Die Exportkontrolle wird noch komplizierter," *Frankfurter Allgemeine Zeitung*, 30 November 1994, p. 16. Germany will also maintain separate national controls on the transfer of knowlege and services for arms projects. See "Die Exportkontrolle in Europa wird harmonisiert," *Frankfurter Allgemeine Zeitung*, 19 December 1994, p. 11.

41. *Congressional Quarterly Weekly Report*, 9 June 1990, p. 1778.

42. *Congressional Quarterly Weekly Report*, 28 April 1990, p. 1253.

43. Michael Wines, "Bush Weighs a Veto of Sanctions For the Spread of Chemical Arms," *New York Times*, 1 November 1990, p. A6; Clyde H. Farnsworth, "U.S. Moves to Cut Chemicals' Spread," *New York Times*, 15 December 1990, p. 5.

44. *Congressional Quarterly Weekly Report*, 25 January 1992, p. 163, 17 October 1992, p. 3256.

45. *Arms Control Today*, November 1993, p. 27.

46. "U.S. Plans to Ease Curbs on Exports of Many Products," *New York Times*, 25 February 1994, p. A1.

47. *Congressional Quarterly Weekly Report*, 23 July 1994, p. 2018.

48. *CQ Weekly Report*, 1 October 1994, p. 2767.

49. Walker and Lönnroth, *Nuclear Power Struggles*, p. 23.

50. Ibid., pp. 34–35.

51. Måns Lönnroth and William Walker, *The Viability of the Civil Nuclear Industry* (New York & London: International Consultative Group on Nuclear Energy, 1980), p. 58.

52. Ibid.

53. West Germany, *Bulletin der Bundesregierung*, no. 36 (15 April 1977), p. 331.

54. Ulrich Albrecht, "West Germany: New Strategies," *Journal of International Affairs* 40 (Summer 1986): 130.

55. Ibid., pp. 131–132.

56. This concept was developed by Richard Rosecrance. According to Richard Rosecrance, there are "two worlds of international relations." In the territorial system states attempt to increase their power through territorial expansion, or in other words, pursue a military political strategy. Economically, they strive for self-sufficiency. Trading states, on the other hand, reject autarky and accept interdependence. They achieve wealth and power through trade. See Richard Rosecrance, *The Rise of the Trading State: Commerce and Conquest in the Modern World* (New York: Basic Books, 1986), p. 16.

57. Ludwig Erhard, *Deutschlands Rückkehr zum Weltmarkt* (Dusseldorf: Econ-Verlag, 1953), p. 5.

58. Ellen Frost and Angela Stent, "NATO's Troubles with East-West Trade," *International Security* 8 (Summer 1983): 180.

59. "U.S. to Allow Sale of the Technology for Spy Satellites," *New York Times*, March 11, 1994, p. A1.

60. Janne E. Nolan, ed., *Global Engagement: Cooperation and Security in the 21st Century* (Washington, D.C.: The Brookings Institution, 1994).

61. Risse-Kappen has argued that the key elements of "common security" became part of the German foreign policy consensus as far back as the early to mid-eighties. See Thomas Risse-Kappen, "Ideas Do Not Float Freely: Transnational Coalitions, Domestic Structures, and the End of the Cold War," *International Organization* 48 (Spring 1994): 185–214.

62. This point broadly follows a line of argument first developed by Henry R. Nau, *The Myth of America's Decline: Leading the World Economy into the 1990s* (New York: Oxford University Press, 1990).

63. Manfred Schmidt, "West Germany: The Policy of the Middle Way," *Journal of Public Policy* 7 (April–June 1987): 148.

64. West Germany, *Verhandlungen des Deutschen Bundestages*, 3. Wahlperiode, Stenographische Berichte 3/142, p. 8100.

65. Peter J. Katzenstein, "Coping with Terrorism: Norms and Internal Security in Germany and Japan," in *Ideas and Foreign Policy: Beliefs, Institutions, and Political Change*, eds. Judith Goldstein and Robert O. Keohane (Ithaca: Cornell University Press, 1993), p. 266–267.

66. Kjell Goldmann, *Change and Stablity in Foreign Policy: The Problems and Possibilities of Détente* (Princeton: Princeton University Press, 1988), pp. 36–37. In recent years cognitive approaches to policy change have emphasized the concept of learning. For introductions to this body of literature see Lloyd S. Etheredge, *Can Governments Learn? American Foreign Policy and Central American Revolutions* (New York: Pergamon Press, 1985); Ernst B. Haas, *When Knowledge is Power: Three Models of Organizational Change in International Organizations* (Berkeley: University of California Press, 1990); Jack S. Levy, "Learning and Foreign Policy: Sweeping a Conceptual Minefield," paper presented to the 1992 Annual Meeting of the American Political Science Association, Chicago, September 3–6; Philip E. Tetlock, "Learning in U.S. and Soviet Foreign Policy: In Search of an Elusive Concept," in *Learning in U.S. and Soviet Foreign*

Policy, eds. George W. Breslauer and Philip E. Tetlock (Boulder: Westview Press, 1991), pp. 22–44.

67. For an important discussion of the institutionalization of ideas in the U.S. context see Judith Goldstein, *Ideas, Interests, and American Trade Policy* (Ithaca: Cornell University Press, 1993).

68. Ibid., p. 259.

69. Risse-Kappen, "Ideas Do Not Float Freely," p. 196. A related line of research is the literature on "epistemic communities." See Peter M. Haas, "Introduction: Epistemic Communities and International Policy Coordination," *International Organization* 46 (Winter 1992): 1–35. One area where the relationship between domestic and transnational sources of new ideas has been debated is the literature on Soviet foreign policy change under Michail Gorbachev. See, for example, Jeff Checkel, "Ideas, Institutions, and the Gorbachev Foreign Policy Revolution," *World Politics* 45 (January 1993): 271–300.

70. Ibid.; Risse-Kappen, "Ideas Do Not Float Freely"; Sarah E. Mendelson, "Internal Battles and External Wars: Politics, Learning, and the Soviet Withdrawal from Afghanistan," *World Politics* 45 (April 1993): 327–360.

71. The German emphasis on acting within multilateral frameworks is typically regarded as a post–World War II phenomenon, but Krüger has suggested that this characteristic of German foreign policy was already present, if only in embryonic form, during the Weimar period. See Peter Krüger, *Die Aussenpolitik der Republik von Weimar* (Darmstadt: Wissenschaftliche Buchgesellschaft, 1985).

72. Katzenstein, "Coping with Terrorism," p. 266.

73. For a more detailed discussion see Clay Clemens, "Opportunity or Obligation? Redefining Germany's Military Role Outside of NATO," *Armed Forces & Society* 19 (Winter 1993): 231–251.

74. Harald Müller, *Nach den Skandalen: Deutsche Nichtverbreitungspolitik*, HSFK-Report 5/1989 (Frankfurt: Hessische Stiftung Friedens- und Konfliktforschung, 1989), pp. 21–23.

75. For a broader discussion of multilateralism see John Gerard Ruggie, ed., *Multilateralism Matters: The Theory and Praxis of an Institutional Form* (New York: Columbia University Press, 1993).

76. Janne E. Nolan, "Cooperative Security in the United States," in *Global Engagement: Cooperation and Security in the 21st Century*, ed. Janne E. Nolan (Washington, D.C.: Brookings Institution, 1994), p. 512.

77. For a more optimistic view of the prospects for multilateralism in U.S. foreign policy see John Gerard Ruggie, "Third Try at World Order? America and Multilateralism after the Cold War," *Political Science Quarterly* 109 (Fall 1994): 553–570.

78. Peter Gourevitch, *Politics in Hard Times: Comparative Responses to International Economic Crises* (Ithaca: Cornell University Press, 1986), p. 54.

79. In a widely read book Arnulf Baring argued quite forcefully that Germany needed to relearn the traditional vocabulary of power politics. But even he did not come out in favor of German nuclear weapons but only suggested the need for a serious discussion of the issue. See Arnulf Baring, *Deutschland, was nun? Ein Gespräch mit Dirk Rumberg und Wolf Jobst Siedler* (Berlin: Siedler, 1991), pp. 209–211.

80. This part of the book draws on work that now carries the label "historical institutionalism." See, most recently, Sven Steinmo, Kathleen Thelen, and Frank Longstreth, *Structuring Politics: Historical Institutionalism in Comparative Analysis* (Cambridge: Cambridge University Press, 1992).

81. Stephen Krasner, *Defending the National Interest: Raw Materials Investments and U.S. Foreign Policy* (Princeton: Princeton University Press, 1978); Eric Nordlinger, *On the Autonomy of the Democratic State* (Cambridge: Cambridge University Press, 1981).

82. Eric Nordlinger, "Taking the State Seriously," in *Understanding Political Development*, eds. Samuel P. Huntington and Myron Weiner (Boston: Little, Brown and Company, 1987), p. 361; Theda Skocpol, "Bringing the State Back In," in *Bringing the State Back In*, eds. Peter Evans, Dietrich Rueschemeyer and Theda Skocpol (Cambridge: Cambridge University Press, 1985), pp. 3–37.

83. Glenn Fong, "State Strength, Industry Structure and Industrial Policy: American and Japanese Experiences in Microelectronics," *Comparative Politics* 22 (April 1990): 275.

84. Ibid.

85. Krasner, *Defending the National Interest*.

86. Peter J. Katzenstein, "Stability and Change in the Emerging Third Republic," in *Industry and Politics in West Germany: Toward the Third Republic*, ed. Peter J. Katzenstein (Ithaca: Cornell University Press, 1989), p. 348.

87. Peter J. Katzenstein, *Policy and Politics in West Germany: The Growth of a Semisovereign State* (Philadelphia: Temple University Press, 1987), p. 370.

88. Ibid., p. 371.

89. Ibid., p. 372.

90. Johannes Preisinger, *Deutschland und die nukleare Nichtverbreitung: Zwischenbilanz und Ausblick*, Arbeitspapiere zur Internationalen Politik no. 76 (Bonn: Europa Union Verlag, 1993), p. 168.

91. Most empirical studies that have attempted to use the strong/weak state distinction and have studied the effect of state centralization have questioned the claims made by Krasner and other statist authors. See, for example, John Kurt Jacobsen and Claus Hofhansel, "Safeguards and Profits: Civilian Nuclear Exports, Neo-Marxism, and the Statist Approach," *International Studies Quarterly* 28 (June 1984): 195–218; Ezra N. Suleiman, "State Structures and Clientelism: The French State Versus the 'Notaires,'" *British Journal of Political Science* 17 (July 1987): 261.

92. G. John Ikenberry, David A. Lake, and Michael Mastanduno, "Introduction: Approaches to American Foreign Economic Policy," *International Organization* 42 (Winter 1988): 10.

93. Stephen Skowronek, *Building a New American State: The Expansion of National Administrative Capacities 1887–1920* (Cambridge: Cambridge University Press, 1982), p. vii.

94. Stephen Krasner, "Approaches to the State: Alternative Conceptions and Historical Dynamics," *Comparative Politics* 16 (January 1984): 234.

95. G. John Ikenberry, "Conclusion: An Institutional Approach to American Foreign Economic Policy," *International Organization* 42 (Winter 1988): 225.

96. William J. Long, *U.S. Export Control Policy: Executive Autonomy vs. Congressional Reform* (New York: Columbia University Press, 1989).

97. Michael Mastanduno, "Trade as a Strategic Weapon: American and Alliance Export Control Policy in the Early Postwar Period," *International Organization* 42 (Winter 1988): 150.

98. *Congressional Quarterly Weekly Report*, 20 November 1993, p. 3211.

99. For a sophisticated and nuanced discussion of the impact of institutional differences on government capabilities see R. Kent Weaver and Bert A. Rockman, eds., *Do Institutions Matter? Government Capabilities in the United States and Abroad* (Washington, D.C.: Brookings Institution, 1993).

100. Kenneth N. Waltz, *Theory of International Politics* (Reading, Mass.: Addison-Wesley, 1979); Peter Gourevitch, "The Second Image Reversed: The International Sources of Domestic Politics," *International Organization* 32 (Autumn 1978): 881–912; Michael Mastanduno, David A. Lake, and G. John Ikenberry, "Toward a Realist Theory of State Action," *International Studies Quarterly* 33 (December 1989): 457–474.

101. In this area the most influential approach has been Putnam's notion of "two-level games." See Robert Putnam, "Diplomacy and Domestic Politics: The Logic of Two-Level Games," *International Organization* 42 (Summer 1988); Howard P. Lehman and Jennifer L. McCoy, "The Dynamics of the Two-Level Bargaining Game: The 1988 Brazilian Debt Negotiations," *World Politics* 44 (July 1992): 600–644; Leonard J. Schoppa, "Two-Level Games and Bargaining Outcomes: Why *Gaiatsu* Succeeds in Japan in Some Cases But Not Others," *International Organization* 47 (Summer 1993): 353–386; Peter B. Evans, Harold K. Jacobson, and Robert D. Putnam, eds., *Double-Edged Diplomacy: International Bargaining and Domestic Politics* (Berkeley: University of California Press, 1993). For a recent critique of narrow realist analyses of grand strategy formation and the formulation of an alternative approach that emphasizes the importance of domestic factors see Richard Rosecrance and Arthur A. Stein, eds., *The Domestic Bases of Grand Strategy* (Ithaca: Cornell University Press, 1993).

102. Bruce W. Jentleson, *Pipeline Politics: the Complex Political Economy of East-West Energy Trade* (Ithaca: Cornell University Press, 1986), p. 41, italics in original.

103. Putnam, "Two-Level Games," pp. 454–456.

104. Schoppa, "*Gaiatsu* and Economic Bargaining Outcomes," p. 385.

105. George P. Shultz, *Turmoil and Triumph: My Years as Secretary of State* (New York: Charles Scribner's Sons, 1993), p. 245.

106. Jentleson, *Pipeline Politics*, p. 118.

107. For broad discussions of German foreign policy since unification see Jeffrey J. Anderson and John B. Goodman, "Mars or Minerva? A United Germany in a Post-Cold War Europe," in *After the Cold War: International Institutions and State Strategies in Europe, 1989—1991*, eds. Robert O. Keohane, Joseph S. Nye and Stanley Hoffmann (Cambridge: Harvard University Press, 1993), pp. 23–62; Wilfried von Bredow and Thomas Jäger, *Neue deutsche Außenpolitik: Nationale Interessen in internationalen Beziehungen* (Opladen: Leske und Budrich, 1993); Harald Müller, "German Foreign Policy after Unification," in *The New Germany and the New Europe*, ed. Paul B. Stares (Washington, D.C.: The Brookings Institution, 1992), pp. 126–173; Karl Kaiser and Hanns W. Maull, eds., *Deutschlands neue Außenpolitik*, vol. 1: *Grundlagen* (Munich: Oldenbourg, 1994).

108. Hanns W. Maull, "Germany and Japan: The New Civilian Powers," *Foreign Affairs* 69 (Winter 1990/91): 91–106; Hanns W. Maull, "Zivilmacht Bundesrepublik Deutschland: Vierzehn Thesen für eine neue deutsche Außenpolitik," *Europa-Archiv* 47 (25 May 1992): 269–278.

109. Gregor Schöllgen, *Angst vor der Macht: Die Deutschen und ihre Aussenpolitik* (Berlin: Ullstein, 1993); Baring, *Deutschland, was nun?*

110. Klaus Naumann, *Die Bundeswehr in einer Welt im Umbruch* (Berlin: Siedler, 1994), p. 217.

111. Anderson and Goodman, "Mars or Minerva," p. 37.

112. Müller, "German Foreign Policy after Unification," p. 162.

113. Arend Lijphart, "Comparative Politics and the Comparative Method," *American Political Science Review* 65 (September 1971): 682–693.

114. "U.S. Backing Work on Czech Reactors by Westinghouse," *New York Times*, 22 May 1994, p. 1.

115. U.S. Nuclear Regulatory Commission, *Annual Report 1980*, p. 171.

2

Persistence and Change: State Institutions, State Strength, and Export Controls

The statist approach makes two broad assertions. First, institutions, once established will tend to persist, and they generally do not adapt to changes in their environment in any kind of automatic or "natural" fashion. Second, advanced industrial nations exhibit significant differences in state structures that affect their ability to achieve state goals or to impose costs on society. Strong states are able to impose such costs, whereas weak states generally fail to overcome predictable societal opposition. Strict export controls impose significant costs on business. Presumably, a state that is relatively well insulated or autonomous from societal pressures should be able to formulate policies imposing such costs more easily than a poorly insulated state. Two institutional factors that may determine the degree of state autonomy are the extent of the state's centralization and the nature of the policy network linking state agencies to society. An analysis of state centralization should consider, first of all, the extent to which the executive branch must share decision-making authority with the legislature and an independent judiciary. Second, is decision-making authority concentrated within the executive branch rather than dispersed among different agencies? Furthermore, besides its advantages for policy formulation, a highly centralized state should find it easier to implement such policies against societal opposition than a fragmented state. This chapter begins with a brief description of the statutory basis of U.S. and German export controls and then compares U.S. and German policies from a historical and state structure perspective.

STATUTORY BASIS FOR EXPORT CONTROLS

The legal basis for German export controls are three acts: the *Außenwirtschaftsgesetz* (foreign trade act), the *Gesetz über die Kontrolle von Kriegswaffen* (war weapons control act), and the *Atomgesetz* (atomic energy act). Overall, the foreign trade act is the most important of the three since it covers the whole range of German exports and imports. The *Außenwirtschaftsgesetz* (AWG) states that foreign trade is principally unrestricted, export controls are the exception.[1] In practical terms, however, more significant than the AWG, which sets out the basic principles of German foreign trade law, are the implementing provisions in the *Außenwirtschaftsverordnung* (foreign trade decree) and one of its appendices, the export list. Since the Libya (Rabta) affair the German government has repeatedly amended the *Außenwirtschaftsverordnung* (AWV) to close loopholes or to counteract potential new embarrassments. For example, the fourth amendment to the AWV made the export of goods for an aerial refueling project in Libya illegal. The seventh amendment dealt with the transit of goods for a long-range cannon in Iraq, whereas the eighth amendment responded to the involvement of German citizens in missile projects in Egypt, Argentina, and Iraq.

One of the most significant changes of the foreign trade decree took place in 1991 with the fourteenth amendment to the AWV. A new section 5 (c) specified that the export of goods and technical documents required a license if the destination was included in the newly created country group H, and if the exporter knew that the intended use was an arms project. The goods themselves may not have been listed on Germany's export control list, but they were subject to export controls in any case if used for arms projects.[2] Among the numerous changes in German export control regulations, representatives of the German business community regarded section 5 (c) and the rather long country list H as particularly onerous. On January 22, 1992, the German cabinet decided to cut the list from fifty-four to thirty-four states, eliminating such countries as Singapore and South Korea. Furthermore, the German government created a new country list I, which included nine countries that had not signed the Nuclear Non-Proliferation Treaty but were not judged to be high proliferation risks, such as Chile, Niger, and Tanzania.[3] In 1995 the law changed again as the German government adjusted its regulations in response to the partial harmonization of European export controls. More specifically, a new country list K was set up to replace country list H. The new K list is considerably shorter than the H list, which shows that on balance the harmonization of European controls will not lead to stricter controls, at least not in Germany.[4]

In the area of arms exports, the *Kriegswaffenkontrollgesetz* (KWKG) regulates the export of war weapons. The KWKG is an act implementing article 26 section 2 of the constitution which states that the production, transportation and sale of war weapons require governmental approval. Although the KWKG only covers war weapons, such as tanks or combat aircraft, the scope of the *Außenwirtschaftsgesetz* includes other armaments, such as armored but unarmed vehicles. Generally, the provisions of the foreign trade act are less stringent than those of the KWKG. In 1982 the German government also issued a revised set of "political principles for the export of war weapons and other armaments" to guide the licensing process.[5] Regarding nuclear energy equipment, export controls are based primarily on the *Außenwirtschaftsgesetz*, whereas the *Atomgesetz* regulates the export and import of nuclear fuel.[6]

On the basis of this legislation the German government constructed export control lists that enumerate the goods and technologies subject to export controls. The most important list is the *Ausfuhrliste* (export list), an appendix to the foreign trade decree. For our purposes, only part I of the *Ausfuhrliste* is relevant, other parts, for example, deal with steel exports to the United States, which are subject to voluntary export restraints. Until July 1995 part I was divided into five sections. Section A covered weapons, munitions, and other armaments, section B goods for the generation of nuclear energy, section C other goods and technologies of strategic importance, whereas sections D and E listed goods for the production of chemical and biological weapons. The *Ausfuhrliste* changed frequently, largely to bring it into line with revisions of the CoCom lists, but other changes reflected unilateral German decisions. After the series of recent scandals, the German government occasionally overreacted, which led to ridicule. For example, Germany now restricts the export and transshipment of hang gliders to Lebanon, Libya, and Syria. The most significant recent change has been to bring the *Ausfuhrliste* into line with the common EU dual-use list. Thus, since July 1, 1995, part I of the new *Ausfuhrliste* consists of section A for weapons, munitions, and other armaments, section B, which implements the weapons embargo against Yugoslavia, and most importantly section C. The new section C corresponds to the European Union's dual-use list. Besides the goods that all EU member states agreed on, section C also includes eleven list positions implementing national German controls. Germany also maintains a separate war weapons list that is considerably shorter than the *Ausfuhrliste*. Whereas the *Ausfuhrliste* takes up over 150 pages, the war weapons list is only 5 pages long.

In the United States, the statutes most relevant for our purposes are the Arms Export Control Act of 1976, the Atomic Energy Act of 1954 as amended by the Nuclear Non-Proliferation Act of 1978, and the Export Administration Act of 1979 (EAA), which has been amended a number of times as well. The Export Administration Act is the most important one of the three, and it forms the counterpart to the German foreign trade act. The EAA recognizes three different grounds for imposing export controls. Exports may be restricted for national security reasons, to further the foreign policy objectives of the United States, or to alleviate problems of short supply.

Regarding armaments, there is no single procedural framework for dealing with arms transfers in the United States. Rather, U.S. arms transfers fall into two broad categories: foreign military sales (FMS) and commercial sales. Foreign military sales are government-to-government transfers. This means that a foreign government requests arms from the U.S. government, which in turn procures the requested items from U.S. arms manufacturers and resells them to the foreign customer. In commercial transactions U.S. companies directly sell military equipment to their foreign customers. The U.S. government regulates these sales through licensing requirements, which are administered by the State Department. As shown in table 6, the FMS program has been the most significant category of U.S. arms transfers, but in 1989 the value of commercial arms export licenses exceeded FMS deliveries. This pattern is different from German arms transfer practices where the vast majority of arms transfers involve commercial exports. It also illustrates the commercial orientation of German arms exports. However, as Smaldone noted, "the volume of [U.S.] commercial sales has grown significantly in both absolute and relative terms in recent years."[7] A comparison of export control lists also shows differences between the United States and Germany. The United States maintains three export control lists: the Commerce Control List, the Munitions List, and the Nuclear Referral List.[8] The Commerce Control List (CCL) broadly corresponds to the German *Ausfuhrliste*, whereas the Munitions List is the U.S. counterpart to the German war weapons list. Until September 1991 the CCL was known as the Commodity Control List. This change involved more than just the relabeling of an acronym since the "new CCL is a 'positive' list specifying those items under control. Under the old CCL, items were controlled unless specifically excluded."[9] In the past at least, the CCL and the Munitions List coexisted rather uneasily because

Broad interpretation of the term "defense article" has resulted in the inclusion on the U.S. Munitions List of many dual use items that are either on the CoCom Industrial List or are not multilaterally controlled at all. As a result, a range of commercially used items, from metal fasteners to air conditioning units to civilian aerospace equipment, are unilaterally controlled as munitions items by the United States.[10]

TABLE 6
U.S. Arms Sales (Dollars in Thousands)

	FY 1983	FY 1985	FY 1987	FY 1989	FY 1991
Foreign Military Sales Deliveries[1]	10,787,581	7,483,492	10,848,875	6,993,144	8,626,696
Commercial Exports	918,386	5,111,157	6,475,610	8,446,535	4,988,730
Military Assistance Program[2]	88,712	54,000	66,111	114,970	177,245

[1]Does not include Foreign Military Construction Sales Deliveries.
[2]Does not include training.

Source: U.S. Defense Security Assistance Agency, *Foreign Military Sales, Foreign Military Construction Sales and Military Assistance Facts, As of September 30, 1993* (Washington, D.C.: DSAA, 1994).

Since the Commodity Control List and the Munitions List are administered by different agencies, exports frequently were caught in disputes over which department exercised jurisdiction in a particular case.[11] In 1992, though, the Bush administration took steps to transfer a number of dual-use items from the Munitions List to the new CCL.[12] More broadly, this illustrates the extreme fragmentation of the American state in this issue area.

The brief discussion of German export control scandals in the previous chapter and differences in the statutory basis of export controls raise the question whether the lapses in German export controls, such as the Libya affair, are related to broader differences in the scope and stringency of U.S. and German export regulations. In regard to the scope of export controls, in 1985 licensed exports represented 5.19 percent of total West German exports.[13] In the United States, about 30 percent of U.S. manufactured goods required export licenses in the mid-1980s.[14] This indicates that the United States intervened more heavily in export controls and imposed more costs on industry than the West German state. It is important, however, to view these figures in a broader context and take into account that the overall significance of exports is greater for the German than for the U.S. economy. Table 7 shows that although U.S. export controls were more extensive than West German controls, their significance for the U.S. and West German economies has been roughly similar. This is due to the fact that the economy of Western Germany has been much more export dependent than the U.S. economy.

TABLE 7
Scope of Export Controls (1985 data)

	West Germany	United States
licensed exports as percentage of total exports:	5.19%	23.0%
export of goods as percentage of GDP:	29.90%	5.9%
licensed exports as percentage of GDP:	1.55%	1.4%

Sources: "Export-Control List Debated," *New York Times,* 14 May 1986; "Liberaler Widerstand," *Wirtschaftswoche,* 5 December 1986, p. 21; Organization for Economic Cooperation and Development, *OECD Economic Surveys: Germany* (Paris: OECD, 1986); U.S. Department of Commerce, *United States Trade: Performance in 1985 and Outlook* (Washington, D.C.: Government Printing Office, 1986), p. 119.

But not only were U.S. export controls more extensive than their German equivalents, even those West German exports that did require export licenses in the mid-1980s received less scrutiny than they would have in the United States. Among the possible indicators for the thoroughness of export controls, I chose the number of export license rejections. Denials of export licenses were not very common in either country, but they occurred more frequently in the United States than in West Germany. Out of 118,135 export license applications the Department of Commerce processed in fiscal year 1984, it rejected a total of 601 applications.[15] In West Germany, of about 80,000 license applications the *Bundesamt für Wirtschaft* in 1985 rejected roughly 100.[16] In 1983 the BAW had received 48,150 export license applications under the foreign trade act, and it rejected 106. A year earlier it had denied 150 out of 44,100 license requests.[17] Overall, this comparison of the scope of export controls and export license denials in the United States and West Germany showed that U.S. controls were more extensive and stringent than West German controls.

We should also consider, however, that although the reform of U.S. export control legislation remains in limbo, export licensing practices have changed in the United States over the past few years. Whereas the Commerce Department had processed 118,135 license applications in fiscal year 1984, by 1989 this dropped to 85,215 cases, and the early 1990s have seen an even more drastic decrease to 38,330 in 1991 and 23,958 cases in 1992, although there was a small increase again in 1993 to 25,376 cases.[18] In Germany the number of export licenses dropped in the early 1990s as well, although not as dramatically as in the United States. In 1991 the number of licenses granted under the foreign trade act stood at 33,455, which does not include temporary and bulk licenses. The following year the number of licenses decreased to 26,237, and in 1993 it went up again to 27,501.[19] Furthermore, both in relative and in absolute terms the number of license denials was higher in Germany in the early 1990s than in the mid-1980s. In 1991 the German government rejected 1016 license applications valued at 1.5

billion marks. The corresponding figures for 1992 were 369 rejections valued at 500 million and 168 rejections valued at 400 million for 1993.[20] So far, however, this comparison of U.S. and German export control policies has not fully taken into account the development and evolution of these policies over time.

HISTORICAL CONSTRAINTS ON EXPORT CONTROL POLICY

Although one can trace the origins of the U.S. export control system back to the Trading with the Enemy Act of 1917, the Export Control Act of 1949 represented "the first comprehensive system of export controls ever adopted by the Congress in peace time."[21] Under this act exports were regarded as a privilege rather than a right. In order words, in principle exports were forbidden unless sanctioned by government licenses. Furthermore, in this act Congress delegated sweeping powers to the executive branch for intervening in the conduct of U.S. foreign trade. The 1970s witnessed several attempts to liberalize this tight control system. An example of that can be seen in the fact that the successor to the Export Control Act has been called the Export Administration Act. Nevertheless, as Bertsch argued, the Department of Defense succeeded in blocking any far-reaching liberalization.[22] According to Long, "[s]ince 1969—although the perceived threat to national security has receded, Congress is more assertive in foreign policy, and the business community's interest in export markets has vastly increased—the executive *still* dominates export control policy."[23]

Turning to arms transfers, after World War II U.S. arms transfers initially took the form of grant military assistance as part of the so-called Military Assistance Program (MAP), institutionalized by the Mutual Defense Assistance Act of 1949.[24] Geographically, U.S. arms flowed primarily to the allies in Western Europe. This started to change in the 1960s, and more and more the United States sold weapons, instead of essentially giving them away. The U.S. involvement in the Vietnam War had a very corrosive influence on domestic political support for U.S. military assistance programs. For example, the Foreign Military Sales Act of 1968 "prohibited arms sales to governments that engage in human rights violations or impede social progress."[25] During the 1970s Congress made further efforts to control U.S. arms sales with the passage of the International Security Assistance and Arms Export Control Act of 1976. Politically, the Carter administration shared this belief in the need for restraints on arms transfers, but the Reagan administration reversed this policy. The three recipient regions that dominated U.S. arms transfers at different times were Western Europe, Southeast Asia, and more recently the

Middle East. Although this very brief historical overview gives the impression of significant changes over the past several decades, Joseph Smaldone argued in regard to commercial arms exports that "historical continuity has been the hallmark of the U.S. arms control system for more than fifty years."[26]

Important institutional changes in U.S. nuclear export policy can also be identified by analyzing the passage of major congressional acts in this issue area.[27] In 1946 Congress passed an Atomic Energy Act, also known as the McMahon Act. At this point, the United States pursued a very restrictive policy on nuclear technology transfer. The McMahon Act stated that "until Congress declares by joint resolution that effective and enforceable international safeguards against the use of atomic energy for destructive purposes have been established there shall be no exchange of information with other nations with respect to the use of atomic energy for industrial purposes."[28] The act also established an Atomic Energy Commission (AEC) and the Joint Committee on Atomic Energy (JCAE).

This restrictive attitude changed under Eisenhower's Atoms for Peace program and its domestic embodiment, the Atomic Energy Act of 1954. This act opened the door for the development of civilian nuclear power by private corporations and permitted private ownership of fissionable material and nuclear facilities, which had been severely restricted under the McMahon Act. Internationally, the United States pursued an aggressive nuclear sales program. The two institutions that controlled and promoted the nuclear energy program were the Atomic Energy Commission and the Joint Committee on Atomic Energy.

In the mid-1970s this institutional framework collapsed. The Energy Reorganization Act of 1974 split the AEC into the Nuclear Regulatory Commission (NRC) as the regulatory authority, whereas the Energy Research and Development Administration (ERDA) had the responsibility for the research and development of nuclear and nonnuclear energy sources. The ERDA later became the Department of Energy. In 1977 Congress abolished the old Joint Committee on Atomic Energy. The following year Congress passed the Nuclear Non-Proliferation Act (NNPA) and increased its own authority in the making of international nuclear policy. Since then, the institutional framework has not experienced major changes. The Reagan administration tried to discover all the loopholes in the NNPA but failed to push through any major structural changes.

American export control laws also provided the philosophical basis of the West German equivalent of the Export Control Act, the *Militärregierungsgesetz Nr. 53* (military government law) of 1949 (MRG 53). The MRG 53 forbade all foreign trade unless specifically authorized.[29] In direct contrast to MRG 53, the *Außenwirtschaftsgesetz* states that in principle German trade is free from government intervention. The act also lists a number of grounds on the basis of which the government may restrict trade, but such restrictions, including export controls, are supposed to be exceptions, not the rule. One institutional oddity remained, however, in the legal treatment of inter-German trade. Since West Germany did not regard trade with East Germany as foreign trade, the *Außenwirtschaftsgesetz* did not cover trade between the two Germanys, and for this area at least the MRG 53 remained on the books.[30]

This shift in West German export control policy did not remain confined to legal principles, but could also be observed in the implementation of West German export controls. The *Bundesamt für Wirtschaft* (BAW), which administered export controls until 1992, was not established until 1955. Until then, different agencies handled export controls on the West German side. In 1950 the West German minister of economics established a *Zentrale Genehmigungsstelle* (central licensing office), which later changed its name to *Zentrale Ausfuhrkontrolle*.[31] In the early 1950s the allies remained heavily involved in West German export control procedures since the majority of license applications had to be cleared with the allied High Commission for Germany.[32] At its peak, the *Zentrale Genehmigungsstelle* employed roughly 150 people. It is instructive to compare that to personnel levels in later years. In 1986 the BAW employed a staff of 60 for work on export controls that actually included a relatively substantial staff increase, compared to the early 1980s.[33] Thus, in the late 1980s the world's largest exporting nation employed less staff for export controls than in the early 1950s when West German exports amounted to a fraction of current trade levels. However, even in the early 1950s the United States had been dissatisfied with the implementation of West German export controls.[34] The wave of reforms beginning in 1989 resulted again in a drastic increase in personnel levels. In April 1992 a newly created *Bundesausfuhramt* took over BAW's export control responsibilities and in June 1992 this new agency provided work for about 300 employees.[35]

In the area of arms transfers, the West German *Bundestag* created a legislative framework for the regulation of arms exports when it passed both the *Außenwirtschaftsgesetz* and the *Kriegswaffen-kontrollgesetz* (war weapons control act) in 1961. The first West German military assistance programs were shrouded in secrecy, however, and only a select group of *Bundestag* deputies knew about them.[36] West Germany concentrated its military assistance on two poor NATO allies, Greece and Turkey, a number of African countries, and Israel. After the existence of the initially secret agreement with Israel had become public knowledge, the West German government decided to cancel the agreement and to prohibit the transfer of war weapons to so-called "areas of tension."

In 1971 the cabinet passed its first set of political principles for the export of arms. To underscore the political sensitivity of these matters, the principles remained confidential until they were leaked and published in a trade journal in 1977.[37] According to these principles, war weapons were not to be sold to areas of tension, whereas exports to NATO allies received favorable treatment. Over time, however, German export licensing practice began to deviate from the relatively restrictive guidelines of 1971. Furthermore, these guidelines did not address issues that became increasingly critical during the 1970s. Most importantly, Germany entered a significant number of arms cooperation agreements with France and Great Britain, both at the governmental and private industrial levels, to jointly develop and produce fighter aircraft, artillery pieces, and the like.[38] The crucial point here is that Britain and France have pursued less restrictive arms export policies than Germany. To use a relatively recent example, in the 1980s Germany did not export Tornado fighter aircraft to Saudi Arabia, but Great Britain did, which benefited the German company MBB as one of the key participants in the Tornado project. In 1982 the West German government took account of some of these developments in a revised set of guidelines and, in contrast to earlier practice, published them in the official bulletin.[39] The 1982 guidelines again distinguish between arms exports to NATO members and non-NATO countries, but the concept of areas of tension was dropped. Regarding coproduction with NATO partners, the government envisioned consultations with its cooperation partners, but principally it regarded arms cooperation and coproduction agreements as more important than adherence to German arms export control standards. The 1982 guidelines remain in effect but in 1994 the federal government decided to "clarify" the guidelines and to treat arms cooperation agreements among private firms similar to agreements between the German government and foreign partners. In practice this will make it easier to obtain export licenses for the shipment of components. Social Democratic opposition politicians charged that this amounted to a loosening of German arms export standards, but the government insisted that it had not changed substantive policy but only simplified procedures.[40]

Of all export control issues, arms exports have received the most political attention in Germany, whereas controversies over nuclear exports have partially faded, unless there has been a clear link to a nuclear weapons program in the recipient country. The *Außenwirtschaftsgesetz* of 1961 and the *Atomgesetz* (atomic energy act) of 1959 have formed the legal framework for the regulation of German nuclear exports. Beyond that, Germany accepted certain obligations as a signatory of the nonproliferation treaty. This legislative framework survived intact until the late 1980s.

Since 1989 the legislatures in both the United States and Germany have worked on revising their respective export control legislation. Since 1990 the German parliament has passed several acts to amend the foreign trade act, the war weapons control act, the atomic energy act, the financial administration act (*Finanzverwaltungsgesetz*), and the code of criminal procedure. The provisions that received the most attention dealt with criminal sanctions against export control violations. Previously, defendants, who had violated provisions of the foreign trade act, could receive sentences of up to three years in prison if their actions had impaired the security of the Federal Republic, disturbed the peaceful coexistence of nations, or had significantly upset the foreign relations of the Federal Republic. In practice it proved to be very difficult to show in court that a specific export control violation had had such an effect. The new legislation eliminated this requirement. In particularly grave cases the maximum penalty now is fifteen years in prison. Amendments to the war weapons control act made it illegal to develop, manufacture, or possess nuclear, chemical, or biological weapons, or to engage in any trading transaction involving such weapons. This may seem somewhat redundant since Germany repeatedly committed itself not to manufacture such weapons. However, in a new paragraph 21 the act applies these prohibitions to acts committed by German citizens abroad. Furthermore, proceeds from illegal exports may now be confiscated, and companies are required to name an "exports officer" who is personally responsible for the company's compliance with export control laws. Other amendments expanded the authority of export control agencies to collect and exchange relevant data.

Furthermore, during the past few years the foreign trade decree has undergone numerous changes, and the export list (*Ausfuhrliste*) has been amended frequently. With the sixty-second amendment of the export list the German government expanded the list of precursor chemicals subject to export controls to seventeen chemicals. Since August 1989 exports of hang gliders to Lebanon, Libya, and Syria require licenses. Later that year the German government added another twenty-five chemical products to its export list. New legislation also allows the economics minister to introduce new restrictions on German foreign trade on the basis of a simple administrative act, rather than a fully fledged decree, which has to be approved by the cabinet.[41] It does appear somewhat excessive for the German cabinet to devote time to the intricacies of exporting hang gliders to Syria, or even just the transshipment of hang gliders through the Frankfurt airport.

In the United States, the House of Representatives on June 6, 1990, passed a bill to reauthorize the Export Administration Act of 1979, which would have eased restrictions on export controls directed against the Soviet Union and Eastern Europe and strengthened the hand of the Department of Commerce at the expense of the Pentagon.[42] The Senate version, though, did not call for institutional changes that would have limited the influence of the Department of Defense.[43] Although the House and Senate eventually agreed on a compromise version, the bill ultimately failed due to a pocket veto by President Bush. Congressional inaction and the efforts of a few determined members of the House of Representatives resulted in the failure of more recent efforts at export control reform. In February and March 1993 the House and Senate passed bills to reauthorize the old Export Administration Act through June 1994 without making any policy changes.[44] Assuming that Congress is more successful in the next round, a new export control system may be in place sometime in the mid-1990s.

Thus, overall we saw a period of significant changes in West German export control policy and institutions during the 1950s until the passage of new legislation in 1961, which replaced military occupation law. Following that, no dramatic changes took place until 1989 when the Libya affair led to a major reevaluation of the West German and now united German system. In the United States, on the other hand, there have been numerous policy changes, but the basic structures underlying U.S. export control policy remained true to their historical roots until recently. During the past few years, though, pressure has been building up in the United States for more than minor policy adjustments. This picture of relatively significant changes in Germany and a slower pace of change in the United States does not hold up equally well in the areas of arms and nuclear exports. However, at the core of the U.S. and German export control systems are the institutions established by the Export Control Act, replaced later by the Export Administration Act, and the foreign trade act in Germany. To illustrate this for the United States, in 1989 the Department of Commerce, which administers the Export Administration Act, approved or denied export licenses valued at $118 billion. The State Department, which handles commercial arms exports under the Arms Export Control Act, processed $56.5 billion worth of munitions licenses in fiscal year 1989.[45] In the following section we will compare the institutions that implement U.S. and German export control legislation in terms of their centralization and the policy networks linking state and societal actors. As we will see, the extreme fragmentation of the American state in this area has been one of the contributing factors to the relative stability of U.S. policy.

INSTITUTIONAL COMPARISON OF U.S. AND GERMAN EXPORT CONTROL AUTHORITIES

State Centralization

First of all, to which extent does the executive enjoy undisputed authority or autonomy from the legislature in this policy area? When discussing the extent of executive autonomy from the legislative branch we need to recognize that Germany has a parliamentary system as opposed to the American presidential system. This means that there are structural differences between the position of the legislative branch in the United States and its counterpart in Germany. However, considerable variation is possible in both systems. To take the example of the United States, the assertiveness of Congress on foreign policy questions has varied greatly since World War II. Thus, to get a full picture of legislative involvement we need to take a closer look at the record in the specific issue areas of concern here.

In contrast to the situation in the United States, the German parliament does not have the power to interfere directly in specific export control decisions. However, there are two exceptions to this general rule. The first exception is based on section 27 part 2 of the *Außenwirtschaftsgesetz*, which states that foreign trade regulations have to be submitted to the *Bundestag*, which can cancel them within three months of their promulgation. There is only one documented case in which this provision played a significant role. It involved a regulation that the federal government had passed on December 14, 1962, requiring export permits for large diameter pipe.[46] Thus, this case was part of the famous pipe embargo of 1962/1963.[47] There was considerable domestic opposition to this embargo, and the government only narrowly avoided defeat of the regulation through a parliamentary maneuver. The other exception to the lack of legislative involvement involves military assistance agreements. After 1966 the annual budget statutes included provisions which required the approval of military assistance agreements by the *Bundestag* committees for foreign affairs and for the budget.[48] Initially, the Social Democrats (SPD) had pressed for these provisions.[49]

In the United States, on the other hand, Congress frequently intervenes in export control policy and in the approval process for particular exports. This is especially the case for arms exports. Since the early 1970s Congress has repeatedly attempted to expand its role in the decision-making process on arms transfers. These congressional attempts have primarily taken the form of the legislative veto and various reporting requirements.[50] In 1983 the Supreme Court struck down the legislative veto in its *Immigration and Naturalization Service v. Chadha* decision. Gibson has argued that in the aftermath of the *Chadha* decision interbranch conflict over arms sales to the Middle East increased. According to Gibson, the legislative veto was an instrument that effectively achieved accommodation between the president and Congress, and with the loss of this tool Congress turned to more confrontational means to oppose presidential proposals.[51]

However, these congressional attempts to gain influence over arms sales decisions have met limited success. Congress has never formally blocked an arms sales proposal of the executive branch. In 1986 Congress came very close to stopping a $265 million sale to Saudi Arabia. Both the House and the Senate had passed joint resolutions disapproving the sale. President Reagan, however, vetoed the Senate resolution, and on June 5, 1986, the Senate failed to override Reagan's veto.[52] Nevertheless, it can be argued that congressional restraints on presidential authority have had some effect by forcing the administration to modify controversial packages. In the case just mentioned, for example, the administration had to drop Stinger anti-aircraft missiles from the package to gain the support of some senators.[53]

Turning to nuclear export policy, in the 1970s and 1980s Congress has been heavily involved in the setting of United States nonproliferation policy.[54] Congress was the driving force behind a number of legislative efforts in the 1970s which culminated in the passage of the Nuclear Non-Proliferation Act of 1978. A significant issue in the debates over the NNPA was the conflict between presidential authority and congressional involvement. The NNPA contains a number of provisions that mandate congressional approval of executive branch activities and that establish procedures for overturning executive actions.[55]

In the area of East-West trade Congress did not reserve itself the right to block specific transactions through legislative vetoes. In this area, executive discretion has been very wide. In 1967 Berman and Garson wrote about the predecessor of the Export Administration Act, the Export Control Act:

Probably no single piece of legislation gives more power to the President to control American commerce. Subject to only the vaguest standards of "foreign policy" and "national security and welfare," he has authority to cut off the entire export trade of the United States, or any part of it, or to deny "export privileges" to any or all persons. Moreover, the procedures for implementing this power are left almost entirely to his discretion, and at the same time heavy administrative and criminal sanctions may be imposed for violation of any export regulation he may introduce.[56]

In recent years, however, Congress has at times expressed irritation at the exercise of presidential authority in imposing export controls. Thus, Congress restricted presidential discretion in the area of export controls imposed for foreign policy reasons, for example, by requiring the president to consider several factors, deemed important by Congress, before imposing export controls. Another example of congressional restrictions is the sanctity of existing contracts clause in section 6 (m) of the Export Administration Act of 1985. This clause was a response to the retroactive imposition of export controls on equipment for the Siberian natural gas pipeline in 1982. However, such restrictions and consultation requirements do not have much bite. In 1990 President Bush vetoed the reauthorization of the Export Administration Act because Congress had included a provision that, in the president's view, unduly restricted executive discretion in imposing sanctions.

Although this discussion of executive autonomy has shown that the extent of legislative involvement may vary considerably across issue areas in both countries, it is clear that the differences between United States and German export control policies cannot be attributed to a lack of executive autonomy vis-à-vis parliament in Germany. Part of the problem may be that the statist literature has paid insufficient attention to differences in the roles legislatures play in different systems. The argument that executive autonomy contributes to the institutional capacity or strength of the state is based on the assumption that the executive officials at the center of the state, such as the U.S. president, pursue broader goals, or what may be called the national interest, whereas legislatures represent more narrow local and society-based interests. The problem is that, at least in the area of German export controls, it does not work that way. To the extent that there has been pressure to tighten German export controls, these pressures usually did not originate within the executive branch but either came from abroad, particularly the United States, or from domestic critics of German policy, including members of parliament. To illustrate this, in 1985 the Social Democratic party, led by its most well known critic of arms exports, Norbert Gansel, introduced a bill to amend the war weapons control act. In explaining this bill, the party argued that in the area of arms export controls the executive enjoyed unusually wide discretion.[57] In order to ensure public accountability of how this discretion was used, the party called for the creation of a commissioner of parliament for arms exports.

However, recently there have been exceptions to the pattern just described. Following press reports that German companies had sold blue prints for submarines to South Africa and allegedly had shipped nuclear fuel to Pakistan, the *Bundestag* set up two fact-finding committees in 1987 and 1988.[58]   Particularly the committee that investigated the activities of the West German company *Transnuklear* brought to light much embarrassing information on West German export controls.[59]

After the scandal over the Libya affair, the German government came under heavy pressure, particularly from the United States, to tighten German controls. In response, the government introduced a number of bills to stiffen criminal sanctions against export control violations, to upgrade the information basis of export control agencies, and to provide for a better coordination of control and enforcement efforts. These bills were drawn up fairly quickly and introduced in the *Bundestag* without prior consultation of members of the Christian Democratic party in parliament. On top of that, these legislative proposals affected five ministries, four of which were led by Free Democrats, the junior coalition partner. As a result, a kind of "backbench revolt," to use British terminology, ensued, and Christian Democratic deputies forced a number of amendments that weakened some of the criminal sanctions provisions. Thus, observers witnessed a rather curious situation in which the opposition Social Democrats defended the original government proposals, while the ruling majority was busy watering down those same proposals.[60] In this particular case, a number of special factors had to come together to produce this outcome, such as inadequate prior consultation of parliament, combined with tensions among the coalition partners.

As a general rule, in the German parliamentary system only the majority parties, which by definition also fill the top executive positions, have a real chance of making a significant impact on policy. The situation gets more complicated, though, when, as is the current case, the opposition party in the *Bundestag* controls the second chamber, the *Bundesrat*. In the episode described above, on May 30, 1989, the federal government led by Christian Democratic Chancellor Kohl introduced a bill to tighten the war weapons control act.[61] The bill specified that anybody who developed, manufactured, or traded nuclear, chemical, or biological weapons would receive a minimum jail sentence of two years. Opposition within the governing party led to the passage of a weakened bill on June 1, 1990.[62] This version lowered the minimum jail sentence to one year and included a clause that limited the criminal liability of scientists, a provision that science organizations had lobbied for. On June 22, 1990, the *Bundesrat*, where the Social Democrats enjoyed a majority at the time, approved two bills to amend the foreign trade act but rejected amendments to the war weapons control act and referred the bill to the conference committee (*Vermittlungsausschuß*).[63] The *Bundesrat* objected specifically to the one-year minimum jail sentence and the science clause.[64] When the act finally went into effect in November 1990 its provisions followed the recommendations of the *Bundesrat*. Thus, the final result followed a general pattern in which the *Bundestag* gives in more frequently than the *Bundesrat*.[65] In 1991 the Social Democrats again used their majority in the *Bundesrat* to block export control legislation.[66] This time, though, the government reacted differently and decided to change the bill in such a way that approval by the *Bundesrat* was no longer necessary.[67] On January 23, 1992, the *Bundestag* passed the revised bill.[68]

Examining evidence not specifically related to export controls, another study found that interest groups attach very little importance to lobbying the German parliament, particularly on foreign policy issues. For example, from 1972 to 1975 the federation of German industry (BDI) addressed 95 percent of all its petitions dealing with foreign and foreign economic policy issues to the federal executive branch and only 1.5 percent to legislative organs. In domestic politics parliament was apparently regarded as more important, since in that area it received 20 percent of all BDI petitions.[69] This has not changed much over the years. For 1986–1988 the BDI listed twenty-one major petitions concerning foreign trade policy. The BDI sent three to the foreign office, 11 to the economics ministry and none to the *Bundestag*.[70]

A study by Aberbach, Putnam, and Rockman, who compared the role orientations of members of parliament and senior civil servants in West Germany, the United States, and four other industrialized countries, further underscores differences between the United States and Germany. Although these authors specifically excluded foreign affairs from their study, their work is helpful for understanding some of the problems we are concerned with here. One of the key findings was that "parliamentary politicians . . . articulate broad demands and thus . . . act as advocates, whereas bureaucrats more frequently are compelled to reconcile . . . the specific interests of the organized clientele affected by their actions."[71] The one country where this relationship did not hold was the United States, where they discovered that members of Congress were more concerned with specific interests than members of parliament in other countries.

Executive autonomy may not only be constrained by legislatures, but provisions for judicial review may have an impact as well. In West Germany in the mid-1980s companies appealed about 40 percent of all export license denials by the *Bundesamt für Wirtschaft*, and occasionally these cases ended up in court. Appeals occurred particularly often in the electronics area.[72] In the United States, on the other hand, opportunities for companies "to seek judicial review of Commerce Department action" are rather limited because the Export Administration Act has been exempted "from the judicial review provisions of the

Administrative Procedure Act."[73] This is not the case, however, for the Arms Export Control Act.[74] The situation may change when Congress reauthorizes the Export Administration Act the next time.[75] Nevertheless, historically the executive has enjoyed unusually wide discretion in implementing the Export Control Act and later the EAA.

Turning to centralization within the executive branch, at the administrative level there has been one agency in Germany that handles export controls, the *Bundesamt für Wirtschaft* (BAW) and after April 1992 the *Bundesausfuhramt* (BAA). In the early 1980s this agency decided on about 40 percent of all license applications itself and sent the other 60 percent to the ministry of economics.[76] In the meantime, though, the relationship between the BAW and the ministry of economics changed, with the consequence that the BAW had to submit more to the ministry than before.[77] License applications for war weapons are never decided by the BAA itself; the BAA forwards them to the ministry of economics, which consults the foreign office.[78] Some war weapons cases do not get settled until they reach the federal security council (*Bundessicherheitsrat*), a cabinet committee.

Essentially, the ministry of economics, the foreign office, and, on occasion, other ministries make export control policy and leave the day-to-day administrative tasks to a detached agency subordinate to the ministry of economics. This mode of operation is characteristic of German administrative practice in general and builds on a tradition that predates the establishment of the Federal Republic, and even the Weimar Republic for that matter.[79] In the United States, on the other hand, administrative business typically is handled either by specialized bureaus in large departments or by independent agencies. Examples in the area of export controls include the Bureau of Export Administration in the Department of Commerce, the Center for Defense Trade in the State Department, and the Nuclear Regulatory Commission as an independent agency. In a statement made in 1940, which is still valid today, Brecht and Glaser observed "that, notwithstanding the incorporation of so many bureaus in their jurisdictions, the German departments are much smaller than their American equivalents, even with due regard to the differences in population, because of the technique of detachment."[80]

From an American perspective, an even more significant contrast is the fact that the ministry of defense plays only a minor role in German export control policy. This holds true, to some extent, even for arms exports. In the 1980s the United States pushed for a greater role of defense officials in CoCom deliberations, but West Germany resisted such demands.

In the United States we do not find a single administrative agency that handles all types of export license applications. Rather, different agencies take responsibility for arms and nuclear exports and trade with the successor states of the Soviet Union. In the area of arms exports, the State Department handles the licensing of commercial sales, whereas the Pentagon implements the foreign military sales program. The volume of commercial arms sales applications reviewed by the State Department has increased considerably since the 1970s. Between the mid-1970s and mid-1980s the case load doubled, reaching "about 45,000 cases a year in the mid-1980s."[81] In fiscal year 1989 the State Department processed 53,780 munitions licenses, valued at $56.5 billion.[82] The State Department relied on its Office of Munitions Control to fulfill this administrative task until 1990, when the department "reorganized the munitions licensing function under the Center for Defense Trade . . . due, at least in part, to repeated complaints from industry of unnecessary time delays and general incompetence."[83] In the Department of Defense the main actors are the Office of the Assistant Secretary of Defense for International Security (OAS/ISA) and the Defense Security Assistance Agency (DSAA). At the level of the individual services, the Air Force, for example, maintains the Air Force Center for International Programs. To further illustrate the fragmentation of the decision-making process, "a single arms case might require as many as twenty signatures before it is cleared and Congress, whose own participation is constantly expanding, is notified."[84] Hammond et al. argue that one of the achievements of the Carter administration in its arms export policy was "[t]he imposition of an enduring managerial discipline over an ad hoc, fragmented, and sometimes chaotic decision making structure."[85]

For East-West trade, licensing authority lies primarily with the Department of Commerce. Until 1987, the Office of Export Administration reviewed license requests. Then the Commerce Department reorganized its export control activities under a new Bureau of Export Administration that is headed by an under secretary, instead of just a deputy assistant secretary. Besides the Department of Commerce, the Pentagon also plays a significant role that adds another player to the decision-making process and further decentralizes it. In fact, during the 1980s Pentagon participation in export control decisions became a hotly contested issue.

In order to prevent the further spread of nuclear weapons technology, the Department of Commerce maintains controls on the export of "dual-use" items that could be used for constructing or testing nuclear explosives. The Nuclear Regulatory Commission licenses the export of production facilities, such as nuclear reactors, and of nuclear fuel. In terms of case load and economic significance, the Department of Commerce plays a more important role than the NRC. For example, in fiscal year 1991 the Commerce Department reviewed 19,741 license

requests for nuclear nonproliferation reasons.[86] In contrast to that,
"[t]he NRC [only] issued 119 new export licenses and 51 minor
amendments to existing licenses" in fiscal year 1989.[87]

Presumably, state centralization will minimize intra-agency
conflict and encourage cohesiveness, while fragmentation contributes to
bureaucratic infighting and to conflicts over policy content. At least for
the issue areas considered here, the German state appears as more
cohesive than the American state. This can be seen most clearly in the
area of East-West trade. Particularly during the Reagan years, intra-
executive conflicts over export controls were rampant, and frequently
the major participants in these conflicts fought their battles not only
behind closed doors but in public forums as well. Typically, such
conflicts pitted the more pro-trade oriented Department of Commerce
against the more restrictive Department of Defense.[88] As Jacobsen
points out, the situation looks rather different in Germany:

There is a basic consensus in the Federal Republic of Germany (FRG) on the
desirability of non-strategic trade with the East. . . . There is virtually no
opposition to improving economic ties with the East. Indeed there has been no
domestic public debate about the necessity or desirability of export control vis-à-
vis the East for decades.[89]

At least in the 1970s the West German state also achieved a
relatively high degree of cohesiveness in the area of nuclear export
policy. Lothar Wilker provided us with a detailed case study of one of
the internationally most controversial West German nuclear exports,
the German-Brazilian deal of 1975. Although this cooperation
agreement received considerable attention and led to diplomatic
tensions between Germany and the United States, the decision-making
and coordination process among West German ministry officials worked
smoothly without major conflicts.[90] Where this cohesiveness has
broken down, however, is in the area of arms exports to the Third
World, including dual-use technologies with potential applications for
chemical and nuclear weapons and ballistic missile programs. For
example, in the 1980s the West German foreign office favored a more
restrictive policy on nuclear technology exports than the ministries for
the economy and for research and technology. Typically, the foreign
office lost in these intra-bureaucratic conflicts.[91] On the whole,
however, the preceding analysis has shown that the laxness of German
export controls relative to their U.S. counterparts is not due to a lack of
centralization in state structures and decision-making processes.

Policy Networks

German state-society relations are characterized by a large number of "parapublic" institutions linking state and societal actors. In the United States we find such institutions less often. This pattern holds true for export control policy. For the issues considered here, the best examples of such close links between state and society operate in the area of East-West trade. The sectors of the German economy, which have an interest in East-West trade, are represented by the *Ostausschuß der deutschen Wirtschaft* (East-West trade committee of the German business community). In 1952 the late economics minister Ludwig Erhard had actively pushed for the creation of the *Ostausschuß*.[92] During the early years of the Federal Republic the formally private institution, the *Ostausschuß*, played the role of an extended arm of the West German executive branch.[93] In fact, the *Ostausschuß* negotiated trade agreements for West Germany with communist nations.[94]

The so-called joint commissions (*gemischte Kommissionen*) represent a more recent example of the blurring of the distinction between state and society in Western Germany. On the basis of cooperation agreements between West Germany and the U.S.S.R and Eastern European countries, joint commissions were formed in the 1970s which, on the West German side, included both high-ranking government officials and representatives of business associations and companies.[95] Below the level of joint commissions, more specialized sections (*Fachgruppen*) were established that discussed specific areas of cooperation before they reached the level of concrete business negotiations.[96]

This pattern of close state-industry cooperation in Germany, compared to a much more distant relationship in the United States, could also be seen in CoCom negotiations and in the list review process, although differences in this area may be decreasing. German industry representatives regularly participated at CoCom meetings in Paris. Beyond that, cooperation between government and business extended to the process of revising the German export control list and of formulating German proposals for the international CoCom list. For example, after the CoCom decision in June 1990 to drastically reduce the CoCom list and to base CoCom controls on a new "core list," the West German government set up eight working groups that were organized by the affected industries. These groups took on the task of formulating a draft of the German proposal for the new core list. According to one participant in this process, the group in charge of propulsion systems finished this task in one day at a meeting in Munich where the major German jet engine manufacturer MTU has its headquarters.[97]

In the United States, Congress in the 1970s mandated the establishment of technical advisory committees (TACs) to make export control policy more responsive to the needs of American exporters. By and large, however, these efforts failed.[98] In 1987 an influential study by the National Academy of Sciences recommended that

A mechanism should be established (or upgraded) to provide effective two-way communication between the highest levels of government and of the private sector on the formulation and implementation of coordinated national policies that balance military security and national economic vitality. One such group already exists: the President's Export Council (PEC) and its subcommittee on Export Controls. However, its advice currently is not receiving appropriate attention at senior policy levels within the government.[99]

In 1991 a successor study again criticized "the lack of sufficient business involvement."[100] Apparently, some progress has been made, though, and the 1989 annual export administration report mentioned that U.S. industry representatives had participated as advisors in CoCom negotiations.[101]

Concerning policy networks, the evidence shows that in the area of export controls state-industry relations have been less strained in Germany than in the United States. Critics of German export control policy argued, though, that it was exactly this collusion between export control authorities and industry, which explained the numerous lapses in German controls, such as nuclear technology exports to Pakistan.[102] The proposition that variation in policy can be explained with differences in state structures receives only limited support here. When we discussed state centralization, however, we primarily examined formal structures. In the following section we will go beyond formal structures and analyze how export control institutions work in practice, and, more specifically, how bureaucrats and unscrupulous businessmen subverted the licensing process.

Subverting Export Controls

In official West German declarations the government always stressed the restrictive nature of German arms export policy. Although it is true that German policies were more restrictive than those in France, for example, over time German arms exporters found ways around such obstacles. German arms manufacturers frequently cooperate with foreign partners, such as the joint venture Euromissile between the German DASA and a French company. This way German arms technology was sold worldwide without running into conflict with German export control laws.

A group of companies linked to the German businessman Alfred Hempel discovered another loophole in German regulations. Hempel repeatedly supplied India with heavy water, which is used as a moderator in natural uranium reactors. If the heavy water had been shipped through Germany, Hempel would have needed a license. Instead, Hempel typically shipped the heavy water through a company in Switzerland. In 1985, for example, Hempel purchased close to six tons of heavy water from a Soviet company. Supposedly, Hempel had lined up customers in several European countries. With one exception, each customer was to receive 990 kilograms heavy water. This is significant because the Soviet Union had agreed to abide by the London Supplier Guidelines, which call for international safeguards for all shipments of heavy water above one ton per year and customer. These shipments did not reach their alleged customers, however, rather they ended up at the Basel/Mulhouse airport, and from there they went via air freight to Bombay, India. Besides the exploitation of loopholes in German regulations, this case also raises questions about potential Soviet collusion.[103]

But even if Hempel's transactions had required the issuance of licenses by the BAW, it is not clear that the BAW would have given those deals the scrutiny they deserved. Before 1986 the BAW did not even have a separate export control division, rather import and export controls were administered in the same division. Since then, however, export and import control functions have been separated. After 1985, BAW's section VI5 assumed responsibility for a large number of product groups, including chemicals, rubber, asbestos, nonferrous and precious metals, ferrous alloys, and radioactive materials. Besides the section head, seven staff members worked in the section, including two clerical workers and two secretaries. According to Manfred Ruck, a former section head, the case load reached such proportions that a thorough treatment of individual license applications was for the most part impossible.[104]

Even if the volume of license applications overwhelmed the BAW in the 1980s, on occasion foreign intelligence services tipped off German authorities about suspicious activities of German companies. Foreign intelligence services, which most often involved the United States and Britain, provided this information in the form of so-called "nonpapers." There is evidence, however, that at least some German bureaucrats processed "nonpapers" rather sloppily. A former BAW section head wrote in 1984 that anonymous papers of that sort usually ended up in his waste basket.[105] Richard Perle charged that German agencies treated "nonpapers" as "demarche-mallows."[106]

In January 1989 the *New York Times* published information that implicated the German company Imhausen in the building of a chemical weapons plant in Libya. Initially, both the German government and Imhausen followed a strategy of denying the allegations. On February 15, 1989, however, the government issued a report that contained a detailed chronology of actions taken in this case. According to this report, as early as July 5, 1985, the West German embassy in Moscow had informed the foreign office of a tip linking Imhausen to the construction of a pharmaceutical plant in Hong Kong. The embassy also indicated that its source suspected that the alleged pharmaceutical plant was really meant to produce chemical warfare agents, and that the ultimate destination was not Hong Kong but possibly Libya.[107]

Although some of the information presented here may suggest that plain bureaucratic blunders caused these lapses in German export controls, other evidence leads to the conclusion that inadequacies in administrative structures simply reflected policy priorities. Hans Rummer, the former president of the BAW, was most well known for his statement that his agency was an office (*Bundesamt*) for (*für*) the economy (*Wirtschaft*), not against it. The head of the foreign trade division in the economics ministry testified at a *Bundestag* hearing that the responsible politicians had always expressed the wish to administer German export controls as quickly and smoothly as possible. There had been no interest in strict controls.[108] Count Lambsdorff, a former economics minister, concurred and noted that during his tenure the prevention of illegal exports was not an acute issue which ended up on the desk of the minister.[109] One of his successors, Haussmann, added that the BAW had been shaped by its historical origins as more of an export than an export control agency.[110]

Nevertheless, although in the 1980s at least Germany was the black sheep of international export control policy, other countries, including the United States, are not immune from such scandals. After the war with Iraq, U.S. export control policy toward that country became a hotly contested issue with Democrats blaming the Republican Bush administration for its laxity up until the Iraqi invasion of Kuwait, and different departments within the executive branch accusing each other. For example, then Under Secretary of Commerce Dennis Kloske testified before a House subcommittee that his department had attempted to slow the export of highly sensitive technology to Iraq during the late 1980s, but the State Department had worked at cross-purposes because of its desire for good diplomatic relations with Iraq.[111] This episode also shows the difficulty in reforming export control policy. On the one hand, the increased export dependency of the U.S. economy and the end of the Cold War call for less strict controls. On the other hand, high technology should not end up in the hands of Saddam Hussein who just a few years ago appeared as a lesser evil than Khomeini's Iran.

Reforming Export Control Policy

Besides the stiffening of criminal sanctions against export control violations, the German government has also sought to strengthen the administrative base of its export control system. Until 1990 the BAW's export control division consisted of six sections. As part of the reforms of 1989/1990 it expanded from six to twenty-two sections, including a special group on missile technology. Staffing of the division increased from around 70 employees in 1988 to 171 by September 1990.[112] In August 1991 the German cabinet debated legislation to transform the BAW's export control division into a separate agency entitled *Bundes-ausfuhramt*. At that time, one of the unresolved questions about this agency was whether it would continue to operate out of its predecessor's offices at Eschborn or move to Bonn as part of an overall effort to compensate Bonn for the loss of its capital status.[113] On January 23, 1992 the *Bundestag* passed the bill creating the *Bundesausfuhramt*.[114] To attract qualified personnel for the new agency the act authorized special bonuses above the regular federal pay scale.[115] One of the problems that the BAW had faced in the past was its low status and pay. Typically, engineers and natural scientists, who actually have some knowledge of chemical or nuclear technology, could find much more lucrative jobs in the private sector. But even ambitious lawyers, who tend to dominate the German civil service, would not necessarily have wanted to work for the BAW since they would be classified in a lower grade than in a ministry, and promotions within the BAW tended to be very slow. The new act represents an attempt to overcome some of these problems. In its recruitment efforts the new agency has placed particular emphasis on the hiring of engineers and natural scientists to expand its base of technical expertise.[116]

Some opposition politicians and academics also suggested more far-reaching organizational changes. Generally, those suggestions either involve a strengthening of the position of the foreign office at the expense of the economics ministry which has in fact taken place, or the creation of an entirely new export control agency under the supervision of the foreign office.[117] The rationale behind these suggestions was that the primary goal of the economics ministry was to support German industry, so in order to sensitize German export control bureaucrats more to foreign policy concerns, the foreign office should supervise export control administration.

Another German export control agency that has undergone a significant expansion and organizational changes is the *Zollkriminal-*

institut (ZKI), a customs agency, and its successor, the *Zollkriminal-amt*. Although the ZKI enjoyed a better reputation than the BAW, export controls did not neatly fit the traditional profile of this agency either. The ZKI was part of the German fiscal administration. Fiscal authorities generally concentrate on generating and administering revenues for the state rather than on the tasks and skills required for the strict enforcement of export controls on high-technology goods. Organizationally, the ZKI was somewhat of an anomaly. Although the agency had responsibility to coordinate export control enforcement at the federal level, its legal status was that of a local customs agency. This was not only a matter of organization charts but also had negative budgetary and personnel consequences. As part of the reform efforts of the early 1990s the agency has been renamed as *Zollkriminalamt* and its status has been upgraded as well. Substantively, one of the most significant recent tasks of German customs agencies has been to set up a data bank called KOBRA (*Kontrolle bei der Ausfuhr*), which would make it easier for customs officials to access information on suspicious export activities. The ZKI became an object of controversy in one of the latest rounds of amendments to Germany's export control laws when the Christian Democratic–led government wanted to give the ZKI the authority to tap phones. The Social Democrats as the main opposition party opposed this proposal on civil liberties grounds and used their majority in the upper chamber, the *Bundesrat*, to block this legislation until the Christian Democrats found a way to overcome this legislative hurdle.[118]   Parallel to changes in the BAW, the ZKI underwent considerable expansion from 94 employees in 1988 to 300 in 1992. Furthermore, the number of investigations conducted by the ZKI rose substantially.[119]

Although in the 1980s the administration of German export controls generally served more as a whipping boy than a model for the United States to adopt, it is interesting to note that some recent U.S. reform proposals would bring U.S. formal administrative structures more in line with the German system. In 1991 a National Academy of Sciences panel suggested that the president issue a "comprehensive national security directive" covering export controls.[120] At the administrative level, the panel proposed that a single agency should handle the export administration (licensing) functions. This agency should be located within the Department of Commerce, which already handles the bulk of all license applications. The panel did not think that the State Department was "an optimal setting for an administrative agency. The State Department is geared primarily to matters of high-level policy and foreign affairs, not the detailed work of a licensing agency."[121]   Furthermore, the panel advocated greater industry input.[122]

Along similar lines, Senators Heinz and Garn introduced legislation in 1990 that called for a consolidation of export control agencies into a new Office of Strategic Trade and Technology.[123] The proposal differed from that of the National Academy of Sciences (NAS) panel, but the underlying thrust toward greater centralization was similar. Heinz concurred with the NAS on the need for improved industry access to export control policy makers in the executive branch. These proposals again raise the question of the links between institutions and policy content. The experience of U.S. and German export control policies suggests that centralized structures may be used for either rather loose or very restrictive controls.

CONCLUSION

In this chapter I compared the institutional basis of U.S. and German export controls in terms of the degree of state centralization and the nature of the policy networks linking state and societal actors. There is no clear link between the extent of state centralization and the direction of German and U.S. export control policy. Centralized institutions are quite compatible with either tight or permissive controls, and a centralized bureaucracy can perform well or poorly, as shown by the example of the BAW. Regarding policy networks, this study did not uncover major surprises. Close government-industry cooperation in Germany contributed to policies that emphasized export promotion, whereas in the United States the access of industry representatives remained limited.

These mixed results regarding the impact of institutional differences on policy content suggest a more general problem with much of the statist literature. As Gourevitch pointed out,

The basic problem with this line of reasoning is that it provides no explanation for the orientation of state policy in the supposedly state-dominated countries. The advantage of looking at politics and the state is that it helps us get away from the well-known problems of pluralist or Marxian reductionism: policy is not simply traceable to the interests of one or another group. . . . But the notion of a strong state as presently used escapes from this trap at the cost of heading into another: instead of explaining society . . . we have to explain the state. Why does the state go in one direction rather than another? Why does it articulate a particular conception of the national interest over another? Why does it use its leverage over particular groups in some ways and not others?[124]

Ikenberry acknowledges that institutions are structures, and structures constrain policy options but they do not determine them.[125] In more general terms, the problem of structure versus agency is not new. The utility of structural explanations in social science research depends on the level of analysis and the particular research problem at issue. Rarely do structures, such as state institutions, constrain policy choices to the extent that only one option is feasible. However, structures may be so constraining that more conjunctural factors explain only trivial residuals. On the other hand, if structural constraints only rule out the most extreme options, structural explanations lose their bite.

Although the primary focus of this study is export control policy, to what extent do the findings presented here correspond to more general characterizations of the U.S. and German states? For the United States, the fragmentation of both the institutions and decision-making processes in the area of export controls fits the conventional wisdom on the American state rather well. German administrative structures in this issue area also correspond to common German administrative practices to the extent that policy formulation takes place in federal ministries, whereas subordinate agencies are responsible for policy implementation. However, although German export control institutions are more centralized than their U.S. counterparts, this pattern does not hold up for a system-level comparison of the U.S. and German states. Both Germany and the United States have federal systems of government. Thus, one measure of state centralization is the percentage of public employees who are on the federal payroll as opposed to state and local employees. In a highly centralized state we would expect many state functions to be concentrated at the central (federal) level, which should find its expression in the distribution of employees at different levels of government. Excluding the postal service, civilian federal employees represented 13 percent of total government employment in the United States in 1990.[126] The comparable German figure was 10.9 percent.[127] But even if we focus on the German federal executive branch, Mayntz and Scharpf found that "[a] major feature of the policy-making process in the federal departments is its considerable decentralization."[128] Most new proposals or policies are initiated and developed at the lowest level, the sections. The political leadership of the individual departments enjoys only very limited central staff support, and thus its capacity for policy initiation is limited as well.

Despite the German state's decentralization, this does not mean that fragmentation has the same consequences as in the United States. In the early 1970s a view of the American foreign policy process gained prominence that asserted that foreign policy decisions reflect organizational constraints and bureaucratic bargaining far more than presidential leadership.[129] According to Krause and Wilker, the utility of Allison's and other American bureaucratic politics models for analyzing German foreign policy is limited because of different government systems (parliamentary versus presidential) and "differences in size, organization and tradition" of German and U.S. bureaucracies and because the "bureaucratic-politics approach puts undue emphasis on the aspect of a bureaucracy in the process of becoming an independent entity."[130] Contrary to the reputed importance of bureaucratic routines and standard operating procedures, Krause and Wilker argue that "the significance of routine is much lower in a non-executive bureaucracy than it is in a purely executive administration."[131] The German federal bureaucracy falls into the first category, whereas its U.S. counterpart is involved in both policy making and purely administrative processes.

Nevertheless, ingrained administrative practices in the BAW/BAA and the ministry of economics made a reorientation of German export control policy more difficult, and there have been intra-executive conflicts over policy direction. Richard Rose, though, argues that parliamentary systems possess means of resolving conflicts among different executive departments and of reaching collective decisions that the contemporary American presidential system lacks.[132] According to Rose, the United States is governed by a coalition of subgovernments that consist of individual departments or bureaus, corresponding congressional committees and subcommittees, and relevant clientele groups. The problem is that nobody, including the president, is really able to pull these subgovernments together and provide an arena for collective decision making. In parliamentary systems, such as the modified version in Germany, the cabinet, which collectively is responsible for government policy, provides a forum for reaching government-wide decisions and for resolving bureaucratic conflicts.

This discussion of state centralization in Germany has shown that what holds at the level of the state as a whole does not necessarily apply to structures in a specific policy area, such as export controls. More broadly, there are interesting parallels to debates on the utility of the weak/strong state distinction. Partly because of its fragmentation, the American state has been regarded as a weak state. However, some recent studies of American foreign economic policy challenged this conventional wisdom and claimed that the American state was not as weak as it was generally made out to be.[133] According to Mastanduno, export control policy represents an area where the American state deviates from the weak state pattern:

None of the presumed characteristics of American state weakness—the effective penetration of the state by interest groups seeking to fulfill private as opposed to national objectives; the decentralization of governmental authority, in particular the deference of the executive to Congress, owing to the latter's Constitutional prerogative to regulate commerce; or the fragmentation of the executive itself along organizational or institutional lines—posed a significant problem for executive officials in the articulation or pursuit of their export control preferences.[134]

If the American state is not as weak as it is often seen, other authors have argued that, contrary to their initial expectations, Japan and France do not fit an idealized strong state pattern.[135] Despite such results, Ikenberry, Lake, and Mastanduno conclude on the basis of findings on the American state that "while the weak/strong state distinction may be appropriate for comparative purposes, it is of limited utility in the analysis of a single case."[136] The logic behind this argument is not clear to me. If strong states are not really strong and weak states are not really weak, the weak/strong state distinction not only tells us little about single cases, but it is useless for comparative purposes as well.

Although state centralization or the lack thereof cannot explain the differences between U.S. and German export control policies, the extreme fragmentation of the American state in this policy area retards policy change.[137] In the past, the exercise of effective veto power by the Department of Defense ensured that security concerns took precedence over economic or foreign policy considerations and helped to block attempts at liberalization.[138] In the German case, a tight policy network, which had been established over the years, inhibited a far-reaching reorientation of German export control policy. Until 1989 German export control policy and its enforcement was handled primarily by a few sections in the ministry of economics, the foreign office, two subordinate agencies, the *Bundesamt für Wirtschaft* and the *Zollkriminalinstitut*, and industry representatives as the primary clients. The issue rarely received much public attention. After the Rabta affair and a series of other scandals this changed, and the policy-making process opened up to some extent. Parliament became involved through investigative committees, a public hearing, and the passage of new legislation. This also meant that political parties made export control policy one of their bones of contention. More broadly, German institutions provided few access channels for new ideas. However, once a series of scandals had created a window of opportunity for change, it was relatively easy to implement a comprehensive set of reforms. In the United States, on the other hand, outsiders face fewer obstacles to making their voices heard, but it is equally easy to block the adoption and implementation of new ideas.

If one takes a longer historical view, the recent policy debates in the United States and Germany show the constraints of past choices. U.S. export controls originated in the highly charged atmosphere of the Cold War period of the 1940s. This set the standard for strict controls. In Germany the foreign trade act of 1961 reflected the credo of free market liberals who had received a boost in the post–World War

II period.[139] But although past choices and their institutionalization may constrain future possibilities for policy change, the pressures for change originate primarily in changes in the international system, such as the end of the Cold War, or in domestic politics.

NOTES

1. Russell Baker and Robert Bohlig, "The Control of Exports—A Comparison of the Laws of the United States, Canada, Japan, and the Federal Republic of Germany," *International Lawyer* 1 (January 1967): 166–167. Oerter has provided a more recent evaluation of changes in German export control laws and compared German practices to the situation in France, the United States, and some smaller European nations. See Stefan Oerter, "Neue Wege der Export-kontrolle im Bereich der Rüstungsgüter," *Zeitschrift für Rechtspolitik* 25 (February 1992): 49–55.

2. Country group H included Egypt, Ethiopia, Afghanistan, Albania, Algeria, Angola, Argentina, Bahrain, Brazil, Bulgaria, Chile, China, Djibouti, Guyana, India, Iraq, Iran, Israel, Jordan, Cambodia, Quatar, Comoro Islands, North and South Korea, Cuba, Kuwait, Laos, Lebanon, Libya, Morocco, Mauritania, Monaco, Mongolia, Mozambique, Myanmar, Namibia, Niger, Oman, Pakistan, Romania, Zambia, Zimbabwe, Singapore, Somalia, South Africa, Syria, Taiwan, Tanzania, United Arab Emirates, Vanuatu, Vietnam, Saudi Arabia, and the Republic of Yemen. Some of these countries were put in group H only because they had not signed the Nuclear Non-Proliferation Treaty. Therefore, restrictions applied only for goods listed in section I B of the *Ausfuhrliste*.

3. "GUS-Staaten ausgespart," *Handelsblatt*, 23 January 1992, p. 8; Germany, Deutscher Bundestag, *Drucksache* 12/2033.

4. The K list includes Afghanistan, Angola, the territory of Yugoslavia according to the boundaries of 22 December 1991, Cuba, Lebanon, Libya, Iran, Iraq, Mozambique, Myanmar, North Korea, Somalia, and Syria.

5. For more detailed discussions of the statutory basis of German arms export controls up to 1989 see Michael Brzoska, "Bundesdeutsche Rüstungs-exporte in die Dritte Welt: Daten—Verfahren—Zusammenhänge," in *Militarismus und Rüstung: Beiträge zur ökumenischen Diskussion*, ed. Bernhard Moltmann (Heidelberg: Forschungsstätte der evangelischen Studiengemeinschaft, 1981), pp. 175–182; Michael Brzoska, "Neue Richtlinien für den Waffenexport aus der Bundesrepublik Deutschland in die Dritte Welt," *Jahrbuch Dritte Welt: Daten, Übersichten, Analysen* 1 (Munich: Verlag C.H. Beck, 1983), pp. 88–89; Eckehart Ehrenberg, *Der deutsche Rüstungsexport: Beurteilung und Perspektiven* (Munich: Bernard & Graefe Verlag, 1981), pp. 66–67; Frederic S. Pearson, "'Necessary Evil': Perspectives on West German Arms Transfer Policies," *Armed Forces & Society* 12 (Summer 1986): 531–534. A more recent analysis is provided by Herbert Wulf, "The Federal Republic of Germany," in *Arms Export Regulations*, ed. Ian Anthony (Oxford: Oxford University Press, 1991), pp. 72–85. The most detailed recent discussion of the war weapons control act has been provided by Klaus Pottmeyer, *Kriegswaffenkontrollgesetz: Kommentar* (Cologne: Carl Heymanns, 1991). However, Pottmeyer works as an attorney for Rheinmetall, a major German arms

manufacturer, and this has biased his interpretation in favor of industry concerns and toward a rather narrow view of the act's criminal provisions.

6. For a more extended legal analysis, which does not cover the most recent changes, however, see Gerhard Meyer-Wöbse, *Rechtsfragen des Exports von Kernanlagen in Nichtkernwaffenstaaten*, Studien zum International Wirtschaftsrecht und Atomenergierecht, vol. 62 (Cologne: Carl Heymanns Verlag KG, 1979). A valuable update has been provided by Harald Müller et al., *From Black Sheep tp White Angel? The New German Export Control Policy*, PRIF Reports No. 32 (Frankfurt: Hessische Stiftung Friedens- und Konfliktforschung, 1994).

7. Joseph P. Smaldone, "U.S. Commercial Arms Exports: Policy, Process and Patterns," in *Marketing Security Assistance: New Perspectives on Arms Sales*, eds. David J. Louscher and Michael D. Salomone (Lexington, Mass.: Lexington Books, 1987), p. 185.

8. John Heinz, *U.S. Strategic Trade: An Export Control System for the 1990s* (Boulder: Westview Press, 1991), pp. 21–25.

9. U.S. Department of Commerce, *Export Administration Annual Report Fiscal Year 1991* (Washington, D.C.: Government Printing Office, 1992), p. 15.

10. National Academy of Sciences, *Finding Common Ground*, p. 87.

11. Ibid.

12. U.S. Department of Commerce, *Export Administration Annual Report 1992* (Washington, D.C.: Government Printing Office, 1993), pp. 19–20.

13. "Liberaler Widerstand," *Wirtschaftswoche*, 5 December 1986, p. 21.

14. "Export Control List Debated," *New York Times*, 14 May 1986, p. 38.

15. U.S. Department of Commerce, *Export Administration Annual Report FY 1984*, p. 12.

16. Personal interview, Michael Waldmann, *Bundesamt für Wirtschaft*, Eschborn, December 16, 1986.

17. Pearson, " 'Necessary Evil,'" p. 534.

18. See annual reports for 1984, 1989, 1991, 1992, and 1993.

19. Author's calculations based on Germany, Deutscher Bundestag, *Drucksachen*, 12/3884, 12/4794, 12/7353.

20. Ibid.

21. Harold J. Berman and John R. Garson, "United States Export Controls— Past, Present and Future," *Columbia Law Review* 67 (May 1967): 792.

22. Gary K. Bertsch, "U.S. Export Controls: The 1970s and Beyond," *Journal of World Trade Law* 15 (February 1981): 78–79.

23. Long, *U.S Export Control Policy*, p. 2.

24. For more in-depth historical overviews see Richard F. Grimmett, "The Role of Security Assistance in Historical Perspective," in *U.S. Security Assistance: The Political Process*, eds. Ernest Graves and Steven A. Hildreth (Lexington, Mass.: Lexington Books, 1985), pp. 1–40; Roger P. Labrie, John G. Hutchins, and Edwin W. A. Peura, with the assistance of Diana H. Richman, *U.S. Arms Sales Policy: Background and Issues* (Washington, D.C.: American Enterprise Institute for Public Policy Research, 1982), pp. 5–18; Paul Y. Hammond, David J. Louscher, Michael D. Salomone, and Norman A. Graham, *The Reluctant Supplier: U.S. Decisionmaking for Arms Sales* (Cambridge, Mass.: Oelgeschlager, Gunn & Hain, 1983), chapters 3, 5, and 6.

25. Labrie et al., *U.S. Arms Sales Policy*, p. 9.

26. Smaldone, "U.S. Commercial Arms Exports," p. 186.

27. For useful discussions of the historical background see Robert L. Beckman, *Nuclear Non-Proliferation: Congress and the Control of Peaceful Nuclear Activities* (Boulder: Westview Press, 1985); Michael J. Brenner, *Nuclear Power and Non-Proliferation: The Remaking of U.S. Policy* (Cambridge: Cambridge University Press, 1981) for the time period of 1974 through the Carter years; and William Epstein, *The Last Chance* (New York: The Free Press, 1976) for the time until the early 1970s.

28. As quoted in Epstein, *The Last Chance*, p. 8.

29. Harald Sieg, Hans Fahning and Karl Friedrich Kölling, *Außenwirtschaftsgesetz: Kommentar* (Berlin: Verlag Franz Vahlen, 1963), p. 1.

30. Gerhard Ollig, "Rechtliche Grundlagen des Innerdeutschen Handels," in *Handelspartner DDR: Innerdeutsche Wirtschaftsbeziehungen*, eds. Claus-Dieter Ehlermann, Siegfried Kupper, Horst Lambrecht, and Gerhard Ollig (Baden-Baden: Nomos, 1975), pp. 149–156.

31. Johannes Hausknecht, *Das Bundesamt für gewerbliche Wirtschaft: Geschichte, Aufgaben, Organisation* (Eschborn: Bundesamt für gewerbliche Wirtschaft, 1975), p. 6.

32. Ibid., pp. 6–7.

33. Personal interview, Waldmann, BAW, December 16, 1986.

34. Adler-Karlsson, *Western Economic Warfare*, pp. 71–74.

35. *Frankfurter Allgemeine Zeitung*, 11 June 1992, p. 16.

36. For a more detailed description of West German arms transfers in the 1960s see Helga Haftendorn, *Militärhilfe und Rüstungsexporte der BRD* (Dusseldorf: Bertelsmann Universitätsverlag, 1971).

37. Brzoska, "Neue Richtlinien," p. 87.

38. Ibid., pp. 94–96.

39. West Germany, Presse- und Informationsamt der Bundesregierung, *Bulletin*, no. 38 (5 May 1982), pp. 309–311.

40. *Woche im Bundestag*, 29 June 1994, p. 59.

41. Germany, Deutscher Bundestag, *Drucksache* 12/104.

42. *Congressional Quarterly Weekly Report*, 9 June 1990, p. 1778.

43. *Congressional Quarterly Weekly Report*, 21 July 1990, p. 2289.

44. *Congressional Quarterly Weekly Report*, 13 March 1993, p. 589.

45. National Academy of Sciences, *Finding Common Ground*, pp. 81, 101.

46. Kurt Tudyka, "Gesellschaftliche Interessen und Auswärtige Beziehungen: Das Röhrenembargo," *Politische Vierteljahresschrift*, vol. 10, Sonderheft, no. 1 (1969), pp. 210–211.

47. Angela E. Stent, *From Embargo to Ostpolitik: The Political Economy of West German-Soviet Relations 1955–1980* (Cambridge: Cambridge University Press, 1980).

48. Christian Loeck, "Die Politik des Transfers konventioneller Rüstung: Strukturen und Einflußfaktoren im Entscheidungsprozess," in *Verwaltete Außenpolitik: Sicherheits- und entspannungspolitische Entscheidungsprozesse in Bonn*, eds. Helga Haftendorn, Wolf-Dieter Karl, Joachim Krause, and Lothar Wilker (Cologne: Verlag Wissenschaft und Politik, 1978), pp. 215, 218.

49. Haftendorn, *Militärhilfe*, p. 68.

50. U.S. Congress, House, Committee on Foreign Affairs, *Executive-Legislative Consultation on U.S. Arms Sales*, Congress and Foreign Policy Series, no. 7 (Washington, D.C.: Government Printing Office, 1982).

51. Martha Liebler Gibson, "Managing Conflict: The Role of the Legislative Veto in American Foreign Policy," *Polity* 26 (Spring 1994): 441–472.

52. *Congressional Quarterly Weekly Report*, 7 June 1986, pp. 1262–1263.

53. *Congressional Quarterly Weekly Report*, 24 May 1986, pp. 1164–1165.

54. Beckman, *Nuclear Non-Proliferation*.

55. Ronald J. Bettauer, "The Nuclear Non-Proliferation Act of 1978," *Law and Policy in International Business* 10 (1978): 1177.

56. Berman and Garson, "United States Export Controls," p. 792.

57. West Germany, *Drucksache* 10/3342, pp. 1–2.

58. West Germany, Deutscher Bundestag, *Drucksache* 11/6141; Holger Koppe and Egmont R. Koch, *Bombengeschäfte: Tödliche Waffen für die Dritte Welt* (Munich: Knesebeck & Schuler, 1990).

59. Germany, Deutscher Bundestag, *Drucksache* 11/7800.

60. West Germany, *Verhandlungen des Deutschen Bundestages*, 11. Wahlperiode, Stenographische Berichte 11/153; West Germany, Deutscher Bundestag, *Drucksache* 11/3995; West Germany, *Verhandlungen des Deutschen Bundestages*, 11. Wahlperiode, Stenographische Berichte 11/215; personal interviews, 25 June and 9 July 1990.

61. West Germany, Deutscher Bundestag, *Drucksache* 11/4609.

62. West Germany, *Verhandlungen des Deutschen Bundestages*, 11. Wahlperiode, Stenographische Berichte 11/215.

63. West Germany, Deutscher Bundesrat, *Stenographischer Bericht* 615.

64. West Germany, Deutscher Bundesrat, *Drucksache* 396/90.

65. Thomas Ellwein, *Das Regierungssystem der Bundesrepublik Deutschland*, 5th edition (Opladen: Westdeutscher Verlag, 1983), p. 290.

66. "Waffenexport-Gesetz scheitert im Vermittlungsausschuß," *Frankfurter Allgemeine Zeitung*, 4 June 1991, p. 1.

67. "Exportkontrollgesetz wird abermals beraten," *Frankfurter Allgemeine Zeitung*, 27 June 1991, p. 17.

68. Stephen Kinzer, "Germany Acts to Curb Arms Exports," *New York Times*, 24 January 1992, p. A3.

69. Wolf-Dieter Karl and Joachim Krause, "Außenpolitischer Strukturwandel und parlamentarischer Entscheidungsprozess," in *Verwaltete Außenpolitik: Sicherheits- und entspannungspolitische Entscheidungsprozesse in Bonn*, eds. Helga Haftendorn, Wolf-Dieter Karl, Joachim Krause, and Lothar Wilker (Cologne: Verlag Wissenschaft und Politik, 1978), p. 79.

70. Bundesverband der Deutschen Industrie, *Bericht 1986–88 des Bundesverbandes der Deutschen Industrie e.V.* (Cologne: BDI, 1988), pp. 450–451. Mann, who has written the most in-depth recent study of the BDI, does not fully agree that there is a clear ranking among the targets of influence attempts by interest groups. Rather, each case is different, the importance of particular institutions and decision makers varies considerably, and the BDI adjusts its strategy accordingly. See Siegfried Mann, *Macht und Ohnmacht der Verbände: Das Beispiel des Bundesverbandes der Deutschen Industrie e.V. (BDI) aus empirisch-analytischer Sicht* (Baden-Baden: Nomos, 1994), p. 247.

71. Joel D. Aberbach, Robert D. Putnam, and Bert Rockman, *Bureaucrats and Politicians in Western Democracies* (Cambridge: Harvard University Press, 1981), pp. 90–91.

72. Personal interview, Waldmann, BAW, December 16, 1986.

73. Franklin D. Cordell for John L. Ellicott, "Judicial Review Under the Export Administration Act of 1979: Is It Time to Open the Courthouse Doors to U.S. Exporters," in National Academy of Sciences, *Finding Common Ground: U.S. Export Controls in a Changed Global Environment* (Washington, D.C.: National Academy Press, 1991), p. 332.

74. Ibid., p. 330.

75. *Congressional Quarterly Weekly Report*, 23 February 1991, p. 455.

76. Stent, *Technology Transfer*, p. 57.

77. Personal interview, ministry of economics, Bonn, June, 21, 1990.

78. Brzoska, "Bundesdeutsche Rüstungsexporte," p. 78.

79. Arnold Brecht and Comstock Glaser, *The Art and Technique of Administration in German Ministries* (Cambridge: Harvard University Press, 1940; reprint ed., Westport, Conn.: Greenwood Press, 1971), pp. 6–12.

80. Ibid., p. 9.

81. Smaldone, "U.S. Commercial Arms Exports," p. 195.

82. National Academy of Sciences, *Finding Common Ground*, p. 81.

83. Ibid., p. 80.

84. Jo L. Husbands, "How the United States Makes Foreign Military Sales," in *Arms Transfers in the Modern World*, eds. Stephanie G. Neuman and Robert E. Harkavy (New York: Praeger, 1979), p. 158.

85. Hammond et al., *The Reluctant Supplier*, p. 98.

86. U.S. Department of Commerce, *Export Administration Annual Report FY 1991*, p. 24.

87. U.S. Nuclear Regulatory Commission, *Annual Report 1989*, p. 116.

88. John McIntyre, "The Distribution of Power and the Interagency Politics of Licensing East-West High Technology Trade," in *Controlling East-West Trade and Technology Transfer: Power, Politics, and Policies*, ed. Gary K. Bertsch (Durham: Duke University Press, 1988), pp. 97–133.

89. Hanns-Dieter Jacobsen, "East-West Trade and Export Controls: The West German Perspective," in *Controlling East-West Trade and Technology Transfer: Power, Politics and Policies*, ed. Gary K. Bertsch (Durham: Duke University Press, 1988), p. 159.

90. Lothar Wilker, "Das Brasilien-Geschäft—Ein 'diplomatischer Betriebsunfall'?" in *Verwaltete Aussenpolitik: Sicherheits- und entspannungspolitische Entscheidungsprozesse in Bonn*, eds. Helga Haftendorn, Wolf-Dieter Karl, Joachim Krause, and Lothar Wilker (Cologne: Verlag Wissenschaft und Politk, 1978), p. 199.

91. Harald Müller, *Nach den Skandalen: Deutsche Nichtverbreitungspolitik*, HSFK-Report 5/1989 (Frankfurt: Hessische Stiftung Friedens- und Konfliktforschung, 1989), pp. 31–32.

92. Otto Wolff von Amerongen, "Außenwirtschaft und Außenpolitik: Aus den Anfängen des deutschen Osthandels nach dem Zweiten Weltkrieg," *Osteuropa* 29 (May 1979): 420. Erhard's initiatives had been preceded by a variety of activities among German business representatives. A key reason why this

committee was not formed earlier was fear of adverse American reactions at a time when West Germany was still subject to occupation law. See the detailed account by Karl-Heinz Schlarp, "Das Dilemma des westdeutschen Osthandels und die Entstehung des Ost-Ausschusses der Deutschen Wirtschaft 1950–1952," *Vierteljahrshefte für Zeitgeschichte* 41 (April 1993): 223–276.

93. Claudia Wörmann, *Der Osthandel der Bundesrepublik Deutschland: Politische Rahmenbedingungen und ökonomische Bedeutung* (Frankfurt: Campus Verlag, 1982), p. 22.

94. Michael Kreile, *Osthandel und Ostpolitik* (Baden-Baden: Nomos, 1978), p. 48.

95. Wörmann, *Der Osthandel*, pp. 172–175.

96. Kreile, *Osthandel und Ostpolitik*, p. 156.

97. Personal interview, ministry of economics, Bonn, July 10, 1990.

98. Long, *U.S. Export Control Policy*, pp. 42–43.

99. National Academy of Sciences, *Balancing the National Interest: U.S. National Security Export Controls and Global Economic Competition* (Washington, D.C.: National Academy Press), p. 176.

100. National Academy of Sciences, *Finding Common Ground*, p. 103.

101. U.S. Department of Commerce, *Export Administration Annual Report FY 1989* (Washington, D.C.: Government Printing Office, 1990), pp. 8–9.

102. Müller, *Nach den Skandalen*.

103. Germany, Deutscher Bundestag, *Drucksache 11/7800*, pp. 750–751.

104. Ibid., pp. 713–714.

105. Ibid., p. 717.

106. Ibid., p. 718.

107. West Germany, Deutscher Bundestag, *Drucksache 11/3995*, p. 5.

108. Germany, Deutscher Bundestag, *Drucksache 11/7800*, p. 712.

109. Ibid.

110. Ibid., p. 714.

111. Clyde H. Farnsworth, "Official Reported to Face Ouster After His Dissent on Iraq Exports," *New York Times*, 10 April 1991, p. A1.

112. Germany, Deutscher Bundestag, *Drucksache 11/8510*, p. 3.

113. "Standort für Exportamt bleibt offen," *Frankfurter Allgemeine Zeitung*, 15 August 1991, p. 9. This question has since been resolved. The BAA will remain in Eschborn, but a branch office has been established in Berlin which is responsible for the import certificate/delivery verification system. See "Zuständigkeiten verlagert," *Frankfurter Allgemeine Zeitung*, 17 August 1993, p. 9.

114. "Der Bundestag beschließt Verschärfung der Exportkontrollen," *Frankfurter Allgemeine Zeitung*, 24 January 1992, p. 1.

115. Germany, Deutscher Bundestag, *Drucksache 12/1461*.

116. "Spezialisten haben bei der Ausfuhrkontrolle jetzt mehr zu sagen," *Frankfurter Allgemeine Zeitung*, 11 June 1992, p. 16.

117. West Germany, *Verhandlungen des Deutschen Bundestages*, 11. Wahlperiode, Stenographische Berichte 11/153, p. 11586; Müller, *Nach den Skandalen*, pp. 43-44.

118. Germany, Deutscher Bundestag, *Drucksache 12/400*.

119. German Information Center, *Focus On Export Controls*, pp. 4–5.

120. National Academy of Sciences, *Finding Common Ground*, p. 140.

121. Ibid., p. 145.

122. Ibid., pp. 151–153.

123. Heinz, *U.S. Strategic Trade*, pp. 146–149.

124. Gourevitch, "The Second Image Reversed," p. 903.

125. Ikenberry, "Conclusion: An Institutional Approach," p. 242.

126. U.S. Bureau of the Census, *Statistical Abstract of the United States: 1992* (Washington, D.C.: Government Printing Office, 1992), p. 305.

127. Germany, Statistisches Bundesamt, *Statistisches Jahrbuch 1992 für die Bundesrepublik Deutschland* (Wiesbaden: Metzler & Poeschel, 1992), p. 541. This figure does not include employees in the new Eastern German states.

128. Renate Mayntz and Fritz W. Scharpf, *Policy-Making in the German Federal Bureaucracy* (Amsterdam: Elsevier, 1975), p. 46.

129. Graham T. Allison, *Essence of Decision: Explaining the Cuban Missile Crisis* (Boston: Little, Brown and Company, 1971).

130. Joachim Krause and Lothar Wilker, "Bureaucracy and Foreign Policy in the Federal Republic of Germany," in *The Foreign Policy of West Germany: Formation and Contents*, eds. Ekkehart Krippendorff and Volker Rittberger, German Political Studies, vol. 4 (Beverly Hills, Calif.: Sage, 1980), p. 148.

131. Ibid., p. 154.

132. Richard Rose, "Government Against Sub-Governments: A European Perspective on Washington," in *Presidents and Prime Ministers*, eds. Richard Rose and Ezra N. Suleiman (Washington, D.C.: American Enterprise Institute for Public Policy Research, 1980), pp. 284–347.

133. Ikenberry et al., "Introduction: Approaches to Explaining American Foreign Economic Policy," pp. 3, 11.

134. Mastanduno, "Trade As a Strategic Weapon," p. 128.

135. Peter A. Hall, *Governing the Economy: The Politics of State Intervention in Britain and France* (New York: Oxford University Press, 1986), p. 17; Helen Milner, "Resisting the Protectionist Temptation: Industry and the Making of Trade Policy in France and the United States During the 1970s," *International Organization* 41 (Autumn 1987): 661–662; Richard J. Samuels, *The Business of the Japanese State: Energy Markets in Comparative and Historical Perspective* (Ithaca: Cornell University Press, 1987), p. 286.

136. Ikenberry et al., "Introduction: Approaches to Explaining American Foreign Economic Policy," p. 11.

137. For a more general discussion of factors which block change see Goldmann, *Change and Stability in Foreign Policy*.

138. Gary K. Bertsch, "U.S. Export Controls," p. 77.

139. Manfred Schmidt, "West Germany: The Policy of the Middle Way," *Journal of Public Policy* 7 (April 1987): 148.

3

Hegemons, Regional Powers, and Trading States

Comparisons of U.S. and German export control policies typically stress that the United States pursues more restrictive policies to further political objectives, whereas German export controls take a backseat to Germany's commercial interests. In the area of arms trade, the United States has used arms exports for the most part as a foreign policy tool, whereas Western European suppliers relied on exports largely to achieve the economies of scale necessary to maintain an independent defense industry. As a recent study by the Office of Technology Assessment put it, "[t]he United States is the only major Western supplier whose arms export policies have been primarily motivated by political considerations."[1] Regarding East-West trade, Beverly Crawford has pointed out that the United States as alliance leader consistently maintained stricter export controls than its alliance partners in part to exercise leadership and thereby send "a signal to Europeans that they should change their preferences for trade promotion and tighten their own export control regulations."[2] To illustrate this point, when the Reagan administration faced severe criticism over its handling of the pipeline controversy of 1982 Vice President Bush responded: "We've heard a lot of protests from our European allies. I am sorry. The United States is the leader of the free world and under this administration we are beginning once again to act like it."[3] For Western Europeans, on the other hand, economic interests in East-West trade weigh much more heavily than for the United States. As Jentleson has shown, "the costs incurred by anti-Soviet export embargoes are . . . distributed highly unequally. The United States bears much smaller relative costs than do Western Europe or Japan."[4]

Civilian nuclear exports became highly controversial in the 1970s. As the United States began to tighten its nuclear export policies in the mid-1970s, West Germany emerged as a significant competitor who was willing to sell not only nuclear power plants but entire nuclear technology packages, such as the agreement to provide Brazil with a complete nuclear fuel cycle. In the late 1980s the West German reputation suffered further due to the lax enforcement of export controls for dual-use technologies.

However, this simple contrast between politically motivated restrictions in the United States and purely commercially oriented policies in Germany does more than just simplify reality but distorts it. In the area of arms exports, "[a] distinctly economic component has entered U.S. international military sales policies in recent years."[5] Furthermore, at least as far as major weapons systems are concerned, German arms export policies in the past showed restraint rather than a purely commercial orientation, although over time restrictive practices have faced a process of erosion.[6] A groundbreaking Stockholm International Peace Research Institute (SIPRI) study distinguished between three patterns of arms transfers: hegemonic, industrial, and restrictive. Whereas U.S. arms transfers fit the hegemonic pattern, West German arms transfers, certainly during the 1970s, corresponded more closely to the restrictive practices of Sweden and Switzerland than the more economically driven policies of France and Great Britain.[7]

Turning to East-West trade, U.S. policies have been restrictive, but this broad label hides the fact that over the past few decades the United States employed different "strategies of economic containment," such as economic warfare, tactical linkage, and strategic embargo.[8] Thus, the principal tasks of this chapter will be to analyze the use of export controls as a tool of economic statecraft and to examine the economic pressures behind export promotion and their impact on U.S. and German policies.

EXPORT CONTROLS AS A TOOL OF ECONOMIC AND MILITARY STATECRAFT

East-West Trade

Over the past 100 years conditions favorable to the exercise of German trade leverage in Eastern Europe have been met twice: under the Nazi regime in the 1930s and since the formation of the Federal Republic in 1949.[9] In 1957, for example, the West German government explicitly tied the negotiation of a trade agreement, which the Soviets had pushed for, to Soviet concessions on the repatriation of ethnic Germans living in the Soviet Union.[10] Similarly, in 1959 West Germany blocked imports from Romania after that country had stopped the emigration of ethnic Germans. In the 1960s, however, the West German government began to pursue at least a partial liberalization of its trade policies toward Eastern Europe.[11] In practice this meant that from the mid-1960s on West German credits to Eastern European customers were eligible for government-backed export credit insurance. Furthermore, the West German government eliminated a large proportion of quotas on imports from Eastern Europe. Easier access to Western credits and import liberalization then helped to prepare the ground for an expansion of West German exports to the Soviet Union and its allies. Although German industry had asked for a "depoliticization" of East-West trade, some of the changes in German trade policies had a political background as well. Gerhard Schröder, who served as German foreign minister from 1961 until 1966, wanted to encourage "polycentric" tendencies in the Eastern bloc and used trade policy toward that end. Thus, Schröder prepared the establishment of diplomatic relations between West Germany and Romania, which occurred under his successor Brandt in January 1967. As an economic reward Romania received officially supported long-term credits and preferential treatment for its exports to the Federal Republic.[12]

Since deténte Germany has viewed East-West trade as a stabilizing influence on relationships otherwise characterized by conflict. German Social Democratic politicians, such as Willy Brandt and Egon Bahr, viewed trade expansion as one instrument to bring about a "transformation of the blocs" and "change through rapprochement," which in the end implied overcoming the division of Europe and of Germany in particular.[13] In regard to export controls, this meant that German policy makers, regardless of party affiliation, recognized the need to maintain controls on militarily relevant technology but opposed the use of export controls for other purposes, such as weakening the economic base of the Soviet Union.

Now, after the fall of the Wall and the revolutionary changes in Eastern Europe, German businesses regard Eastern Europe as a key target for investments.[14] Beyond that, Germany has more at stake in the successful rebuilding of the East European economies than the United States because Germany would feel the failure of Eastern European restructuring efforts more immediately. One concern, in particular, is the fear of increased immigration pressures as a possible result of economic failure and social unrest. In this context, German policy makers at the end of the 1980s regarded extensive and tight CoCom controls as an increasingly intolerable anachronism.

Whereas West Germany was willing to support a policy of strategic embargo against the former Soviet Union, the United States at times used export controls for a variety of other purposes. A strategic embargo seeks to deny the target goods and technology which have direct military significance. One of the difficulties in implementing such a policy is to determine which goods and technologies in fact directly enhance the military capabilities of the target country.

In the 1950s, 1960s, and again during the first Reagan administration, the United States used export controls to pursue a strategy of economic warfare. Compared to a strategic embargo, economic warfare is more ambitious as it seeks to weaken the adversary's economic base. In chapter 6, I will analyze one specific attempt to utilize such a strategy, the efforts of the Reagan administration to block the construction of the Urengoi-Uzhgorod pipeline in the early 1980s. A third strategy, tactical linkage, uses the economic instrument of export controls to achieve political ends. For example, the Nixon administration at various times linked the granting of export licenses to progress in the negotiations over the SALT agreement and the Quadripartite Agreement on Berlin in 1971.[15] In 1978 the United States imposed controls on exports of oil and gas equipment primarily to signal U.S. displeasure over the trial of two prominent dissidents, Anatoly Shcharansky and Aleksandr Ginzburg.[16] Even more well known has been the attempt to link Soviet emigration policies to the granting of most-favored nation status and access to Export-Import Bank credits through the famous Jackson-Vanik amendment, although this link by Congress in fact undermined the policies pursued by Nixon and Kissinger.

To the extent that the United States remains concerned about technology transfer after the end of the Cold War, the focus of that concern has shifted. Rather than attempting to prevent the flow of weapons technology to the East, the United States has embarked on efforts to stem the outflow of Eastern European technology to the Irans, Iraqs, and North Koreas of the world. For example, the United States pressured the Czech Republic to prevent the completion of an Iranian nuclear power plant by Skoda.[17] Nevertheless, there are parallels to U.S. policies during the Cold War when the United States pushed Western Europe to restrict trade with Eastern Europe and the Soviet Union. One tool that the United States used with some success until the 1960s was to offer economic compensation for the trade forgone with the Soviet Union.[18] More recently, the United States apparently succeeded in getting Russia to exercise restraint in transferring missile technology to India. As a reward for such restraint the United States held out the prospect of "space projects with the United States . . . and potential contracts for launching American satellites on Russian rockets."[19] To summarize, whereas Germany and other European states in the past agreed to a limited strategic embargo coordinated by CoCom, the United States tended to employ export controls for more ambitious goals as well.

This contrast also holds true for a comparison of U.S. and German arms transfers.

Arms Exports

Former Secretary of State Cyrus Vance provided us with a rather long list of goals served by U.S. arms transfers:

1. To support diplomatic efforts to resolve major regional conflicts by maintaining local balances and enhancing our access and influence vis-à-vis the parties;
2. To influence the political orientation of nations that control strategic resources;
3. To help maintain regional balances among nations important to us in order to avert war or political shifts away from us;
4. To enhance the quality and commonality of the capabilities of major allies participating with us in joint defense arrangements;
5. To promote self-sufficiency in deterrence and defense as a stabilizing factor in itself and as a means of reducing the level and automaticity of possible American involvement;
6. To strengthen the internal security and stability of recipients;
7. To limit Soviet influence and maintain the balance in conventional arms;
8. To enhance our general access to and influence with government and military elites whose political orientation counts for us on global or regional issues;
9. To provide leverage and influence with individual governments on specific issues of immediate concern to us; and
10. To secure base rights, overseas facilities, and transit rights to support the development and operations of our forces and intelligence systems.[20]

Although some of these rationales, particularly those pertaining to the containment of Soviet influence, have been overtaken by events, many others continue to play a role in U.S. arms transfer policy. For example, in 1994 the Clinton administration justified the decision to sell jet fighters to Argentina by referring to the need to "help preserve the balance of power in the southern part of Latin America."[21] A year later President Clinton unveiled the principles of his administration's arms export policy. According to this policy, "the United States continues to view transfers of conventional arms as a legitimate instrument of U.S. foreign policy . . . when they enable us to help friends and allies deter aggression, promote regional security, and increase interoperability of U.S. forces and allied forces."[22]

In their historical overview of U.S. arms sales policies Hammond et al. argue that three broad factors account for the emergence of arms sales as a major tool in U.S. foreign policy in the 1950s and thereafter. First, U.S. policy makers, and members of Congress in particular, were looking for a way to ease the U.S. foreign assistance burden, and converting grant military aid to foreign military sales appeared as a promising avenue. Second, in the late 1950s the United States began to experience significant balance-of-payments deficits. Arms sales to increasingly affluent allies, such as West Germany, served to partially offset the costs of stationing troops in Europe, which had contributed to U.S. deficits. Third, U.S. arms sales to its allies helped to deal with the problem of "logistics cooperation and weapons standardization within the Atlantic Alliance."[23] At the end of the 1960s President Nixon provided additional impetus to U.S. arms sales through the formulation of the so-called "Nixon Doctrine." According to this doctrine, the United States would no longer use its own military manpower to directly support its regional allies but called on regional powers to provide for their own defense bolstered by U.S. arms sales.[24] The military buildup of Iran constitutes one example of this policy.

German arms transfers have not served such ambitious foreign policy goals as those of the United States. In fact, restrictions on German arms exports represent an attempt to avoid getting involved in political and military conflicts outside of Europe. The official policy of the 1970s to not export arms to so-called "areas of tension" was one concrete example of this restrictive approach. However, German arms export policies did not neatly fit a clearly restrictive pattern in the past, nor do they now. In the 1960s West Germany linked some arms transfers or their cutoff to Third World recipients to the West German claim that the *West* German government was the only legitimate representative of the German people.[25] For example, West Germany provided military aid to a variety of African countries. In 1965 Tanzania agreed to the opening of a consulate general for East Germany in Daressalam, and the West German government promptly cut off the military aid program.[26] In the mid-1980s Frederic Pearson detected a trend toward a more autonomous German foreign policy that included a willingness to use arms transfers as a political instrument:

The point here is not that Bonn has carefully associated arms transfer policies with well-defined and well-ordered political priorities. . . . Rather, the Federal Republic has more or less stumbled into using arms in connection with a more assertive foreign policy. Arms increasingly are seen as a policy instrument offered in part to shore up relations with cooperative states. . . . German business interests are likely to continue to dominate FRG weapons trade in most areas, but as a pivotal European power with independent security concerns, Bonn will feel pressure to assert more autonomous defense agreements abroad and participate in joint European approaches, especially in regions designated as high security priorities.[27]

Nevertheless, despite the fact that German foreign policy may have become more autonomous since the mid-1980s, German arms exports continue to reflect largely, but not exclusively, commercial considerations. Arms exports as a foreign policy instrument can also be linked to the issue of nuclear nonproliferation. To the extent that the desire to acquire nuclear weapons reflects genuine security concerns of would-be proliferators, some analysts have suggested that conventional arms transfers may help to alleviate such fears.[28]

Nuclear Exports

Although arms exports and restrictions thereof may serve a variety of different goals, the purpose of nuclear export controls is rather straightforward and simple, to prevent the spread of nuclear weapons capabilities. U.S. and German policies in this area have differed less in terms of the desirability of nuclear proliferation than in the methods to achieve this end. Underlying the differences in policy is the fact that the United States was the first nation to develop nuclear weapons and to lead the Western world in the commercialization of nuclear energy, whereas Germany renounced the possession of nuclear weapons as early as 1954 but at the same time spent considerable diplomatic effort to fend off restrictions on its civilian nuclear energy program. Essentially the U.S. approach has varied between strict denial and a more liberal policy of controlled cooperation. Right after World War II the United States followed a course of strict denial as expressed in the McMahon Act of 1946. The United States at that time even refused to cooperate with the British who had contributed to the Manhattan project. In 1953 the United States reversed course with Eisenhower's "Atoms for Peace" plan. In the following years, the United States concluded numerous nuclear cooperation agreements with foreign governments and exported both research and power reactors.

During the mid-1960s nonproliferation again became a major item on the U.S. foreign policy agenda under President Johnson, which made possible the successful conclusion of the NPT negotiations. Nonproliferation was a promising avenue along which to pursue détente with the Soviet Union as both superpowers discovered that they had common interests in limiting the number of additional nuclear powers. At the same time, however, incipient cooperation between the United States and the Soviet Union on arms control matters raised fears among the Western allies, and German conservatives in particular, about a superpower "condominium" at Germany's expense. But the NPT represented a high point for U.S. nonproliferation policy. In the late 1960s and early 1970s when the United States looked for a way out of Vietnam and a general reduction in its global security commitments the Nixon administration attached less significance to a vigorous pursuit of nuclear nonproliferation. When India tested a nuclear device in 1974

Henry Kissinger "resisted any action that would place the United States in the position of committing itself to taking severe retaliatory measures against all proliferators present and prospective. In his judgment, the acquisition of a crude nuclear device should not be endowed with great intrinsic value."[29]

In another policy shift beginning in the mid-1970s the United States attempted to impose restrictive trading standards on civilian nuclear commerce, including stricter export controls. Under President Carter the United States backed away from the development of breeder reactors and pressured other countries to forego the use of plutonium as well. The attempts of the Carter administration to gain international agreement on strict nuclear trading standards and the nuclear fuel cycle were only partially successful, however.

In the early 1980s the Reagan administration showed a willingness to relax nuclear trade rules to some extent, but on the whole the United States continued to follow a relatively strict export control policy. An example of the Reagan administration's renewed emphasis on supporting the depressed U.S. nuclear industry and on China's geopolitical significance was the nuclear cooperation agreement between the United States and China in 1985. During the mid-1980s nuclear industry executives around the world hoped to gain access to the Chinese market for nuclear power generating equipment. As a Westinghouse executive put it in congressional testimony in 1984, "the People's Republic of China represents the last major untapped market for the world vendors of nuclear power reactors."[30] The U.S.-People's Republic of China nuclear cooperation agreement laid the legal groundwork for American companies to compete in this market. In the end, however, these hopes were disappointed because the anticipated orders never materialized.

Under President Reagan there was also a clear link between a renewed emphasis on East-West issues and a lower priority for nonproliferation concerns in Asia, the Middle East, South Africa, and Latin America. Reagan succeeded in revitalizing CoCom, although at some cost, but the United States also did not press threshold countries, such as Pakistan, particularly hard to stop their nuclear weapons programs. Israel's, Pakistan's, and South Africa's value in containing Communism was ultimately more important to the Reagan administration than nuclear nonproliferation.[31] With the Cold War clearly over, the Clinton administration appears committed to make nonproliferation a priority concern of its foreign policy, although there is the danger that Clinton will fall into similar traps as the Carter administration and not recognize that a forceful and effective U.S. nonproliferation policy requires an expansive view of U.S. security interests and the commitment of substantial resources rather than retrenchment.

Turning to Germany, in 1954 the Western allies ended the occupation status of West Germany, and the Federal Republic committed itself not to manufacture atomic, biological and chemical weapons.[32]   In the late 1960s the Nuclear Non-Proliferation Treaty became a hotly debated issue in Germany. By the end of 1966 the U.S. and Soviet co-chairmen of the Eighteen-Nation Disarmament Committee (ENDC) came to a tentative agreement on the NPT. On December 20, 1966, the U.S. Ambassador to the Federal Republic McGhee delivered a draft text to the West German government headed by the Christian Democratic Chancellor Kurt Georg Kiesinger and his Social Democratic Foreign Minister Willy Brandt.[33] Within West Germany the proposed NPT generated heated debate. Former Chancellor Adenauer called the treaty a "devilish repetition of the Morgenthau plan."[34] Beyond the hyperbole, at the end of 1966 West German leaders clearly were irritated about the lack of prior consultation between the United States and its allies on this matter.[35] On April 27, 1967, Foreign Minister Brandt answered a series of questions involving the NPT in the German *Bundestag*. He grouped German concerns under four headings. First of all, a nonproliferation treaty should not present obstacles to the peaceful use of nuclear energy. Second, a link should be established to general disarmament, and the willingness of nonnuclear weapons states to renounce the acquisition of nuclear weapons had to be accompanied by the nuclear powers' own disarmament efforts. The third concern involved security guarantees, and fourth, a nonproliferation treaty should not stand in the way of European integration efforts.[36]

In essence, in the 1960s "[t]he Federal Republic's opposition to a nonproliferation arrangement stemmed primarily from Bonn's determination to keep open major options for German foreign policy, all of which seemed in danger of being foreclosed or narrowed by the NPT: German participation in a jointly owned NATO nuclear force and in NATO's nuclear planning and crisis management, the creation of a European nuclear force, and the possibility of retaining (or obtaining) bargaining leverage in future negotiations on the German question."[37] Thus, the issue of German accession to the NPT was part of the larger problem of the role of nuclear weapons in defending Germany and in deterring an attack on the country, a problem that predated international negotiations on the NPT. The West German desire to be more closely involved in NATO nuclear decision making than before reflected concerns about the reliability of American nuclear deterrence and deep skepticism toward the doctrine of "flexible response."[38] Although some German politicians may have had broader nuclear ambitions, "[r]eservations about the nonproliferation treaty stemmed not so much from a desire to own nuclear weapons as from a reluctance to be deprived of the threat of acquiring them."[39] As summarized by Kelleher, Adenauer's foreign policy consisted of three fundamental goals: "security against the Soviet Union, equality within the Western alliance, and the eventual unity of the Germany of 1937."[40] It was not always easy, though, to reconcile these three overarching goals, and in the second half of the 1960s some of the premises on which Adenauer's foreign policy had been based began to unravel. Most importantly, the Cold War lost some of its intensity. West German hesitation in supporting the NPT led to strains in German relations with the United States, and this policy provided Moscow with a useful propaganda tool. As long as West German politicians insisted on keeping increasingly illusory nuclear options open, the Soviet Union could always use German revanchism and potential nuclear ambitions as a bogeyman to keep its own allies in line.

On July 1, 1968, sixty-two countries signed the NPT, but the West German federal government did not sign until November 28, 1969, under a new chancellor. Together with its signature the West German government submitted a note that stated that the Federal Republic would not ratify the treaty until the conclusion of a satisfactory verification agreement between the International Atomic Energy Agency (IAEA) and EURATOM. Following successful negotiations on a model IAEA safeguards agreement and on the relationship between the IAEA and EURATOM, the German *Bundestag* ratified the treaty on February 20, 1974.[41]

Although the NPT as such no longer generated controversy in German politics and Germany remained firmly committed to the treaty, in the mid-1970s German and U.S. nonproliferation policies diverged again. West Germany countered U.S. nonproliferation initiatives by advocating what Walker and Lönnroth call a "spider's web" approach.[42] Rather than isolating proliferation risk countries, this approach called for engaging countries, such as Argentina and Brazil, in a web of cooperative agreements and thereby tying them to the nonproliferation regime. More specifically, the United States and Germany repeatedly clashed over the question of whether nuclear suppliers should require that customers place all nuclear activities under IAEA safeguards. West Germany resisted U.S. and Canadian attempts to include such "full-scope safeguards" in the London suppliers' guidelines of 1976.[43] During the third NPT review conference in 1985 West Germany, Switzerland, and Belgium actively resisted the inclusion of a provision in the conference's final declaration that would have urged all nuclear suppliers to require full-scope safeguards for their exports.[44] In 1990, however, the German government reversed its long-standing policy and decided to require full-scope safeguards as a condition for future German nuclear exports. The second part of this chapter will address the question of whether policy differences between the United States and the Federal Republic of

Germany, and changes in these policies over time, reflect the influence of commercial pressures.

EXPORT CONTROLS AND ECONOMIC COMPETITION

Although the economic costs of export controls have received considerable attention in the United States in recent years, few studies have addressed this issue in more than an impressionistic fashion. Both Germany and the United States publish licensing statistics, but the value of export license denials is not a good indicator of the trade forgone because of export controls. Whereas some companies have their export license requests rejected, others do not even apply either because they expect to be turned down or because the complexity of licensing procedures itself has a deterring effect.

In 1987 the National Academy of Sciences published one of the best studies available which contained a rough estimate of the economic costs of U.S. national security export controls at the time. Table 8 presents the components of this estimate, which totaled $9.3 billion annually. This figure represented only the short-run direct costs and left out other potential cost factors.[45] According to this study, the total impact on employment amounted to 188,340 lost jobs "based on a value of 25,800 jobs lost per $1 billion of exports lost."[46] These costs resulted in an estimated overall gross national product (GNP) loss of $17.1 billion for 1985.[47]

A comparison of the individual components of table 8 shows that although U.S. national security export controls aimed at preventing the former USSR from acquiring strategic technology, the main economic impact was on West-West exports. At the basis of these estimates is the observation that U.S. export controls are stricter and more comprehensive than those of other exporting nations. This puts U.S. exporters at a competitive disadvantage, and some potential U.S. exports will be lost to competitors. Empirically, the estimate of $5.9 billion in lost West-West export sales rests on an analysis of trade data for exports of analytic instruments.[48] In the case of analytic instruments the Commerce Department in April 1984 relaxed regulations for unilaterally controlled exports but tightened regulations again late that year. Observed changes in the level of U.S. analytic instruments exports in 1984 and 1985 form the basis of an estimate of the economic effects of these regulatory changes.[49] The overall $5.9 billion estimate essentially represents an extrapolation of the findings for analytic instruments.[50] The estimate of lost West-East export sales rests more on a number of rough assumptions than on actual empirical data.[51] Thus, one should treat these numbers only as ballpark estimates.

TABLE 8
Components of the Estimated Economic Impact of U.S. National Security
Export Controls in 1985 (in billion dollars)

Component	Impact
Administrative cost to firms	0.5
Lost West-West export sales	5.9
Lost West-East export sales	1.4
Reduced research and development spending	0.5
Value of licenses denied	0.5
Lost profits on export and foreign sales	0.5
TOTAL	9.3

Note: Employment loss = 188,000 jobs.

Source: William F. Finan, "Estimate of Direct Economic Costs Associated with U.S. National
       Security Controls," in National Academy of Sciences, *Balancing the National Interest:*
       U.S. National Security Export Controls and Global Economic Competition (Washington,
       D.C.: National Academy Press, 1987), p. 266.

Furthermore, we also have to consider that export licensing practices
have changed since the mid-1980s. Export license applications dropped
from over 100,000 in the mid-1980s to less than 25,000 in 1992. In
addition, the annual reports by the Commerce Department for 1991 and
1992 contain separate figures for license applications to CoCom
countries. These figures show that between 1991 and 1992 the share of
CoCom license applications fell from 21.7 percent to 15.4 percent. Since
CoCom includes the most important Western trading partners of the
United States, estimates of lost West-West sales due to export controls
may be particularly unreliable. This is confirmed by a recent study on
U.S. export disincentives.[52] The results of Richardson's regression
analysis support the claim that U.S. national security export controls
have had a significant impact on U.S. exports. According to this report,
in 1989 national security export controls cost the United States between
$1.7 and $19.9 billion in lost exports.[53] In contrast to the National
Academy of Sciences study, however, Richardson did not find evidence
for lost West-West sales, but his figures represent lost exports to targeted
countries, including the Soviet Union, Eastern Europe and China.
Furthermore, his analysis suggests that even after the reforms of 1990
national security export controls remained a significant impediment to
U.S. exports.[54]

Despite the very rough nature of these estimates they show that the
economic costs of the U.S. export control system aimed at the former
Soviet Union were substantial. These are not the only costs, however.
Besides national security export controls, the United States also restricts
trade with a variety of countries, such as Iran, Libya, and North Korea,
for foreign policy reasons. Stanley Nollen analyzed one example of such

foreign policy controls and examined the costs to companies in the United States from the use of American sanctions against the Urengoi natural gas pipeline. He estimated that for the time period 1982–1987 these business costs totaled between $3.605 and $4.085 billion.[55] Nollen admits, however, that there may be an upward bias in some of the figures he used.[56] Richardson's study estimates that all foreign policy controls resulted in lost exports totaling $2.4 to $3.1 billion in 1989.[57]

Unfortunately, there are no comparable studies for the economic impact of German export controls. Until fairly recently the German government did not even publish basic licensing statistics. In 1987 the *Bundesamt für Wirtschaft* issued licenses for the export of armaments valued at 6.3 billion Deutsche Mark (DM). Export licenses for goods listed in the nuclear energy section of the *Ausfuhrliste* came to 2.7 billion DM, whereas licenses for other strategic goods reached a level of 19.4 billion DM.[58] As shown in table 9, exports subject to licensing requirements represent a significant but still relatively small proportion of Germany's overall exports. However, as discussed above, the value of export licenses or license denials does not represent a valid indicator of the economic costs of export controls. Another approach to this issue, though, is to analyze trade in those sectors specifically targeted by export controls.

East-West Trade

At the surface level the question of the economic significance of East-West trade for the U.S. and German economies is easy to answer. Although East-West trade is more important for the German economy than for its U.S. counterpart, it is not vital for the health of either the U.S. or German economies. For a more thorough assessment, however, we have to consider several complicating factors. First of all, we should not only examine the overall situation but analyze sector-specific variations as well; and there we find that for some sectors of the German steel and machinery industries the former Soviet Union was one of the best customers. On the other hand, German industry has had much more extensive economic and technological ties to the United States than the former Soviet Union/Russia, and to the extent that the United States used its economic and technological leverage to influence allied East-West trade policies, this created countervailing economic pressures. In the American case it is true that trade with the former Soviet Union was at best only of marginal significance for U.S. trade overall, but the controls that the United States had instituted to limit East-West trade did not only affect U.S. trade with Eastern Europe but resulted in significant economic costs for U.S. trade with Western countries as well.   However,

TABLE 9
Summary of German Export Licensing Statistics (in billion Deutsche Mark)

Year	Total Exports	Value of Export Licenses	Export Licenses as Percentage of Total Exports
1988	568	32**	5.6
1989	641	46**	7.2
1990	643*	21**	3.1
1991	662	33	5.0
1992	671	29	4.3
1993	604	40	6.6

* Does not include the five new (former East German) states.
** Does not include bulk licenses.

Sources: Germany, Deutscher Bundestag, *Drucksachen*, 12/1140, 12/3884. 12/4794, 12/7353.

European observers also raised suspicions that the United States was using national security export controls for its own commercial advantages and that U.S. controls on technology transfers were linked to American efforts to protect its own high-technology sector from other Western competitors.

Examining the empirical evidence, table 10 shows that although exports to the former U.S.S.R. and the European members of Comecon as a whole made up a significantly higher proportion of overall West German exports than of U.S. exports in the 1980s, none of these figures were very high. Furthermore, in the case of West Germany trade with the former Eastern bloc countries constituted a smaller proportion of overall German trade at the end of the decade than at the beginning. Thus, the health of the German economy does not appear to depend on exports to the East. Tables 11 and 12 present data on the value of U.S. and German export licenses to Central and Eastern European destinations in 1989 and the early 1990s. It is somewhat problematic, however, to relate the licensing data to actual export figures because exports may take place during a different year than when the license was granted, or not at all.

An analysis of more disaggregated trade figures shows that the United States tended to export quite different products to the former Soviet Union and Eastern Europe than Germany did. Tables 13 and 14 provide data on U.S. and West German exports to the former Soviet Union and Eastern Europe broken down by broad commodity categories. Whereas U.S. exports to the Soviet Union consisted largely of agricultur-

TABLE 10
Percentage Share of Exports to the CMEA in Total
U.S. and West German Exports

USSR	United States	West Germany
1981	1	1.9
1982	1.2	2.2
1983	1	2.6
1984	1.5	2.2
1985	1.1	2.0
1986	.6	1.8
1987	.6	1.5
1988	.9	1.7
1989	1.2	1.8
Comecon Europe*		
1981	1.9	4.3
1982	1.7	4.3
1983	1.4	4.6
1984	1.9	4.2
1985	1.5	4.0
1986	.9	3.7
1987	.9	3.4
1988	1.1	3.5
1989	1.4	3.8

*Does not include intra-German trade.

Source: Calculations based on OECD, *Monthly Statistics of Foreign Trade*, Series A.

al products, German exports consisted primarily of machinery, steel products, and chemicals. From an export control perspective, the catch is that CoCom rules restricted the export of sophisticated machinery but not of American grain. Furthermore, although Germany conducts considerably more trade with some of its small Western European neighbors than with the former Soviet Union, the Soviet Union played a more significant role for certain sectors of the West German economy. In 1989, for example, exports to the Soviet Union represented 7.2 percent of total West German exports of iron and steel (SITC 67) and 8.9 percent of West German metalworking machinery exports, which includes machine tools. If we analyzed trade figures at the three-digit SITC level or even looked at export sales of certain companies, such as Mannesmann or Salzgitter, the weight of the former Soviet Union as a customer would appear even greater. In regard to West German exports of machinery and transportation equipment as a whole, however, exports to the Soviet Union accounted for only 1.6 percent of all West German SITC 7 exports. Thus, although manufactured products make up the bulk of German exports to Russia and the other Soviet successor states, this fits   the over-

TABLE 11
**Value of German Export Licenses for Eastern European Destinations in 1989
and 1993 (in Deutsche Mark)**

1989

Sections of the Export List (Ausfuhrliste)

Country	A	B	C	D
Bulgaria	483,657	*	28,172,981	290,378
Czecho-slovakia	652,877	*	110,452,222	2,741,313
Hungary	388,384	*	51,144,303	89,003,078
Poland	552,235	*	63,111,940	1,926,680
Romania	10,537	-	2,740,807	182,286
Soviet Union	30,982	*	279,125,722	75,941,467

1993

Sections of the Export List (Ausfuhrliste)

Country	A	B	C	D
Bulgaria	337,135	143,813	91,453,161	460,967
Czech Republic	1,186,118	20,339,471	623,255,833	30,169,205
Slovakia	3,045,518	1,651,081,338	1,721,381,032	1,273,468
Hungary	2,716,130	555,796	705,100,362	7,795,681
Poland	1,289,610	703,095	126,542,538	6,607,671
Romania	105,581	112,464	265,546,859	16,850,014
Russia	29,698,624	3,123,776	467,289,062	239,074,188
Ukraine	1,520,667	*	115,794,926	4,816,219

* For legal reasons the German Federal government does not provide information if there are less than three licensees.

Sources: Germany, Deutscher Bundestag, *Drucksachen*, 12/1140, 12/7353.

all profile of Germany's export oriented industries rather than implying a dependence on Eastern European markets.

There have been years in the recent past, though, when the Soviet Union and Eastern Europe played a more important role as customers of West German industrial goods. As Claudia Wörmann reported, in 1977

TABLE 12
Value of U.S. Export Licenses Granted for Eastern European Destinations in Fiscal Year 1989 and 1992 (in U.S. dollars)

	FY 1989
Albania	28,038
Bulgaria	43,724,766
Czechoslovakia	69,019,490
Hungary	238,130,014
Poland	69,084,601
Romania	327,860,769
USSR	1,279,298,895

	FY 1992
Albania	201,120
Bulgaria	5,652,387
Czechoslovakia	65,925,473
Poland	43,121,831
Romania	4,478,635
Russia	318,156,572
Ukraine	10,064,250

Source: U.S. Department of Commerce, *Export Administration Annual Report FY 1989, FY 1992.*

West Germany sent 17.7 percent of its iron and steel exports and 5.6 percent of its machinery and transportation equipment exports to Comecon nations.[59] On the basis of such figures, Wörmann came to the conclusion that East-West trade played a quite significant role for the German economy and would most likely continue to do so in the future. As more recent developments have shown, her predictions were wrong.

For the United States, exports of steel or machinery to the former Soviet Union were clearly insignificant in relative terms. This was not the case for agricultural exports, however, where the Soviet Union and now its successor states have played an important role as customers. In 1989, for example, 18.9 percent of U.S. cereals and cereals preparations exports (SITC 04) went to the Soviet Union.

TABLE 13
Composition of U.S. Exports to Eastern Europe by Commodity in 1990 (in million U.S. dollars)

	Comecon Europe	USSR
SITC 0 (Food and Live Animals)		
value	2415.023	2157.242
percentage	57%	70%
SITC 1 (Beverages and Tobacco)		
value	70.529	47.558
percentage	2%	2%
SITC 2 (Crude Materials, except Fuels)		
value	264.732	80.092
percentage	6%	3%
SITC 3 (Mineral Fuel, Lubricants)		
value	131.178	29.032
percentage	3%	1%
SITC 4 (Animal and Vegetable Oils etc.)		
value	22.809	22.648
percentage	1%	1%
SITC 5 (Chemicals)		
value	338.576	280.442
percentage	8%	9%
SITC 6 (Manufactured Goods Classified Chiefly by Material)		
value	89.517	44.154
percentage	2%	1%
SITC 7 (Machinery and Transport Equipment)		
value	661.289	331.328
percentage	16%	11%
SITC 8 (Miscellaneous Manufactured Goods)		
value	137.233	62.948
percentage	3%	2%
SITC 9 (Commodities Not Classified Elsewhere)		
value	84.774	16.196
percentage	2%	1%
Total Value of Exports	**4215.660**	**3071.640**

Source: OECD, *Foreign Trade by Commodities*, 1991, Series C, vol. 3 (Paris: OECD, 1992).

One way in which trade dependency becomes a politically volatile issue is through its impact on employment. Jochen Bethkenhagen analyzed the employment effects of exports to Council for Mutual Eco-

TABLE 14
Composition of West German Exports to Eastern Europe by Commodity in 1990 (in million U.S. dollars)

	Comecon Europe	USSR
SITC 0 (Food and Live Animals)		
value	1092.166	508.165
percentage	8%	8%
SITC 1 (Beverages and Tobacco)		
value	80.374	18.752
percentage	1%	0%
SITC 2 (Crude Materials, except Fuels)		
value	248.677	57.391
percentage	2%	1%
SITC 3 (Mineral Fuel, Lubricants)		
value	148.480	19.343
percentage	1%	0%
SITC 4 (Animal and Vegetable Oils etc.)		
value	30.424	9.465
percentage	0%	0%
SITC 5 (Chemicals)		
value	1835.882	732.781
percentage	13%	12%
SITC 6 (Manufactured Goods Classified Chiefly by Material)		
value	2658.210	954.966
percentage	18%	15%
SITC 7 (Machinery and Transport Equipment)		
value	6684.293	3352.099
percentage	46%	53%
SITC 8 (Miscellaneous Manufactured Goods)		
value	1410.499	563.681
percentage	10%	9%
SITC 9 (Commodities Not Classified Elsewhere)		
value	269.552	142.430
percentage	2%	2%
Total Value of Exports	**14458.557**	**6359.073**

Source: OECD, Foreign Trade by Commodities.

nomic Assistance (CMEA) countries for the West German economy by economic sector. As table 15 shows, the overall employment effects of East-West trade were not very high for the West German economy in the

TABLE 15
The Impact of Exports to the CMEA Countries[a] on Employment in the FRG by Sector (in percent of those employed in the sector)

	CMEA (6)				USSR			
	1970	1975	1980	1982	1970	1975	1980	1982
Agriculture & forestry	0.9	0.6	1.2	1.1	0.0	0.1	0.5	0.5
Energy supply & mining	1.0	2.8	1.9	1.7	0.3	1.4	1.0	1.0
Chemicals & oil refining	1.7	3.2	2.6	2.5	0.5	1.0	0.9	0.9
Quarrying, ceramics, glass	0.5	1.4	1.0	1.0	0.1	0.5	0.3	0.4
Metals, manufacture & production	1.8	7.1	4.5	4.6	0.6	3.7	2.7	3.3
Steel & mech. eng., EDP[b]	2.3	5.6	3.8	4.0	0.8	2.7	2.0	2.3
Transport equipment	0.2	1.5	0.4	0.4	0.0	0.8	0.1	0.2
Electrical	0.9	2.1	1.5	1.4	0.3	0.8	0.6	0.6
Precision eng., optics, EBM[c]	1.7	1.3	1.1	1.2	1.1	0.5	0.4	0.5
Wood & paper	0.4	0.8	0.7	0.8	0.1	0.3	0.3	0.4
Textiles & Clothing	0.5	1.4	1.5	1.7	0.2	0.3	0.4	0.5
Food & Drink	0.4	0.4	1.0	1.1	0.0	0.1	0.6	0.6
Trade	0.2	0.5	0.4	0.4	0.1	0.2	0.2	0.2
Transport & postal serv.	0.4	1.0	0.6	0.6	0.1	0.5	0.3	0.3
Other sectors[d]	0.1	0.3	0.2	0.2	0.0	0.1	0.1	0.1
Total	**0.6**	**1.3**	**0.9**	**0.9**	**0.2**	**0.6**	**0.4**	**0.5**

[a]Exclusive of inter-German trade.
[b]Electronic data processing.
[c]Sheet iron and metal products.
[d]Construction, service companies, public sector services, private households.

Source: Jochen Bethkenhagen, "Soviet-West German Economic Relations: The West German Perspective," in *Economic Relations with the Soviet Union: American and West German Perspectives,* ed. Angela E. Stent (Boulder: Westview Press, 1985), p. 76.

1980s, and this was true for most individual sectors as well. The two areas in which exports to the USSR/Commonwealth of Independent States have had a relatively significant impact are the manufacture and processing of metals and steel/mechanical engineering.

A different way to analyze the impact of export controls, and of the Cold War more generally, on German-Russian/Soviet trade is to compare trade patterns during the Cold War to earlier periods in German-Russian relations. The Cold War, and CoCom in particular, disrupted established trade patterns. To the extent that Germany lost traditional markets due to export controls this represented costs to the German economy. It is, of course, impossible to produce reliable estimates of what German-Soviet trade might have amounted to if CoCom had not existed. Nevertheless, it is instructive to discuss the history of German-Russian and German-Eastern European trade not only for historical reasons. With the end of the Cold War, the transition to market economies in Eastern Europe, and the liberalization of export controls to the region many observers expressed expectations (or fears) that Germany, partly because of historical ties to the region, would again dominate Eastern Europe economically. Thus, what role did Germany play?

German-Russian trade relations began shortly after the end of the Thirty Years War when elector Friedrich Wilhelm of Brandenburg sent a mission to Moscow to ask for grain shipments to Brandenburg.[60] In 1726 Prussia and Russia concluded a treaty that protected merchants from high tariffs and which included a "most-favored nation" clause.[61] The nineteenth century witnessed drastic changes in both German and Russian trade policies. In 1865 Germany became the largest exporter to Russia and maintained this position until 1914.[62] Table 16 provides more detailed information on the development of German-Russian trade from the 1880s until the outbreak of World War I. The percentage figures show that the two countries played a much more significant role in each other's trade relations in this time period than after World War II. Nevertheless, trade relations were not smooth then either. In 1893 Russia and Germany waged a trade war that led to a contraction in trade volume. The following year, however, the two countries successfully concluded negotiations on a new trade treaty and, as table 16 shows, the volume of German exports to Russia more than doubled between 1894 and 1898. In the nineteenth century the commodity composition of German-Russian trade changed and began to resemble the current pattern. In 1913 barley, wheat, eggs, butter, bran, wood, and flax accounted for over 50 percent of German imports from Russia, while machinery, hides and leather, textiles, electro-technical products, vehicles, and chemicals made up more than 50 percent of German exports to Russia.[63] What has changed since then is that Russian agri-

TABLE 16
The Relative Significance of German-Russian Trade before World War I

Year	*Imports from Russia*		*Exports to Russia*	
	Million Marks	Percentage of German Imports	Million Marks	Percentage of all German Exports
1880	331.4	11.7	231.8	7.8
1881	335.3	11.2	200.6	6.5
1882	388.8	12.4	204.0	6.2
1883	408.1	12.6	188.4	5.7
1884	412.1	12.6	167.9	5.2
1885	342.9	11.5	132.9	5.3
1886	264.3	9.0	148.4	4.9
1887	362.3	11.4	131.6	4.1
1888	456.5	13.3	199.6	5.9
1889	551.8	13.5	196.9	6.0
1890	541.9	12.7	206.5	6.1
1891	580.4	13.2	262.6	7.9
1892	383.4	9.1	239.5	7.6
1893	353.4	8.5	184.6	5.7
1894	544	12.7	195	6.4
1895	569	13.4	221	6.5
1896	635	13.9	364	9.7
1897	706	14.6	372	9.8
1898	737	13.5	441	11.0
1899	716	12.4	437	10.0
1900	730	12.1	359	7.5
1901	730	12.8	346	7.7
1902	774	13.3	372	7.7
1903	842	13.3	413	8.1
1904	837	12.2	352	6.6
1905	1,112	15.0	412	7.0
1906	1,091	13.6	457	7.2
1907	1,131	13.0	501	7.3
1908	964	12.5	521	8.1
1909	1,388	16.3	507	7.6
1910	1,413	15.8	621	8.3
1911	1,669	17.1	701	8.6
1912	1,565	14.7	763	8.5
1913	1,470	13.6	978	9.7

Source: Jürgen Kuczynski and Grete Wittkowski, *Die deutsch-russischen Handelsbeziehungen in den letzten 150 Jahren*, 2d ed. (Berlin: Die Wirtschaft, 1947)).

cultural exports have lost in significance and have been replaced by energy deliveries.

After World War I the new Soviet Union and the Weimar Republic became the "pariah states of Europe." In this situation both countries benefited from close relations and established what could be called a special relationship symbolized by the infamous "Rapallo" treaty of 1922. This special relationship lasted until the early 1930s. In this decade Germany again emerged as the largest trading partner of Russia/Soviet Union.[64] However, for much of this decade exports to the Soviet Union only amounted to about 3 percent of total German exports.[65] Thus, with the exception of the depression years of 1931 and 1932, German-Soviet trade did not assume the significance this trade had had for Germany before World War I.

Now that political restrictions on East-West trade have fallen and Eastern European countries have begun to (re-)establish market economies, will Germany expand its trade position in Central and Eastern Europe to reach levels last achieved before World War II, or in the case of Russia before World War I? A detailed attempt to answer this complex question is beyond the scope of this project, but there is room for a few preliminary remarks. One of the consequences of German unification was that eastern German exports to its traditional trading partners in Central and Eastern Europe essentially collapsed.[66] On the other hand, in 1991 western German exports to Central and Eastern Europe, including the Soviet successor states, represented 5.6 percent of western German exports overall, compared to 3.7 percent in 1990. For the United States, however, we do not see similar changes as the comparable figures remained at 1.1 percent for both years. We also need to consider that the trade relationships between Germany and Eastern European countries tend to be highly asymmetrical. Poland, Hungary, and the Czech Republic, for example, do not rank among Germany's most significant trading partners, but by 1992 Germany had replaced the former Soviet Union as East Central Europe's largest supplier and customer. German dominance may take other forms as well, such as the penetration of Eastern European economies through foreign direct investment and, less tangibly, the emulation of German policies and institutions.[67] In the area of export controls Germany committed itself to assist successor states of the former Soviet Union in establishing export control systems. In June 1993, for example, the German government promised such assistance to Georgia and Ukraine.[68] Nonetheless, the rapid pace of change in Europe during the past few years has shown that it is rather risky to extrapolate past trends far into the future.

Arms Exports

Most treatises of arms export policy contain at least a short discussion of the economic benefits of arms exports to the supplier nations. There is very widespread agreement that among the Western arms suppliers, the United States, in the past at least, participated in this trade primarily for political and strategic reasons, whereas for Western European arms exporters economic considerations were more important. This assessment is shared by many analysts regardless of their position on the utility of arms transfers for foreign policy purposes, on the desirability and practicality of restraints on arms exports, or on the ethical implications of arms exports.

Beyond that, there is considerable disagreement on the magnitude of the economic benefits of arms exports. American analysts who are sympathetic to the goal of restraining arms exports tend to downplay the economic significance of arms exports. A prominent example is Andrew Pierre who argued that

the economic significance of arms sales—the explanation most often given for their existence and expansion—is not so great as it is often believed to be. The widespread perception that high levels of arms sales are necessary for the national economies of the principal suppliers is based upon vague, general notions rather than on hard data. Closer investigation . . . suggests that the economic benefits are less than is generally assumed. Accordingly, limited restraints on sales may have a relatively small economic impact, except for the particular companies or regions directly affected.[69]

Hammond et al. take just the opposite position. They argue that a

prevalent misconception about arms sales is that they are not critical to the economies of Western suppliers. This misconception has resulted in naive proposals for limiting arms exports from industrial suppliers to Third World recipients. A failure to comprehend the national political and economic importance of arms sales for America's European allies was a major reason for the collapse of the Carter administration's multilateral effort to restrain arms transfers.[70]

Although the world has changed significantly since these words were written over a decade ago, many of the arguments made in the early 1990s sound rather familiar. Thus, William Hartung argued in 1994 "that when public and private subsidies and indirect costs are included, arms exports may actually harm the American economy."[71] On this basis Hartung then proposed legislative initiatives to curb the arms trade. Unfortunately, an independent assessment of this dispute is hampered by a number of factors. Prominent among them is the fact that accurate and reliable comparative data on arms transfers do not exist. The two most often used data sources, which I rely on as well, are annual publications by ACDA and SIPRI. These two sources differ in their coverage of arms exports and their data collection methodology. SIPRI, for example, only covers arms transfers of major weapons but not small arms. The quality of some of the data presented in ACDA's *World Military Expenditures and Arms Transfers* and SIPRI's *World Armaments and Disarmament* yearbook is suspect.[72] In general, it can be said that although some hard data are available for evaluating the economic significance of arms exports for the United States, for other countries we often have to rely on more or less reasonable estimates and guesses.

Despite these qualifications it is possible to reach some conclusions about economic motives behind arms transfers. Besides analyzing the economic significance of arms exports, another approach to this question is to examine who receives U.S. and German arms. If an arms supplier's policy is primarily based on political and strategic considerations, most of his arms exports should go to his close allies, and for the United States and the major Western European arms suppliers this means other NATO countries. If the vast majority of arms exports go to countries outside the alliance, this may be taken as an indication of economic motives behind arms exports. This argument applies primarily to Western European arms exporters, less so to the United States since, in contrast to Western European nations, the United States is a global power with global interests. Table 17 presents data on the percentage of Western arms exports going to other NATO countries. According to these data, Germany appears as the least commercially motivated among the major Western European arms suppliers. To the extent that this is the case, it is not the result of a grand German political strategy, however, but reflects the fact that at least some German restrictions on arms exports have not completely eroded (yet).

Lewis Snider has done some of the methodologically most sophisticated work on explaining levels of arms exports. He hypothesized that during economically difficult times governments will increase the "butter side" of the budget more than the "gun side," and as a result the share of the defense budget in central government expenditures will decrease. This will lead to increased pressures to expand arms exports. Using multiple regression he found that "[f]or the European countries, arms exports expand in proportion to total exports in response to declines in the defense budget's share of central government expenditures."[73] For the United States his results show just the opposite, which for him "underscores what is generally assumed: that for the United States increases in arms exports occur mainly to serve broader security objectives, not just economic ones."[74]

The next question is whether these findings correspond to the economic significance of arms exports for the U.S. and German economies. A broad indicator of the economic importance of arms exports is the share of total exports taken up by arms exports. Here ACDA reports that in 1988 arms transfers made up 4.6 percent of total U.S. exports, whereas in 1989 this figure dropped to 3.1 percent. The comparable West German figures are 0.4 percent for both years.[75] We have to take into account, however, that Germany is far more export dependent than the United States. In 1989 arms exports represented 0.2 percent of the GNP of the United States and 0.1 percent of West German GNP.[76]

TABLE 17
Proportion of Total Arms Transfers to Other NATO Member Countries and to Developing Countries, 1985–1989

	NATO	developing countries*
United States	31%	58%
West Germany	41%	56%
France	16%	89%
United Kingdom	22%	75%

*Includes NATO members Greece and Turkey.

Source: ACDA, World Military Expenditures, table III.

Nevertheless it may be that arms exports are more important for the German arms industry than its U.S. counterpart. Krause has argued that the international arms production and arms transfer system is characterized by a historical division between different tiers of arms producers and suppliers with the United States as the prime example of a first-tier supplier, while Germany represents a second-tier supplier state.[77] In the 1940s the United States and the Soviet Union emerged as first-tier producers capable of manufacturing weapons at the technological frontier. Their domestic procurement base dwarfed that of all other producers and political considerations dominated their arms export decisions. Second-tier producers, such as Britain, France, and Germany, eventually caught up technologically, but since their domestic markets were relatively small they were pushed to rely on arms exports to spread research and development (R&D) costs and to lower unit costs of production. Second-tier states have also been more willing to transfer technology than first-tier states who tried to preserve their technological advantage.[78]

Although Krause has given us the theoretically most sophisticated account of historical changes in arms transfers, the utility of his model for explaining differences between U.S. and German arms export policies is limited by the fact that his characterization of second-tier suppliers is geared toward the French and British cases rather than the more complex German experience. Among other factors, "Germany has not sought a high degree of industrial self-sufficiency in defense (in marked contrast to France and the UK)."[79]

One measure of the economic importance of arms exports for the arms industry is the percentage of arms produced for exports. According to one estimate, from 1984 until 1989 Germany exported about 10 percent of its defense production compared to 45 percent for France, 33 percent for Britain, and 10 percent for the United States.[80] Given that exports account for about a third of German GDP, this shows that the German arms industry depends less on exports than the German economy as a whole. However, these figures are averages for the defense industry as a whole which hide substantial intra-industry variation. For example, according to industry sources, roughly 65 percent of all military orders received by German shipyards in the last few years involved exports to foreign navies.[81]

Another way to analyze the problem of the economic significance of arms exports is to examine the budgetary savings that accrue to the United States and Germany from arms exports. These savings can be divided into several major categories: learning curve effects, savings on overhead costs, and savings resulting from the avoidance of production line gaps.[82] It is generally assumed that these savings are of greater significance for Western European arms industries than for the United States. Besides the fact that there appears to be fairly widespread agreement in the literature on the validity of this argument, this line of thinking seems very plausible. The domestic U.S. arms market is larger than Western European defense markets, and thus the United States enjoys a natural advantage over Western Europe in terms of learning curve effects and the possibility to spread R&D costs for advanced fighter jets, for example, over considerably more units. European producers may try to overcome the handicap of small domestic markets through exports. However, although there is some fairly solid empirical evidence for these kinds of savings in the United States, there is no systematic and rigorous empirical study comparing the extent of these savings for the United States and the major European suppliers. Furthermore, the most often cited American studies of this issue are now somewhat dated.

For the United States, a Congressional Budget Office study reported that savings from foreign military sales occur, and that the largest single source of savings consisted of the recoupment of R&D costs. However, according to this study, the extent of savings depended less on the absolute level of foreign military sales than on the weapons mix of these sales. Although the sale of high-technology weapons, such as fighter aircraft or missiles, could result in substantial savings, this was not the case for many other weapons systems, such as ships or ammunition, which are either less R&D intensive or do not involve substantial learning curve effects and economies of scale.[83] In the case of Germany, naval exports, which have played an important role in German arms exports, probably do not result in substantial savings. On the other hand, exports of Tornado aircraft, which by way of Britain are ending up in such places as Saudi Arabia, may result in significant savings.

Overall, Brzoska came to the conclusion that savings realized from arms exports were probably higher for the United States than for western Germany.[84] At a minimum this suggests the need for a solid empirical study of this issue which would require data on the weapons mixes of different suppliers, how they have changed over time and estimates of savings for different weapons categories.

To conclude, our analysis supported the argument that German arms export policy is more commercially oriented than is the case in the United States but it also questioned some of the broad generalizations frequently made in the literature. Furthermore, given shrinking defense budgets both in Western Europe and the United States, defense industries on both sides of the Atlantic are undergoing a restructuring process.[85] Besides consolidation and diversification, defense companies, including those in the United States, also face even greater pressure than before to gain international business and to enlist government support in securing foreign orders. In the German case employment in the defense industry decreased from 280,000 employees in 1988 to 180,000 in 1993, and in the long run it may decline further to less than 100,000 jobs.[86] This has to be seen in light of the fact that "German military procurement is being cut 60% from Cold War levels."[87] As a result representatives of the German defense industry began to ring alarm bells in the early 1990s. One of their key political demands involved changes in German arms export policy. The leading German trade journal *Wehrtechnik* went as far as claiming that arms export controls could seal the fate of the German aerospace industry.[88] More specifically, industry representatives charged that strict German controls had earned German manufacturers a reputation as unreliable partners. This in turn meant that British and other European defense firms were becoming reluctant to enter into cooperation agreements with German companies. Particularly in the aerospace sector, though, international cooperation was essential for the industry's survival.[89]

If we examine the economic significance of arms exports at the industry level, there is some, but limited evidence to suggest that economic pressures for exports are greater for the German industry than for its U.S. counterpart. This would support the reasoning that the relaxation of political restrictions on western German arms exports, which took place in the late 1970s and 1980s, can be attributed in large part to increased economic pressures at the industry level. However, such economic pressures do not explain specific decisions or the fact that there still are substantial restrictions on the export of some weapons but not on others. For example, whereas just about any country may buy German war ships, as long as it can come up with the money to pay for them, this is not the case for tanks. In the 1980s the western German shipbuilding industry experienced severe problems, but German tank manufacturers faced tough times as well.[90] The primary reasons why German war ships are sold almost indiscriminately all over the world while German tanks are not, or at least not to the same extent, are less of an economic and more of a political nature. Despite the somewhat problematic nature of the distinction between offensive and defensive weapons, tanks are generally perceived as offensive weapons. Furthermore, tanks can and often are used not only against enemy soldiers but to put down internal unrest. War ships, on the other hand, do not face the same stigma. Thus, although economic factors are important, there is no economic determinism at work.

Nuclear Exports

When considering this area it is important to note that the international market for nuclear power equipment more or less collapsed in the 1980s. Thus, to the extent that we will discuss this area of trade we will be dealing with events that took place in the 1970s and early 1980s, and many of the sources used here were written during this time period. In more recent years Iraqi imports of nuclear technology, particularly from Germany, received considerable attention. Some of the equipment imported by the Iraqis had very specific nuclear applications, but German companies and a number of other suppliers also sold machine tools and other dual-use equipment to Iraq, which have a variety of civilian and bomb making uses. Restricting this kind of trade means more than limiting "nuclear" exports but calls for stricter scrutiny of machine tool and other precision equipment exports more generally. For the United States, former President Bush noted in his 1991 nuclear nonproliferation report that "[w]hereas the number of uniquely nuclear commodities and technology transfer cases are approximately one to three hundred a year, the number of Commerce [Department] licenses reviewed annually for non-proliferation control purposes are over 12,000."[91]

In the late 1970s and early 1980s West German nuclear exports made up less than one half percentage point of total West German exports.[92] In 1987 the West German government granted export licenses for nuclear goods valued at 2.7 billion DM.[93] That year total West German exports came to 528.3 billion DM, which shows that relatively speaking nuclear exports have been insignificant for the western German economy as a whole. Due to a lack of data it is impossible to make direct comparisons to the United States, but there is no reason to assume that, in the 1980s at least, U.S. nuclear exports were significantly higher than those of German suppliers.

This would imply that such exports have been insignificant for the two economies. In the past, however, not all analysts agreed with this assessment. Erwin Häckel argued for the West German case that

in contrast to the two leaders in the field, the USA and the USSR, the stakes in nuclear export competition are for Germany very high indeed. West Germany is today the largest exporting nation in the world. Its dependency on foreign sales is greatest among all major industrial countries, and the necessity to earn a large share (presently, in fact, more than one fourth) of their national income abroad has become a deeply ingrained truism in the minds of the German people.

Nuclear exports contribute directly as well as indirectly to the country's total industrial exports. Indirectly, they help to hold down production costs for the German manufacturing industry. Nuclear exports improve the economies of scale for German reactor production and devolve some of the costs of domestic nuclear electricity upon the shoulders of foreign nuclear customers. The availability of low-cost energy at home is important for German exporters in their own competition with foreign industries that have the benefit of competitively priced nuclear energy, as in France, or of relatively cheap fossil energy, as in the United States.

Directly, nuclear exports contribute to foreign earnings as part of the assortment of high-quality industrial products which account for the major share of Germany's total exports. As the international commerce in relatively simple industrial products is increasingly taken over by aspiring countries of the Third World, it becomes requisite for the German industry to specialize in highly sophisticated export products. The actual contribution of the nuclear industry to total German exports may not be very impressive in quantitative terms. . . . But its symbolic value as a showpiece of Germany's leadership in advanced technology is considerable.

The function of nuclear industry as a trailblazer or booster for international commerce is difficult to gauge but impossible to overlook.[94]

Although the expectations of Häckel and others in the end turned out to be wishful thinking, these arguments played a significant role historically and may have helped shape nuclear export policies of European suppliers.

Furthermore, Häckel was correct in pointing out that the western German nuclear industry has been more export dependent than its U.S. counterpart. Table 18 presents some evidence for the relatively high export dependence of the West German nuclear industry compared to its major Western competitors. Although West Germany's cumulative share of the world market was considerably smaller than that of the United States at the end of the 1970s, it was twice as export dependent as the U.S. industry.

As subsequent events showed, everybody miscalculated market trends. One way in which reactor suppliers responded to the depressed nuclear power market was to increase their presence in nuclear services.

TABLE 18
National Shares in World Nuclear Exports

Country   Nuclear Power Plant Production by 31 December 1980

	total production (MW)	total exports (MW)	share of production exported %	share of world exports %
USA	228 888	36 442	15.9	51.6
France	56 124	3 644	7.0	5.2
USSR	55 975	15 470	27.6	21.9
W. Germany	36 239	11 192	33.7	15.8
Canada	17 926	2 354	13.1	3.3
UK	15 682	200	1.3	0.3
other	31 045	-	-	-
World	450 039	70 622	15.7	100.0

Note: Table shows total net capacity in electric MW for nuclear power plants in operation, under construction, or ordered; percentages rounded.

Source: Atomwirtschaft-Atomtechnik 26 (1981): 217, as cited in Häckel, "The Politics of Nuclear Exports," p. 70.

This appears to have increased pressure on established American companies as European and Japanese competitors increasingly entered the U.S. market.[95] For example, in 1987 the Bechtel corporation of San Francisco and Kraftwerk Union of Germany agreed to cooperate in the nuclear services market in the United States.[96] *Businessweek* reported in 1983 that

Equipment manufacturing now accounts for only about 25% of Westinghouse's nuclear business, down from more than 50% more than five years ago. It is expected to fall to 15% within a few years. Servicing now makes up 40% of the company's nuclear business.[97]

This strategy, though, had its problems as well since, as Westinghouse's annual report for 1986 noted, "the more price competitive service activities generally result in lower profit margins causing operating profit to decline."[98] In the case of Kraftwerk Union the decline of nuclear power clearly shows in company figures for the balance between nuclear and conventional business. In the business year 1980/81 nuclear power accounted for 48 percent of the company's revenues. In 1982/83 nuclear power generating equipment contributed 74 percent to total revenues. By 1992/93 the comparable figure had decreased to 30 percent.[99]

In the face of contracting markets one also would have expected to see a consolidation process in the industry. But as Lönnroth and Walker pointed out, for a long time the nuclear industry did not experience a

wave of international mergers or other forms of international collabo-
ration to cope with excess capacity. Rather,

In the absence of strong commercial competition and open markets, the tendency
towards increasing concentration that has been a characteristic of many
industries in recent years, and of the nuclear industry in the 1960s, has been
lacking—indeed, the tendency has if anything been towards greater
fragmentation and reduced commercial efficiency.

There are other reasons why it is unlikely that a more "rational" international
division of labor will develop in this industry. For reasons of sovereignty and
security of supply, countries for right or wrong place self-sufficiency before
economy and resist increased foreign influence over reactor supplies. In all
major industrial countries the trend in thermal reactor production has been
towards trying to reduce foreign involvement.[100]

In more recent years, though, some restructuring has taken place at the
international level. In 1989 the French reactor supplier Framatome and
the German company Kraftwerk Union, a subsidiary of Siemens,
announced the establishment of Nuclear Power International (NPI). The
two partners agreed to jointly develop a pressurized water reactor for the
international market.[101]

To summarize, although nuclear exports are of marginal significance
for both the U.S. and German economies, they have historically been
important for the western German nuclear industry, while this has not
been the case for all U.S. reactor manufacturers. Furthermore, in its
attempts to prevent future export control scandals, such as the German
involvement in Iraq's nuclear program, the German government has
taken steps that had effects beyond the nuclear industry. German
machine tool manufacturers, for example, frequently mentioned the
negative impact of the "H list" on their export sales.[102]

CONCLUSION

This chapter began with the widespread assertion that U.S. export
control policies have been motivated primarily by strategic and political
considerations, whereas German policies reflect the needs of an industry
that is highly export dependent. The evidence presented in this chapter
suggests the need for a more nuanced explanation of policy differences.
First of all, U.S. policies have not been uniformly restrictive, as we saw in
the case of nuclear export policy which has undergone considerable
change over time. Furthermore, after World War II western Germany
frequently used economic instruments not only to increase German
wealth but to achieve a variety of foreign policy goals as well. This has
been particularly important for German policies toward Eastern Europe.
Finally, the simple contrast between strict U.S. policies and loose German

ones is insufficient to explain more subtle differences in the way German authorities have treated the export of different weapons categories, such as tanks and naval vessels.

Besides the need for a more nuanced analysis, the evidence presented in this chapter also suggests some broader patterns. In the 1990s nonproliferation export controls will receive the most attention. An analysis of the historical record of U.S. nonproliferation and nuclear export policy shows that two conditions have been essential for a strong nonproliferation policy.[103] First of all, periods of decreasing tensions between the United States and the Soviet Union were conducive to effective U.S. nonproliferation efforts. Thus, the United States and the Soviet Union negotiated the NPT during the latter half of the 1960s. Under the first Reagan administration, on the other hand, non-proliferation took a backseat. Second, successful U.S. nonproliferation initiatives took place under administrations committed to an expansive view of U.S. national security interests. Thus, the post-Vietnam retrenchment of the 1970s undermined U.S. nonproliferation policy. To apply this to the Clinton administration, the end of the Cold War favors strong U.S. initiatives in this area, but such initiatives may not be forthcoming if they involve significant diplomatic, military, or economic costs.

For Germany this chapter showed that German policies on East-West trade and arms transfers did not consistently follow a commercial logic. Until the 1960s the Federal Republic made various attempts to use economic leverage in its relations with the Soviet Union and Eastern Europe. Similarly, West German governments, occasionally at least, pursued political objectives in the area of arms transfers. Such efforts were not crowned with notable success, however. Rather, in the 1970s the West German government depoliticized trade relations with the Soviet Union and attempted to stay out of diplomatic trouble by restricting highly visible arms sales to the Middle East. Thus, Germany's "trading state strategy" was not fully in place until the 1970s.

The data presented in this chapter show that in a number of cases percentage of exports or of GNP (GDP) or employment figures do not correspond to the results on the commercial versus political orientation of export policy. An example of this lack of fit is the difference between U.S. and German arms export policies, which does not correspond to the overall significance of arms exports for the two economies. A general problem with arguments about the economic importance of particular areas of trade is that just about any area of trade matters to somebody and thus potentially assumes political significance as well. Germany is much more dependent on foreign trade than the United States, and this means that the interests of export promotion have received greater priority in Germany than in the United States although the United States has begun to catch up on this score under the Clinton administration. This is an across-the-board generalization, though, and raises the question of how to explain issue-specific variations. Furthermore, a general problem with interest-based explanations of policy or policy change is that quite often a range of specific policies is compatible with a given set of economic or political interests. For example, German companies can live with either liberal or restrictive export control policies as long as licensing criteria are clear and as long as their competitors face similar rules. Which specific policy is adopted depends less on objectively defined interests than on the domestic political process and on ideas that serve as focal points around which expectations converge.[104]

NOTES

1. U.S. Congress, Office of Technology Assessment, *Global Arms Trade*, OTA-ISC-460 (Washington, D.C.: U.S. Government Printing Office, June 1991), p. 47.

2. Beverly Crawford, "Western Control of East-West Trade: The Role of U.S. Power and International Regimes," in Gary K. Bertsch, ed., *Controlling East-West Trade and Technology Transfer: Power, Politics, and Policies* (Durham: Duke University Press, 1988), p. 284.

3. Angela E. Stent, *Technology Transfer to the Soviet Union: A Challenge for the Cohesiveness of the Western Alliance*, Arbeitspapiere zur Internationalen Politik no. 24 (Bonn: Europa Union Verlag, 1983), p. 29.

4. Bruce W. Jentleson, "The Western Alliance and East-West Energy Trade," in Gary K. Bertsch, ed., *Controlling East-West Trade and Technology Transfer: Power, Politics, and Policies* (Durham: Duke University Press, 1988), p. 320.

5. OTA, *Global Arms Trade*, p. 13.

6. Michael Brzoska, "The Erosion of Restraint in West German Arms Transfer Policy," *Journal of Peace Research* 26 (May 1989): 165–177.

7. Stockholm International Peace Research Institute, *The Arms Trade with the Third World* (Stockholm: Almqvist & Wiksell, 1971); Gregory S. Sanjian, "Great Power Arms Transfers: Modeling the Decision-Making Processes of Hegemonic, Industrial, and Restrictive Exporters," *International Studies Quarterly* 35 (July 1991): 173–193.

8. Michael Mastanduno, "Strategies of Economic Containment: U.S. Trade Relations with the Soviet Union," *World Politics* 37 (July 1985): 503–531.

9. Robert Mark Spaulding, Jr., "The German Trade Policy in Eastern Europe, 1890–1990: Preconditions for Applying International Trade Leverage," *International Organization* 45 (Summer 1991): 344.

10. Stent, *From Embargo to Ostpolitik*, pp. 59–67.

11. Kreile, *Osthandel und Ostpolitik*, chapter 3.

12. Ibid., pp. 102–104.

13. Wörmann, *Der Osthandel*, pp. 109–111.

14. Stephen Engelberg, "Eager if Uneasy, East Europe Accepts German Investments," *New York Times*, 23 January 1992, p. 1.

15. Mastanduno, *Economic Containment*, pp. 145–146.

16. Kenneth W. Abbott, "Linking Trade to Political Goals: Foreign Policy Export Controls in the 1970s and 1980s," *Minnesota Law Review* 65 (1981): 790–791.

17. "U.S. and East European Weapons Dealers Clash," *New York Times*, 13 February 1994, p. A14.

18. Jentleson, *Pipeline Politics*.

19. "Russia Is Halting Arms-Linked Sale," *New York Times*, 17 July 1993, p. 4.

20. Hammond et al., *The Reluctant Supplier*, pp. 32–33.

21. "U.S. Approves Sale of Warplanes to Argentina," *New York Times*, 6 February 1994, p. A8.

22. *U.S. Department of State Dispatch*, 27 February 1995, p. 155.

23. Ibid., p. 61.

24. Ibid., p. 75.

25. Haftendorn, *Militärhilfe*, pp. 21–22.

26. Ibid., p. 21.

27. Pearson, "Necessary Evil," p. 546.

28. Lewis A. Dunn, *Controlling the Bomb: Nuclear Proliferation in the 1980s* (New Haven: Yale University Press, 1982), pp. 128–130.

29. Brenner, *Nuclear Power and Non-Proliferation*, p. 69.

30. Testimony by John Moore in U.S. Congress, House Committee on Energy and Commerce, *Nuclear Energy Cooperation with China*, 98th Cong., 2d sess., p. 3.

31. For a more detailed account of U.S. nonproliferation policy in the 1980s see Peter A. Clausen, *Nonproliferation and the National Interest: America's Response to the Spread of Nuclear Weapons* (New York: HarperCollins College, 1993), chapter 7.

32. Chancellor Adenauer had made this commitment on October 1, 1954, at a diplomatic conference in London that discussed a German contribution to the Western alliance in the wake of the French National Assembly's rejection of the European Defense Community. The conference laid the groundwork for the formation of the Western European Union, German membership in NATO, and the end of the occupation status for West Germany. In his memoirs Adenauer recalled that after he had made his famous statement John Foster Dulles had approached him saying that this commitment was, of course, subject to the standard caveat of "rebus sic stantibus." There is evidence, however, that Adenauer's account of this exchange was not quite accurate. See Konrad Adenauer, *Erinnerungen 1953–1955* (Stuttgart: Deutsche Verlags-Anstalt, 1966), p. 347; Hans-Peter Schwarz, "Adenauer und die Kernwaffen," *Vierteljahrshefte für Zeitgeschichte* 37 (October 1989): 578; Hanns Jürgen Küsters, "Souveränität und ABC-Waffen-Verzicht: Deutsche Diplomatie auf der Londoner Neunmächte-Konferenz 1954," *Vierteljahresschrift für Zeitgeschichte* 42 (Ocober 1994): 499–536.

33. George McGhee, *At the Creation of a New Germany: An Ambassador's Account* (New Haven: Yale University Press, 1989), p. 208.

34. As quoted in Waldemar Besson, *Die Außenpolitik der Bundesrepublik: Erfahrungen und Maßstäbe* (Frankfurt: Ullstein, 1973), p. 363.

35. Theo Sommer, "Bonn Changes Course," *Foreign Affairs* 45 (April 1967): 483.

36. Statement by Brandt as reprinted in West Germany, Presse- und Informationsamt der Bundesregierung, *Vertrag über die Nichtverbreitung von Kernwaffen: Dokumentation zur deutschen Haltung und über den deutschen Beitrag* (Bonn: Presse- und Informationsamt der Bundesregierung, 1969), p. 17.

37. Hanrieder, *Germany, America, Europe*, p. 91.

38. Kurt Birrenbach, *Meine Sondermissionen: Rückblick auf zwei Jahrzehnte bundesdeutscher Außenpolitik* (Dusseldorf: Econ Verlag, 1984), p. 178.

39. Hanrieder, *Germany, America, Europe*, p. 93.

40. Catherine McArdle Kelleher, *Germany & The Politics of Nuclear Weapons* (New York: Columbia University Press, 1975), p. 3.

41. Erwin Häckel, *Die Bundesrepublik Deutschland und der Atomwaffensperrvertrag*, Arbeitspapiere zur Internationalen Politik, no. 53 (Bonn: Europa Union Verlag, 1989), p. 24.

42. Walker and Lönnroth, *Nuclear Power Struggles*, p. 141.

43. Lothar Wilker, "Nuklearexport- und Nichtverbreitungspolitik—ein Prioritätenkonflikt für die Bundesrepublik?" in *Nuklearpolitik im Zielkonflikt: Verbreitung der Kernenergie zwischen nationalem Interesse und internationaler Kontrolle*, ed. Lothar Wilker (Cologne: Verlag Wissenschaft und Politik, 1980), p. 83.

44. Spector, *The New Nuclear Nations*, pp. 246–247.

45. National Academy of Sciences, *Balancing the National Interest*, p. 121.

46. Finan, "Estimate of Direct Economic Costs," p. 275.

47. Ibid., p. 264.

48. Ibid., p. 266.

49. Stephen A. Merrill, "Operation and Effects of U.S. Export Licensing for National Security Purposes," in National Academy of Sciences, *Balancing the National Interest: U.S. National Security Export Controls and Global Economic Competition* (Washington, D.C.: National Academy Press, 1987), pp. 247–249.

50. Finan, "Estimate of Direct Economic Costs," pp. 266–267.

51. Ibid., pp. 272–274.

52. J. David Richardson, *Sizing Up U.S. Export Disincentives* (Washington, D.C.: Institute for International Economics, 1993).

53. Ibid., p. 120.

54. Ibid., pp. 105–106.

55. Stanley D. Nollen, "Business Costs and Business Policy for Export Controls," *Journal of International Business Studies* 18 (Spring 1987): 8.

56. Ibid., p. 9.

57. Richardson, *U.S. Export Disincentives*, p. 120.

58. West Germany, Deutscher Bundestag, *Drucksache* 11/2120, p. 1.

59. Wörmann, *Der Osthandel*, p. 180.

60. Jürgen Kuczynski and Grete Wittkowski, *Die deutsch-russischen Handelsbeziehungen*, 2nd ed. (Berlin: Die Wirtschaft, 1948), p. 15.

61. Ibid.

62. Ibid., p. 24.

63. Ibid., p. 33.

64. Werner Beitel and Jürgen Nötzold, *Deutsch-sowjetische Wirtschaftsbeziehungen in der Zeit der Weimarer Republik* (Baden-Baden: Nomos, 1979), pp. 100–101.

65. Ibid., p. 93.

66. András Inotai, "Economic Implications of German Unification for Central and Eastern Europe," in *The New Germany and the New Europe*, ed. Paul B. Stares (Washington, D.C.: Brookings Institution, 1992), p. 283.

67. In the literature this theme has been emphasized most strongly by Andrei S. Markovits and Simon Reich, "The Latest Stage of the German Question: Pax Germanica in the New Europe," *Arms Control* 12 (September 1991): 60–76; Andrei S. Markovits and Simon Reich, "Should Europe Fear the Germans?" in *From Bundesrepublik to Deutschland: German Politics after Unification*, eds. Michael G. Huelshoff, Andrei S. Markovits, and Simon Reich (Ann Arbor: University of Michigan Press, 1993), pp. 271–289. Whether increased German influence will constitute "hegemony," as Markovits and Reich claim, is doubtful, and their assertion that German prosperity was achieved at the expense of other Europeans is rather dubious.

68. *Deutschland Nachrichten*, 25 June 1993, p. 2, Germany, Presse- und Informationsamt der Bundesregierung, *Bulletin*, no. 53 (17 June 1993), p. 558.

69. Andrew J. Pierre, *The Global Politics of Arms Sales* (Princeton: Princeton University Press, 1982), p. 25.

70. Hammond et al. *The Reluctant Supplier*, p. 13.

71. William Hartung, "The Phantom Profits of the War Trade," *New York Times*, 6 March 1994, sec. 3, p. 13.

72. Brzoska, "Arms Transfer Data Sources."

73. Lewis W. Snider, "Arms Exports for Oil Imports? The Test of a Nonlinear Model," *Journal of Conflict Resolution* 28 (December 1984): 694.

74. Ibid.

75. ACDA, *World Military Expenditures*, 1990, table II.

76. Ibid., tables I and II.

77. Keith Krause, *Arms and the State: Patterns of Military Production and Trade* (Cambridge: Cambridge University Press, 1992).

78. Ibid., p. 32.

79. James B. Steinberg, *The Transformation of the European Defense Industry*, R-4141-ACQ (Santa Monica: RAND Corporation, 1992), p. 33.

80. Martyn Brittleson, *Co-operation or Competition? Defence Procurement Options for the 1990s*, Adelphi Papers 250 (London: International Institute for Strategic Studies, 1990), p. 25.

81. "Die Vielfalt der deutschen Wehrtechnik-Branche," *Frankfurter Allgemeine Zeitung*, 6 September 1993, p. 15.

82. U.S. Congressional Budget Office, *Budgetary Cost Savings To the Department of Defense Resulting From Foreign Military Sales* (Washington, D.C.: Government Printing Office, May 1976), pp. 3–5.

83. U.S. Congressional Budget Office, *Foreign Military Sales and U.S. Weapons Costs* (Washington, D.C.: May 1976), pp. vii–viii.

84. Brzoska, *Rüstungsexportpolitik*, p. 176.

85. Michael Brzoska and Peter Lock, eds., *Restructuring of Arms Production in Western Europe* (Oxford: Oxford University Press, 1992).

86. "Die Rüstungsindustrie muß weiter schrumpfen," *Frankfurter Allgemeine Zeitung*, 25 August 1993, p. 14.

87. *Aviation Week & Space Technology*, 31 January 1994, p. 45.

88. *Wehrtechnik*, June 1994, p. 6.

89. *Wehrtechnik*, May 1994, pp. 9–12, 22–24, June 1994, pp. 5–8.

90. In 1994 big export orders from Western European customers alleviated some of the concerns of German tank builders. See "Der Spanien-Auftrag würde die Panzer-Industrie sichern," *Frankfurter Allgemeine Zeitung*, 17 November 1994, p. 23.

91. U.S. Congress, House, *Report to Congress Pursuant to Section 601 of the Nuclear Non-Proliferation Act of 1978 for the Year Ending December 31, 1991* (Washington, D.C.: Government Printing Office, 1992), p. 24.

92. *Atomwirtschaft*, November 1981, 1984.

93. West Germany, Deutscher Bundestag, *Drucksache* 11/2120, p. 1.

94. Erwin Häckel, "The Domestic and International Context of West Germany's Nuclear Energy Policy," in *Nuclear Policy in Europe: France, Germany and the International Debate*, eds. Erwin Häckel et al., Arbeitspapiere zur Internationalen Politik, no. 12 (Bonn: Europa Union Verlag, 1980), pp. 108–109.

95. "Big Stakes in Nuclear 'After-Market,'" *Nuclear News Buyers Guide*, Mid-March 1985, p. 20.

96. *Nuclear News*, August 1987, p. 107.

97. *Businessweek*, 5 December 1983, p. 130.

98. Westinghouse Corporation, *Annual Report* 1986, p. 29.

99. *Atomwirtschaft*, April 1983, p. 176; *Atomwirtschaft*, March 1984, p. 116; *Frankfurter Allgemeine Zeitung*, 9 February 1994, p. 14.

100. Lönnroth and Walker, *The Viability*, p. 72.

101. "Siemens/KWU and Framatome Form PWR Group," *Nuclear Engineering International*, June 1989, p. 2; "NPI's New Reactor Takes a Further Step Along the Evolutionary Road," *Nuclear Engineering International*, April 1992, pp. 48–49.

102. "Traub schneidet besser als die Branche ab," *Frankfurter Allgemeine Zeitung*, 15 May 1993, p. 16.

103. Clausen, *Nonproliferation and the National Interest*, chapter 8.

104. Geoffrey Garrett and Barry R. Weingast, "Ideas, Interests, and Institutions: Constructing the European Community's Internal Market," in *Ideas and Foreign Policy: Beliefs, Institutions, and Political Change*, eds. Judith Goldstein and Robert O. Keohane (Ithaca: Cornell University Press, 1993), pp. 173–206.

4

The Domestic Politics of Export Controls

The first striking difference between domestic political debates in Germany and the United States is that in Germany political parties play a critical role in articulating more or less coherent positions on export control issues and in shaping the political debate. In the United States, on the other hand, we do not find party-based but interest-based politics. This does not mean that interest group politics is marginal for understanding the German policy-making process or that Democrats and Republicans, liberals and conservatives have always fully agreed on the outlines of U.S. export control policy. However, there remain qualitative differences in the roles political parties and interest groups play in the two countries. Furthermore, any discussion of the domestic politics behind U.S. export controls has to consider institutional interests and turf battles among and within different branches of government pitting Congress against the presidency, as in the case of arms exports, or the Department of Defense against the Commerce Department, as in the area of East-West trade in the 1980s.

Substantively, strict export controls enjoyed greater domestic political support in the United States than in Germany after 1945. Strong anticommunist sentiments in the 1940s and 1950s provided an ideological and moral basis for export controls that at that time were directed against the Soviet Union and its allies. In this context one of the important features of the politics of export controls in the United States until the 1980s was the relative inactivity of business. As Angela Stent put it, "[i]t is noteworthy that organized United States business, which lobbies so effectively in some areas, has been virtually impotent in arguing its case for East-West trade."[1] This changed in the 1980s. One can argue that ultimately this change reflected the increasing export dependency of the U.S. economy. Politically, business interests received a big boost from a widely read and influential report by a National Academy of Sciences panel of academics, former administration officials, and high-level business executives.[2] The bottom line was that export controls should not only enhance national security but also protect the economic and technological vitality of the United States. According to the panel, the current export control system hurts U.S. exporters and thus undermines the economic health of the United States. In 1990 the House of Representatives verbally expressed this political shift by calling its version of the bill to reauthorize the Export Administration Act of 1979 an "Export Facilitation Act."[3] In 1991 a business executive argued at a congressional hearing on export control policy that "[i]f the demand is there, the demand will be met sooner or later by someone else if not us. . . . So any technology that is available now or shortly will be, why constrain ourselves? Why not go ahead and take the benefits right here in this country and create the jobs for our benefit?"[4] At the peak of the Cold War this executive probably would have been accused of trading with the enemy.

In the early 1990s congressional initiatives on export control policy often reflected regional economic interests. Thus, California legislators from Silicon Valley pushed for the liberalization of controls on computers, whereas lawmakers from Massachusetts, Utah, Washington, and California as well, opposed export controls on encryption software.[5] In the area of arms exports major New England arms manufacturers, such as Raytheon of Massachusetts, and members of Congress from the region supported legislation in 1993 to set up a loan guarantee program supporting U.S. arms sales. Technically, the legislation would have diverted funds from a defense conversion program to offer subsidized loans for arms exports.[6] More generally, these examples show how the relative fragmentation of American society and the state encourage and make it fairly easy for interest groups to pursue special deals. This may well increase the incoherence of U.S. export control policy, particularly now in the absence of anticommunism as an ideological glue.

In Germany during the post–World War II period a broad consensus supported the export orientation of the West German economy, and export controls were a nuisance, necessary at times but nonetheless a nuisance. This consensus united all the major established political parties, including the Christian Democrats, the Social Democrats, and the Free Democrats. In the 1980s this consensus was challenged by some Green politicians. Eckhard Stratmann, a Green deputy in the *Bundestag*, supported a reorientation of the German economy toward the domestic market instead of the world market.[7] In a speech to the *Bundestag* in 1989 he explicitly linked this broad proposal to the issue of export controls by arguing that West Germany had achieved its trade surpluses to a considerable extent by fueling the war machinery of other countries.[8] More important for changes in official policy has been the fact that the German foreign office under Hans-Dietrich Genscher pushed for a tightening of German controls at the end of the 1980s. However, increased support for strict export controls remains fragile. In early 1994 some of the most important German industry associations, such as the machinery association (VDMA), the electronics industry association (ZVEI), and the aerospace industry (BDLI), expressed strong irritation with German controls on dual-use goods and the complicated licensing process. These associations accused the German government of preventing a harmonization of European export controls by insisting on controls unacceptable to Germany's European partners.[9]

More broadly, in the past both German and U.S. export controls rested on a fairly clear normative basis, although the substance of this normative basis differed between the two countries. To begin with the United States, export controls were a product of the Cold War. Over time first deténte and then the end of the Cold War undermined the moral vision of U.S. export controls. In the absence of an alternative vision that resonates as deeply as containment of communism did in the late 1940s and 1950s advocates of strict U.S. export controls will most likely be on the defensive, and many such controls with some possible exceptions, such as sanctions directed against Iran, will become subordinate to commercial self-interest. The situation was more complex in Germany. The export orientation of the German economy was more than just an economic strategy but also represented a break with autarkic traditions of the past. On the other hand, the experience of German militarism in the 1930s and 1940s called for more restrictions on the German use of military statecraft than of its less tainted European neighbors. As mentioned above, the Greens challenged German "export myths" in the 1980s. The Green critique of Germany's integration into the world market rested on normative grounds, although not necessarily sound economic analysis. Stratmann argued that German export surpluses meant the elimination of jobs among Germany's trading partners. Furthermore, German exports contributed to the Third World debt crisis, and the highly export dependent automobile and chemical industries did not only create jobs but also environmental damage.[10]

Pointing in a different direction, more and more restrictions on German foreign policy have fallen in recent years, including, most recently, restrictions on the use of German troops abroad. Thus, despite the tightening of German export controls after 1989, the normative basis for "special" German arms export restraints has partially disintegrated. Evidence for a shift in values also shows up in public opinion data. According to polls conducted by the Allensbach institute, in October 1990 57 percent of West German respondents agreed with the statement that it was sufficient for Germany to be strong economically and that Germany should heed the concerns of its neighbors by not attempting to become the leading political power in Europe. By 1992 support for this statement had dropped to 34 percent of West German and 51 percent of East German respondents.[11] A more in-depth discussion of the politics of export controls needs to be sensitive to variations across specific issue areas.

EAST-WEST TRADE

Even during the Cold War there was a consensus in western Germany supporting East-West trade, which "include[d] the business and banking communities, the labor unions, and all of the major political parties. There [was] . . . virtually no opposition to improving economic ties with the East."[12] In 1953 Ludwig Erhard, who has been idolized as the father of the West German economic miracle, lamented that West Germany had suffered even more from the collapse of East-West trade than other Western European countries and that Western export controls hindered West German exports more than those of other countries.[13] In fact, until 1952 western German trade with Eastern Europe was subject to tighter export controls than the CoCom lists, but apparently German businesses frequently circumvented these controls through illegal exports.[14]

However, Chancellor Adenauer's foreign policy emphasized the Western integration of the Federal Republic, and this implied, among other things, loyalty to the Western embargo. Furthermore, leading representatives of the German business community supported the primacy of Western integration over traditional East-West trade interests. In 1954 Fritz Berg, the powerful president of the federation of German industry (BDI), stated in an interview

We have always without reservation supported German integration policy, and I thus declare in the name of German industry that our preference for the West is definitive. . . . In the relations between us and the countries of the East politics enjoys unconditional primacy over economics. This is what I have stressed repeatedly.[15]

Berg did not speak for the entire German business community, though, parts of which advocated an expansion of East-West trade. Furthermore, the Social Democratic party (SPD) at the time was more interested in reunification than Western integration, and SPD politicians believed that expanded trade and a liberalization of export controls could contribute to achieving that goal.[16] In the 1960s and 1970s West-East export controls did not generate much political controversy in western Germany except for the 1961/62 oil pipeline embargo, which will be discussed briefly in chapter 6. Export controls became a highly contentious issue among NATO allies in the 1980s, but for the most part all major political parties and interest groups in the Federal Republic agreed in their opposition to American economic warfare policies. Toward the end of the 1980s politicians within the German Social Democratic party voiced strong objections to CoCom restrictions and even recommended ignoring CoCom rules if the United States did not come to its senses. The Christian Democratic–led government did not go that far but this domestic opposition to CoCom provided the German government with ammunition for playing what Putnam calls "two-level games" in CoCom negotiations with the United States.[17]

For the future, it appears likely that export controls will cease to be a major bone of contention, but German trade with Eastern Europe may continue to generate controversy because of German investment in the East and rising imports from Eastern Europe. Although the net welfare gains or losses from a liberalization of European Community trade with Eastern Europe may be relatively small for the EC, affected industries in the EC will push for protectionist measures.[18] For example, Mannesmann has been one of the world's largest suppliers of large-diameter pipe and in the past the Soviet Union was a major customer. Now, however, the pipe activities of Mannesmann are facing severe problems because of cheap Eastern European imports, and Mannesmann asked for more protection against Eastern European pipe imports.[19]

For the United States, we pointed out earlier that business was not particularly effective in pressing its interests in this area. To some extent, this was due to the fact that the United States traded very little with the Soviet Union and Eastern Europe after the onset of the Cold War, and, in contrast to the situation facing Western Europe in the late 1940s and early 1950s, the United States did not depend on supplies from Eastern Europe. Besides the marginal economic significance, business representatives also confronted a political climate in which East-West business contacts were considered as "trading with the enemy."[20] These sentiments did have serious consequences for some companies targeted by boycotts. In one example the Firestone Rubber Company in 1964 planned to construct a synthetic rubber plant in Romania. An anticommunist group, "Young Americans for Freedom," picketed the company's headquarters and eventually urged dealers not to sell the company's products. In the end Firestone canceled the contract with Romania.[21]

In the 1960s the Johnson administration pursued a trade liberalization policy with the East. Business interests, however, showed themselves to be somewhat reluctant followers. In fact, "[c]orporate officials who were willing to speak publicly in favor of expanded East-West trade generally stressed its potential political benefits. Rather than defending

trade on the grounds of economic opportunity, they followed the State
Department in emphasizing the utility of trade as an instrument to
extract political concessions from, and to bring political change to, the
East."[22]   In the 1970s U.S. trade with the Soviet Union expanded
considerably, and business lobbied for a further loosening of restrictions.
Much of the growth in U.S. exports to the Soviet Union, however,
consisted of increased agricultural exports, and East-West trade, for the
most part, remained marginal for U.S. industry.   The 1970s also
witnessed a number of efforts at export licensing reform that presented
opportunities as well as risks for U.S. industry.

In 1976 a Defense Department advisory panel led by Fred Bucy, an
executive at Texas Instruments, published the very influential Bucy
report. Although the report primarily addressed export controls aimed
at the Communist bloc, one of its most significant aspects was its
position on intra-Western technology restrictions. In fact, the report
argued that the United States should not continue a policy of unlimited
access by U.S. allies to the most advanced U.S. technology.[23] Under the
Reagan administration this eventually resulted in stricter licensing
procedures for intra-Western trade. These restrictions did not only meet
with protest in Western Europe but they also had a more profound
impact on U.S. industry than East-West controls. U.S. companies gained
a reputation as unreliable suppliers, and the U.S. faced the prospect of
customers shifting to non-U.S. technology and suppliers to avoid U.S.
export controls. According to a 1986 survey, "38 percent [of respondents]
had existing customers actually express a preference to shift to non-U.S.
sources of supply to avoid entanglement in U.S. controls."[24] The extent
to which such shifts actually occurred is debatable but U.S. industry and
Western European governments pushed for an elimination of intra-
Western controls.

Since then the politics of East-West controls has changed dramatically. This is also reflected in the attitudes of U.S. companies toward trade
with the former Soviet Union and Eastern Europe. For example, on
September 24, 1991, an AT&T executive testified at hearings on the
reauthorization of the Export Administration Act. She argued that lifting
restrictions on the sale of telecommunications equipment was not only
important for U.S. competitiveness but also for encouraging economic
development in the Soviet Union and for assisting the democratization
process.[25] This is a far cry from the economic warfare of the 1950s and
early 1980s.

Throughout the Cold War opponents of East-West trade and advocates of strict export controls included conservatives in Congress, the
conservative national security establishment, including such groups as
the Committee on the Present Danger, and prominent labor leaders, such
as George Meany of the AFL-CIO.[26] The Committee on the Present

Danger and related groups were not primarily interested in East-West trade but focused more on arms control issues, such as SALT II or the Strategic Defense Initiative. To understand the position of American labor on East-West trade one has to consider the strong anticommunist stance of the AFL-CIO, particularly under the leadership of George Meany. In Congress early opponents of East-West trade under the Truman administration included conservative isolationist Republicans. A prominent example was Senator James Kem of Missouri who, among other things, authored the Kem amendment, which sought to punish Western European allies for trading with the Soviet Union.[27] Advocates of tight trade restrictions did not only include Republicans, though. In the 1970s Democratic Senator Henry Jackson succeeded in pushing through Congress the Jackson-Vanik amendment, which probably was the most important legal obstacle to trade between the United States and the Soviet Union.[28] A key staff member working for Jackson at the time was Richard Perle who later became President Reagan's point man on export controls in the Pentagon.

With the demise of the Soviet Union traditional justifications for national security export controls and CoCom have become obsolete. However, such controls have won new friends. For example, Gary Milhollin, who frequently publishes on nuclear nonproliferation issues and who testified at hearings on both sides of the Atlantic, argued at a Senate hearing in 1991 that the United States had made a mistake in cutting the CoCom list:

If you talk about this subject with the Europeans and you ask them specifically what things they control and under what methods, they basically get out the CoCom list . . . once we drop all this stuff off the CoCom list, it's going to be gone. . . . So I think we've made a big mistake in agreeing so easily to get rid of most of the things controlled by CoCom.[29]

In fact, some nonproliferation advocates have pursued their cause with the same fervor as Cold War warriors held up the banner of anticommunism a few decades earlier.

ARMS EXPORTS

Although East-West controls were an emotionally charged issue in the United States during the Cold War, the same has been true for arms trade restrictions in Germany. In the Federal Republic the primary societal group supporting arms exports and their expansion is, of course, the arms industry. After World War II, however, German militarism and the arms industry were discredited and this produced certain distinct features of the German arms industry. For example, until the 1970s West German companies that produced weapons for the military labeled their defense divisions *Sondertechnik* (special technology) to disguise their arms production.[30] In the 1950s some members of the West German government expressed reservations about increasing the defense capacities of German industry. Thus, economics minister "Erhard was opposed to having more contracts, especially for heavy weapons, awarded to German manufacturers, since the required expansion of capacity would then lead to a dangerous boom and to 'first class' waste in the economy."[31] Furthermore, in Germany, and in contrast to the United States, no industry association represents the interests of arms exporters.[32] In a country known for its "organized private enterprise" this is an anomaly.[33] Interest groups that oppose German arms exports or a further relaxation of export restrictions include mainly the unions, the peace movement, and religious groups. The unions are caught in an uncomfortable position, however. On the one hand, their ideological position pushes them toward opposing arms exports. On the other hand, unions are active in the arms industry and they have to represent the interests of workers employed by arms manufacturers. The metal workers union (IG Metall), where most workers in the arms industry are organized, favors a restrictive arms export policy. But the union has had problems in dealing with workers and union representatives who in the past bypassed official union channels and argued for increased arms exports.[34]

Turning to political parties, positions on the arms export issue reflect a left-right continuum along which German parties can be aligned. The Greens oppose arms exports in principle, whereas the left wing of the Social Democratic party argues for very strict limits on arms exports. In 1994, for example, Green deputies introduced a resolution in the German *Bundestag* that called for a constitutional ban on arms exports.[35] Among individual legislators, the Social Democrat Norbert Gansel built his reputation by uncovering questionable arms export practices, most notably the illegal export of blue prints for German submarines to South Africa. On the right, the Christian Democrats (CDU), and particularly their Bavarian affiliate, the Christian Social Union (CSU), tend to favor expanded arms exports and a loosening of restrictions. Even within the CDU, though, we find differences between the positions of the late Manfred Wörner, the former NATO secretary general and German defense minister, and of Heiner Geißler who is a prominent representative of the party's left wing.[36] The Free Democrats conform to their overall swing position and fall in between the SPD and the CDU/CSU.

In January 1994 a controversy developed within the Christian Democratic party delegation in the *Bundestag*. Karl Lamers, the group's foreign policy spokesman, had suggested that Germany revise its strict 1982 guidelines for arms exports to correspond to the more liberal rules of its European partners. He claimed that the 1982 guidelines made it difficult for German arms manufacturers to participate in cooperative ventures with other European companies, and as a result the guidelines threatened the loss of thousands of jobs and technological know how. A solid industrial basis, however, was important for Germany to be able to influence a common European security and armaments policy. Almost immediately, a number of other Christian Democratic deputies objected, including Rainer Eppelmann, the former East German defense minister, and deputy Stercken, the chairman of the *Bundestag*'s foreign affairs committee. Stercken argued that in view of the number of wars in the world it should not be a goal of European foreign assistance policy to revive the arms market. The deputy chairman of the Christian Democratic parliamentary group Gerster admonished that before discussing a liberalization of German arms export policy, the government should take steps to combat the illegal arms trade. Foreign Minister Kinkel and Economics Minister Rexrodt, both Free Democrats, stated that the guidelines would not be changed, but Germany would continue to work for common European Union rules on "dual-use" goods, which in practice would mean a loosening of German standards. The Social Democrats predictably opposed a liberalization of German arms export policy.[37]

However, we should also recognize that throughout the 1970s and 1980s the basis for a restrictive arms export policy eroded more and more even under a SPD-led government, and "[t]he change of power from the SPD to a conservative government in 1982 speeded the erosion process somewhat, but did not change its structure or dynamics."[38] Furthermore, economic concerns may override political differences. One of the most recent major arms export proposals involved the supply of submarines to Taiwan. This sale would have benefited the shipyards on the North Sea coast, which happens to be a stronghold of Germany's Social Democrats. Despite party resolutions against arms exports, Gerhard Schröder, the Social Democratic premier of Lower Saxony and one of Brandt's most prominent political "grandchildren" (*Enkel*), openly pushed for an export license. At the insistence of Free Democratic foreign minister Klaus Kinkel, the federal security council denied the request.[39]

Some of the arguments over arms exports and their regulation in Germany are similar to the arguments made elsewhere. For example, German advocates of expanded arms exports emphasize the positive employment effects of an increase in exports, whereas critics deny that arms exports can help to solve Germany's unemployment problems.[40] Arms made in Germany raise more sensitive issues, though, in Germany than arms exports do in the United States, touching off painful memories. In the 1980s a heated discussion raged in Germany over how Germany should treat the Holocaust. Was the Holocaust a unique event in history or just one example of genocide in the twentieth century, including the genocide against Armenians by Turkey, the Soviet Union's Gulag and elimination of Kulaks, and the "killing fields" of Cambodia? This debate started as a dispute among professional historians and dealt with such concrete issues as the proposed building of a museum of German history in (West) Berlin.[41] The passions that this fight set free involved more, however, than a tempest in the academic ivory tower but dealt with fundamental issues of German national identity and the role of history in providing such an identity, and it had implications for the way Germans viewed their role in international affairs.

In 1985 the German political scientist Hans-Peter Schwarz published a book in which he charged that although German politicians from the Wilhelmine period to Hitler had been obsessed with power, contemporary Germans had learned the lessons of the Nazi period too well and tended to deny the relevance of power politics to international relations.[42] To use his own terminology, the Germans had been tamed and had changed from ferocious beasts to harmless pets, which were easily frightened and taken advantage of. According to Schwarz, this tendency was particularly pronounced, although not limited to, the German left and it manifested itself, for example, in the Green demand to stop all German arms exports. Similar arguments have been made by prominent conservative politicians, such as Franz-Josef Strauß, who in 1987 told a *New York Times* reporter that

Germany must be once again willing to assume a certain measure of world political responsibility. . . . We must gradually come out from the shadow of the past. I'm no proponent of an unbridled or unrestrained weapons export policy. But where we can contribute to stability, we should not shy away from acting like a normal nation. We want no priority, but where the English, French and Italians are active, the Germans must be prepared to accept the same responsibility.[43]

The German Social Democrat Dietrich Stobbe, on the other hand, argued that "[w]e won't forget the lessons to be drawn from Hitler's Germany, when songs were sung about Germany the arms forge."[44] Although the issues are somewhat different, arguments over out-of-area operations for German troops, such as German participation in UN operations in Somalia or the former Yugoslavia, stress similar themes. To put this in broader terms, one of the goals of the Kohl government has been to turn Germany into a "normal nation" again and to make Germans feel like being part of a normal nation rather than referring to Germany as a "troublesome fatherland" as the former German President Gustav Heinemann had done. Constructing a "normal nation" implies a healthy patriotism, including a positive attitude toward national symbols such as the national anthem, and the possible use of German power abroad. In this view Germany took a big step toward normality when it reunited in 1990. As Klaus Naumann, the inspector general of the German armed forces, put it in a recent book,

the united Germany must confront its responsibilities and must not permanently remain simply a net importer of security. Neither our European nor our Atlantic partners will allow us to sit on the moral throne in partially self-righteous arrogance and to let others take risks. Foreign countries are not so much afraid of possible new German desires to great power status, but they fear new German *Sonderwege* and German unreliability in crises.[45]

This normalization still reaches its limits, however, when it comes to the sale of weapons to Israel and its Arab neighbors.[46]

In the early 1990s the politically most sensitive German arms transfers involved weapons shipments to Turkey. West German military aid to Turkey began as early as 1964 and represented a form of burden sharing within the NATO alliance.[47] This aid was fairly significant for the Turkish military, particularly after 1974 when the United States instituted an arms embargo against Turkey following the Turkish invasion of Cyprus.[48] In 1991 the oppression of the Kurdish minority in Turkey became a political issue within Germany, and in November 1991 the *Bundestag* budget committee temporarily blocked funds for military assistance to Turkey because of allegations that Turkey had used German weapons in operations against its Kurdish minority. In March 1992, however, German media reported that the defense ministry had continued to ship German tanks to Turkey. As a result Defense Minister Gerhard Stoltenberg, who had already come under fire for secret arms shipments to Israel in 1990 and 1991, resigned, and Germany temporarily stopped military aid to Turkey. The controversy heated up again in 1994 when reports circulated that Turkey had used German-supplied armored personnel carriers and other German arms against Kurds. This again resulted in a temporary stop of arms shipments, and Kurdish activists in Germany staged a number of violent protests against German government policy.[49] During the parliamentary debates over this issue in 1992 deputies representing the Party of Democratic Socialism (PDS) called for a weapons embargo against Turkey, whereas Social Democrats advocated the conversion of military aid to Turkey into an economic aid program. The Christian Democrats supported a continuation of military aid to Turkey but emphasized that the German parliament expected Turkey to honor its contractual obligations.[50]

Although arms exports as such have been highly controversial in Germany, this is not the case in the United States, at least not to the same extent. Here Mahoney and Wallace found that few groups are interested in the security assistance program in its entirety. Instead, they focus on portions of the program. Their activities often involve the potential use of security assistance programs as a means through which other facets of foreign policy can be affected, rather than an interest in security assistance, per se.[51]

The one group that consistently favors U.S. arms transfers is, not surprisingly, a trade promotion group, the American League for Exports and Security Assistance, Inc.   Its members include both defense contractors and unions.   According to Mahoney and Wallace, the two handicaps that the group faced were, first of all, that its members at times had divergent interests and, second, the lack of strong trade union involvement.[52]   Prominent among groups that become active on only specific parts of the U.S. arms transfer program are groups with ties to a particular nation or region.   Here the American Israel Public Affairs Committee (AIPAC) stands out as an important example.   In regard to political parties, it is more difficult to classify the positions of parties in the United States than in Germany.   Nevertheless, it is safe to say that in the past efforts to restrain arms exports struck a more responsive chord among Democrats than Republicans.   This can clearly be seen in the differences between Carter's and Reagan's arms export policies. President Carter instituted a variety of changes in U.S. policy and attempted to exercise more restraint in this area.   These measures included, for example, the prohibition of coproduction agreements for major weapons systems, no permission for the development of advanced weapons exclusively for the export market, and a quantitative ceiling on arms transfers.   Although it is debatable whether these efforts, and the quantitative ceiling in particular, enjoyed much success, the Reagan administration had no interest in restraint at all and viewed arms sales as an essential part of U.S. foreign policy.[53]

Yet, in the wake of the Gulf War the Bush administration called for restraint in arms transfers, but it failed to follow through on those declarations by announcing billion dollar arms sales to the Middle East shortly thereafter.[54]   In Congress Republican Senator John McCain introduced a War Prevention and Arms Transfer Control bill and wrote in early 1991 that "the current thawing of the Cold War offers a priceless opportunity to reduce those arms sales that threaten world peace."[55]   But McCain did not advocate cutting back on arms transfers to friendly countries, rather control efforts should be focused on "a few rogue nations" including Iraq, Iran, Cuba, North Korea, Vietnam, Afghanistan, Syria, and Libya.[56]   Furthermore, he argued that "the United States sold virtually no arms to aggressor states during the 1980s" who instead "obtained their arms from Communist bloc countries."[57]

At the end of 1993 Republican Senator Mark Hatfield and Democratic Representative Cynthia McKinney introduced a bill entitled the Code of Conduct on Arms Transfers Act of 1993. This bill would block U.S. arms transfers to countries that do not have democratic political institutions, violate human rights, engage in armed aggression, or do not fully participate in the UN Arms Register.[58] As is standard in sanctions legislation, the bill allows for presidential waivers, but in a new twist such waivers would have to be approved by Congress. In a statement for the Congressional Record, Hatfield argued that "[t]here is one significant sector of our export economy which not only undermines our own security but contributes to destabilization in the developing world. I am talking about conventional arms transfers."[59]

NUCLEAR EXPORTS

Although the problem of restrictions on arms exports forms a quite contentious issue in German politics, the situation has looked different in the area of nuclear exports. Most of the major parties in the past supported a nuclear export policy which was considerably less restrictive than that of the United States. Nuclear nonproliferation became a major issue in West Germany in the 1960s. Between 1967 and 1969 the controversy over the NPT showed splits between the major political parties in Germany, and also within parties. Opponents of the NPT included parts of the Christian Democratic party, and particularly the CSU. To some extent, splits within the CDU/CSU on this issue reflected the old division between Gaullists and Atlanticists.[60] Among the opponents or skeptics of the treaty different politicians stressed different themes. Science Minister Stoltenberg emphasized technical aspects of concern to the German nuclear industry, such as the safeguards and inspection issue.[61] Chancellor Kiesinger, at least in a meeting with the American Ambassador McGhee, argued that his "principal concern lay in the possible effect of the treaty on the development of European political unification."[62] Vocal opponents of the treaty also included high-level German diplomats, such as the German ambassador to NATO Wilhelm Grewe.[63] In his memoirs Grewe stresses the discriminatory intent and impact of the NPT which, at least from the Soviet point of view, was directed specifically against the Federal Republic. In January 1969 Grewe and Ambassador Schnippenkoetter, who represented West Germany on disarmament and arms control questions, criticized the NPT at a conference in Munich. The foreign office then prohibited these diplomats from making public speeches.[64]

The Social Democratic party led by Brandt did not join the chorus of vehement anti-NPT rhetoric initiated by the CSU and parts of the CDU, but as foreign minister, Willy Brandt pushed for revisions in the treaty to make it more acceptable to Germany. Brandt's main claim to fame, however, was his *Ostpolitik* and acceptance of the NPT helped to open

the door to improved relations with the Soviet Union and Eastern
Europe. The Free Democrats as early as 1958 proposed that Germany be
free of nuclear weapons and the party objected to the German acquisition
of nuclear delivery systems. During the NPT debate, though, the party
failed to take a clear position.[65]

At the end of 1966 the SPD and the CDU/CSU formed the so-called
Grand Coalition, which meant that on some issues, such as the NPT, the
government found it difficult to reach common positions. To turn to
non-governmental actors, representatives of the West German nuclear
industry, such as the German atomic forum (*Deutsches Atomforum*)
expressed some criticisms of the treaty at the beginning of the domestic
debate. On the whole, however, the German nuclear industry supported
the German signature of the NPT. Industry representatives did not share
the strong anti-NPT sentiments of some conservative politicians and
even called the opposition to the NPT "hysterical."[66]

The deadlock over the NPT was not broken until after the election of
September 1969, but then as one of its first actions the Brandt govern-
ment signed the NPT. During the debate over the ratification of the NPT
in 1973 and early 1974 the Christian Democrats were again divided. On
February 20, 1974, a majority of Christian Democratic deputies, led by
Karl Carstens and Helmut Kohl, voted in favor of ratification. However,
the ranks of the NPT opponents included such prominent politicians as
Alfred Dregger, Alois Mertes, Theo Waigel, and Manfred Wörner.[67]
After the controversy over the NPT had died down, nuclear nonproliferation issues ceased to be significant objects of German political
debates until the end of the 1980s. In the international arena, however, in
the 1970s the West German government again found itself in opposition
to U.S. nonproliferation policy and specifically nuclear export practices.
Whereas the United States pressed for tighter controls and safeguards,
West German officials pointed to article IV of the NPT, which states that
all treaty signatories "have the right to participate in the fullest possible
exchange of equipment, materials and scientific and technological
information for the peaceful use of nuclear energy." Domestically, all
three major parties, the CDU/CSU, the SPD, and the smaller Free
Democratic Party (FDP), stood behind a government policy that broadly
supported the principle of nonproliferation but also favored relatively
few restrictions on nuclear trade.[68] This changed with the rise of the
Greens. The Greens opposed both civilian nuclear power and nuclear
weapons, and consequently they also criticized German nuclear exports.
Furthermore, in the 1980s the Social Democratic party changed its
position on full-scope safeguards. In the 1970s SPD-led governments
had opposed American pressure to require full-scope safeguards of all
nuclear customers, but as the largest opposition party in the 1980s it
shifted its stance.[69]

In 1987 a scandal rocked the German nuclear industry. The key participants included a set of companies that are all located in Hanau and play a crucial role in the German nuclear fuel cycle. The scandal started with reports of irregularities in the transport of nuclear waste. Some media accounts speculated about the diversion of radioactive material to Libya and Pakistan.[70] In 1988 the *Bundestag* set up an investigative committee that began hearings on a range of related issues, including German nuclear nonproliferation policy and nuclear export controls.[71] While this committee conducted its work, other scandals broke. Most importantly, the *New York Times* began a series of articles on German involvement in a chemical weapons project in Libya that William Safire referred to as "Auschwitz-in-the-sand."[72] Jolted to action, the federal government initiated a series of legislative and administrative changes in German export control policy. For our purposes particularly important is the fact that in 1990 the German government decided to require full-scope safeguards as a condition for future German nuclear exports. This decision also requires a renegotiation of the notorious German-Brazilian nuclear cooperation agreement.[73] Furthermore, in September 1990 the two Germanys committed themselves in article 3 of the so-called Two-plus-four Treaty to maintain the nonnuclear status of a unified Germany and to honor the obligations of the NPT. In contrast to the late 1960s, this renewed renunciation of a nuclear option caused hardly a ripple in German politics.

In contrast to Germany, in the United States the division between advocates of strict nuclear export controls and proponents of more liberal policies does not neatly correspond to partisan differences. Considering the legislative politics of this issue, support for strong nonproliferation and tight nuclear export policies

cuts across party lines. It is based upon a tacit coalition of liberal antinuclear constituencies and the more right-wing constituencies that are preoccupied with national security and preserving the USA's geopolitical dominance.[74]

While Walker and Lönnroth's analysis primarily dealt with the 1970s and early 1980s, conservative concerns over the spread of nuclear weapons have been evident much longer. In fact, during the 1950s opposition to Eisenhower's Atoms for Peace program and the dissemination of American nuclear technology and material came primarily from conservative Republicans, such as Senators Joseph McCarthy, John W. Bricker, William F. Knowland, and Bourke B. Hickenlooper.[75] Conservative opposition to the Atoms for Peace program in both the Democratic and Republican parties surfaced in 1957 during the debate on the ratification of the International Atomic Energy Agency's (IAEA) statute.[76] In a *National Review* article David Shea Teeple warned that China could become a member of the agency, nuclear material supplied to the agency by the United States could end up in the Soviet Union, and he doubted that the agency could prevent the diversion of nuclear material for military purposes. IAEA inspections would most likely be ineffective.[77]

Both in Germany and the United States domestic conflict over nuclear export and nonproliferation policy at times pitted one executive branch agency against another. In the 1960s during the NPT negotiations, proponents of such a treaty included the Arms Control and Disarmament Agency (ACDA) and the Atomic Energy Commission (AEC), whereas Europeanists in the State Department were concerned about the strain the NPT put on intra-alliance relations, particularly the relationship between Washington and Bonn. Former AEC Chairman Seaborg criticized that "there was a great reluctance in the administration, from President Johnson on down, to treat the Germans other than with kid gloves."[78]

In the 1970s and 1980s nuclear power became a hotly contested issue both in Germany and the United States. However, one of the key differences between the politics of nuclear exports in Germany and the United States has been that, for the most part, opposition to nuclear energy in Germany remained separate from the nonproliferation issue and the larger concerns of the peace movement in the 1980s.[79] In the United States, on the other hand, environmentalist groups, such as the Sierra Club or the Natural Resources Defense Council, not only opposed civilian nuclear power projects in the United States but directly linked nuclear energy to nuclear weapons. This meant that they also became active on nuclear nonproliferation and nuclear export issues. Anti-nuclear activists achieved some success under the Carter administration which engaged in heated political battles against reprocessing and the plutonium economy at home and abroad. The Carter administration included a few strong opponents of nuclear power, such as Jessica Mathews who served on the National Security Council and Gustave Speth who won a seat on the Council on Environmental Quality. According to Brenner, these "purists" in the Carter White House "were unrelenting in pressing for the severest licensing terms on nuclear exports and in resisting any trimming of non-proliferation sails to political winds, and they were unyielding on concessions to technically proficient states desirous of undertaking commercial reprocessing."[80]

One of the most controversial nuclear export issues during the Carter administration involved the shipment of nuclear fuel to the Tarapur nuclear power station in India. In May 1980 the Nuclear Regulatory Commission turned down licenses for fuel shipments to India, but the Carter administration decided to overrule the NRC, a decision that then became subject to a legislative veto. The fight in the Senate was rather close, but on September 24, 1980, the Senate voted 46–48 to reject a resolution blocking the shipment. The supporters of the resolution challenging the president included such odd couples as Ted Kennedy of Massachusetts and North Carolina's Jesse Helms, and Colorado's Gary Hart and South Carolina's Strom Thurmond. This again shows that the politics of nuclear proliferation and nuclear exports does not follow simple partisan or ideological divisions.[81]

President Carter's successor in the White House did not continue Carter's high-profile nonproliferation policy and viewed the plight of the American nuclear industry more sympathetically than his predecessor. However, Richard Perle, Reagan's point man on export control policy, did not only push for a tightening of East-West controls but also fought for strict nonproliferation controls that, on occasion, led to squabbles with the State Department. In a prepared statement for a hearing on nuclear nonproliferation issues in 1987 Perle stated that

export controls are politically costly, and the costs are much more immediate than the benefits. Export controls require that a nation forgo commerce and may cause diplomatic irritation. Export controls require that one apply general policies to a specific case where the friendship and the relationship with another country are highly valued. It is regrettable that this must be done, but it is the only way to maintain an effective nonproliferation regime.[82]

A good illustration of the complexity of the politics of these issues is the odyssey of a bill that Senators Pell and Jesse Helms first introduced in 1989. S195 required the executive branch to impose a variety of sanctions on countries that used chemical weapons and on companies that contributed to the proliferation of chemical weapons. Although the bill dealt with chemical rather than nuclear weapons, the political issues involved are closely related. The fact that this piece of legislation was cosponsored by Pell and Helms yet again demonstrates the crossing of partisan and ideological lines on this issue. Although the measure enjoyed broad support in the Senate it failed to pass in 1989 because of a jurisdictional dispute between the Foreign Affairs and Banking committees. In 1990 the Senate attached the provisions of S195 to the Export Administration Act reauthorization bill, but President Bush pocket-vetoed the bill because of the chemical sanctions provisions. Pell and Helms tried again in 1991 and attached their bill to a measure authorizing funds for the State Department, but this time passage of the bill was delayed by opposition from the House Ways and Means committee.[83]

In the 1990s the key question will continue to be how to reconcile the goals of economic competitiveness and export promotion with continued vigilance on nonproliferation issues. As the Clinton administration formulates its policies in this area it will face conflicting pressures from Congress. Some members of Congress, such as Senator John Glenn of

Ohio who has played a prominent role in nonproliferation policy since the 1970s, favor a strict export control policy. Others, such as former House Subcommittee Chairman Sam Gejdenson of Connecticut, have been more concerned with the negative impact of tight controls on U.S. trade.

CONCLUSION

To summarize, until the late 1980s the domestic political environment in the United States was more hospitable to strict export controls than in Germany. Furthermore, an important difference between the domestic politics of our three issue areas is that whereas in the United States all have been quite controversial during the 1970s, 1980s and early 1990s, in Germany this has been true of arms exports, but not of East-West trade and only intermittently in the case of nuclear exports. In the areas of East-West trade and nuclear exports, where there has been a considerable degree of consensus among the major actors, German policies generally reflected the goal of supporting an economy for which exports are vital. In regard to the issue of arms exports, however, we found conflict, and this is reflected in the tension between an official rhetoric, which still espouses the value of a restrictive export policy, and denials of particularly sensitive and publicly visible export requests, on the one hand, and a less restrictive policy on less sensitive weapons and on transfers which are more difficult to control and trace, on the other hand. During the past few years, however, different political developments in the two countries have occurred that may result in at least a partial convergence of their policies. In Germany the domestic political climate has shifted in favor of tighter export controls, at least for Third World customers. In the United States, on the other hand, pressure has been mounting to relax national security export controls.

Another major difference between the politics of export controls in Germany and the United States concerns the number of relevant political actors who articulate policy demands. In Germany export control policy usually does not make the headlines, and in the past, policy generally was hashed out between executive agencies and industry as the primary client. To the extent that controversies arise, political parties articulate the major policy alternatives. In the United States, on the other hand, different ethnic groups, environmentalists, other public interest groups, and individuals employed by various think tanks enjoy at least limited access to the policy-making process. This suggests that Germany and the United States differ in their political opportunity structures. As Kitschelt has argued, the German political system with "its centripetal party system, organized along class and religious cleavages, weak legislature, and inaccessible executive" is relatively closed.[84] In the United States, on the other hand, "[t]he comparatively strong position of the Congress, the lack of tightly integrated political parties, the relative openness of a deeply fragmented administration, all" contribute to a fairly open system.[85] However, this is a description of how the U.S. and German political systems typically work. At critical junctures, such as 1989 for export control policy, even the relatively closed German system opened up to create windows of opportunity for change. The following two chapters will show whether these broad generalizations hold at the level of concrete case studies.

NOTES

1. Stent, *Technology Transfer to the Soviet Union*, pp. 27–28.
2. National Academy of Sciences, *Balancing the National Interest*.
3. U.S. Congress, *Congressional Record*, House, 6 June 1990, p. 3284.
4. U.S. Congress, House Committee on Foreign Affairs, *The Reauthorization of the Export Administration Act*, 102d Cong., 1st sess., 1991, p. 87.
5. *Congressional Quarterly Weekly Report*, 28 May 1994, p. 1374.
6. *Arms Control Today*, July/August 1993, p. 24; October 1993, p. 20; December 1993, p. 22.
7. Eckhard Stratmann, "Made in Germany: Vom Weltmarkt zum Binnenmarkt," in Frank Beckenbach, Jo Müller, Reinhard Pfriem, and Eckhard Stratmann, eds., *Grüne Wirtschaftspolitik: Machbare Utopien* (Cologne: Kiepenheuer & Witsch, 1985), pp. 327–349.
8. West Germany, *Verhandlungen des Deutschen Bundestages*, 11. Wahlperiode, Stenographische Berichte 11/153, p. 11585.
9. "Vorsichtiger Optimismus im deutschen Maschinen- und Anlagenbau," *Frankfurter Allgemeine Zeitung*, 21 January 1994, p. 17; "Luftfahrtindustrie will stärkere Förderung," *Frankfurter Allgemeine Zeitung*, 18 January 1994, p. 11; "Gegen nationale Exportkontrolle," *Frankfurter Allgemeine Zeitung*, 28 February 1994, p. 15.
10. Stratmann, "Made in Germany," pp. 333–335.
11. As reported in Ludger Kühnhardt, "Wertgrundlagen der deutschen Außenpolitik," in *Deutschlands neue Außenpolitik*, eds. Karl Kaiser and Hanns W. Maull, vol. 1 (Munich: Oldenbourg, 1994), p. 118.
12. Jacobsen, "East-West Trade and Export Controls," p. 159.
13. Erhard, *Deutschlands Rückkehr zum Weltmarkt*, pp. 195–197.
14. Wörmann, *Der deutsche Osthandel*, pp. 16–17.
15. Tudyka, "Gesellschaftliche Interessen," p. 208. The BDI maintained this position into the 1980s. In its 1988 report to its members the BDI stated in regard to CoCom that German industry had always agreed to the primacy of security interests. In the following sentence the report also supported a reduction of CoCom lists, though. See BDI, *Bericht 1986–88*, p. 287.
16. Stent, *From Embargo to Ostpolitik*, pp. 35–40.
17. Putnam, "Diplomacy and Domestic Politics."
18. Jim Rollo and Alasdair Smith, "EC Trade With Eastern Europe," *Economic Policy*, no. 16 (April 1993): 140–181.

19. "Mannesmann rechnet mit Betriebsverlust im ersten Halbjahr," *Frankfurter Allgemeine Zeitung*, 2 June 1993, p. 19.

20. Mastanduno, *Economic Containment*, pp. 73–74.

21. Samuel Pisar, *Coexistence and Commerce: Guidelines for Transactions Between East and West* (New York: McGraw Hill, 1970), pp. 84–85.

22. Mastanduno, *Economic Containment*, p. 136.

23. For a more detailed discussion of the Bucy report and its implementation see Mastanduno, *Economic Containment*, chapter 6.

24. National Academy of Sciences, *Balancing the National Interest*, p. 116.

25. Congress, *Reauthorization of the EAA*, pp. 50–53.

26. Reinhard Rode, *Sicherheit versus Geschäft: Die Osthandelspolitik der USA von Nixon bis Carter* (Frankfurt: Campus, 1986), chapter 2.

27. For a more detailed discussion of the legislative politics of East-West trade during this time see Philip J. Funigiello, *American Soviet Trade in the Cold War* (Chapel Hill: University of North Carolina Press, 1988), chapter 3.

28. For an intricate account of the politics behind the Jackson-Vanik amendment see Paula Stern, *Water's Edge: Domestic Politics and the Making of American Foreign Policy* (Westport, Conn.: Greenwood Press, 1979).

29. U.S. Congress, Joint Economic Committee, *Arms Trade and Non-proliferation*, 101st and 102d Cong., pp. 294–295.

30. Brzoska, *Rüstungsexportpolitik*, p. 162.

31. Gerard Braunthal, *The Federation of German Industry in Politics* (Ithaca: Cornell University Press, 1965), p. 298.

32. Brzoska, *Rüstungsexportpolitik*, p. 167.

33. Andrew Shonfield, *Modern Capitalism: The Changing Balance of Public and Private Power* (Oxford: Oxford University Press, 1965). There are interest groups, though, that represent the interests of the German defense industry, and of arms exporters in particular. The best example is the BDLI, the association of the German aerospace industry.

34. Christian Wellmann, "Gewerkschaftliche Alternativplanstrategie," in *Das Geschäft mit dem Tod: Fakten & Hintergründe der Rüstungsindustrie*, eds. Michael Brzoska et al. (Frankfurt: Eichborn, 1982), pp. 123–161.

35. *Woche im Bundestag*, 2 March 1994, p. 40.

36. Brzoska, *Rüstungsexportpolitik*, pp. 29–30.

37. "'Nachteile für deutsche Rüstungsfirmen müssen verschwinden'," *Frankfurter Allgemeine Zeitung*, 5 January 1994, p. 1; "Unerwarteter Protest gegen vereinfachte Rüstungsexporte," *Frankfurter Allgemeine Zeitung*, 6 January 1994, p. 1; "Kanzleramt befürwortet einfachere Waffenexportrichtlinien," *Frankfurter Allgemeine Zeitung*, 10 January 1994, p. 1; "'Harmonisierung in Europa ist nötig,'" *Frankfurter Allgemeine Zeitung*, 12 January 1994, p. 5.

38. Brzoska, "The Erosion of Restraint," p. 165.

39. *Der Spiegel*, 25 January 1993, pp. 23–25; *Der Spiegel*, 22 February 1993, pp. 30–31; *Woche im Bundestag*, 31 March 1994, p. 44, 8 December 1993, p. 36.

40. For a discussion of these issues from a leftist perspective see Ulrich Albrecht, Peter Lock, and Herbert Wulf, *Mit Rüstung gegen Arbeitslosigkeit?* (Reinbek: Rowohlt Taschenbuch Verlag, 1982), pp. 115–141.

41. Charles S. Maier, *The Unmasterable Past: History, Holocaust, and German National Identity* (Cambridge: Harvard University Press, 1988).

42. Hans-Peter Schwarz, *Die gezähmten Deutschen: Von der Machtbesessenheit zur Machtvergessenheit* (Stuttgart: Deutsche Verlags-Anstalt, 1985).

43. John Tagliabue, "Marketing West German Arms," *New York Times*, 29 March 1987, sec. 3, p. 4.

44. Ibid.

45. Naumann, *Bundeswehr*, p. 141, author's translation.

46. For a Social Democratic critique of this "normalization thesis" see Peter Glotz, *Die falsche Normalisierung: Die unmerkliche Verwandlung der Deutschen 1989 bis 1994* (Frankfurt: Suhrkamp, 1994).

47. Haftendorn, *Militärhilfe*, pp. 14–15.

48. Brzoska, *Rüstungsexportpolitik*, p. 136.

49. *Der Spiegel*, 30 March 1992, pp. 18–20; 11 April 1994, pp. 22–23; 9 May 1994, pp. 51–55.

50. Germany, Deutscher Bundestag, *Drucksachen*, 12/2498, 12/3216, 12/3434.

51. Robert B. Mahoney, Jr., and David L. Wallace, "The Domestic Constituencies of the Security Assistance Program," in *U.S. Security Assistance: The Political Process*, eds. Ernest Graves and Steven A. Hildreth (Lexington, Mass.: D. C. Heath, 1985), p. 126.

52. Ibid., pp. 143–144.

53. Pierre, *The Global Politics of Arms Sales*, pp. 52–68.

54. William D. Hartung, "Curbing the Arms Trade: From Rhetoric to Restraint," *World Policy Journal* 9 (Spring 1992): 219–247.

55. John McCain, "Controlling Arms Sales to the Third World," *Washington Quarterly* 14 (Spring 1991): 80.

56. Ibid., pp. 81–82.

57. Ibid., p. 82.

58. *Arms Control Today*, March 1993, pp. 36–37.

59. *Congressional Record*, 18 November 1993, p. S16219.

60. Besson, *Die Außenpolitik*, p. 364. Gaullists, such as chancellor Adenauer in his last few years and leading politicians in the CSU, favored closer ties with France and feared American détente policies. Atlanticists, such as Adenauer's successor Erhard, realized the illusions of that approach and, occasionally with reluctance, followed Washington's diplomatic line.

61. Ibid.; McGhee, *At the Creation*, pp. 210–212.

62. McGhee, *At the Creation*, p. 210

63. Wilhelm G. Grewe, *Rückblenden 1976–1951* (Frankfurt: Propyläen, 1979), pp. 689–703.

64. Besson, *Die Außenpolitik*, p. 398.

65. Matthias Küntzel, *Bonn und die Bombe: Deutsche Atomwaffenpolitik von Adenauer bis Brandt* (Frankfurt: Campus, 1992), pp. 129–131.

66. Joachim Radkau, *Aufstieg und Krise der deutschen Atomwirtschaft 1945–1975: Verdrängte Alternativen in der Kerntechnik und der Ursprung der nuklearen Kontroverse* (Reinbek: Rowohlt Taschenbuch Verlag, 1983), pp. 329–333.

67. Küntzel, *Bonn und die Bombe*, pp. 236–239.

68. Lothar Wilker, "Nuklearexport- und Nichtverbreitungspolitik," pp. 92–93.

69. Lothar Wilker, "Bundestag und Außenpolitik," in *US-Kongreß und deutscher Bundestag: Bestandsaufnahmen im Vergleich* (Opladen: Westdeutscher Verlag, 1988), p. 394.

70. Holger Koppe and Egmont R. Koch, *Bomben-Geschäfte: Tödliche Waffen für die Dritte Welt* (Munich: Knesebeck & Schuler, 1990).

71. Germany, Deutscher Bundestag, *Drucksache* 11/7800.

72. William Safire, "The German Problem," *New York Times*, 2 January 1989, p. 19.

73. Germany, Deutscher Bundestag, *Drucksache* 11/8512, p. 5.

74. Walker and Lönnroth, *Nuclear Power Struggles*, p. 155.

75. Jack M. Holl, "The Peaceful Atom: Lore and Myth," in *Atoms for Peace: An Analysis After Thirty Years*, eds. Joseph F. Pilat, Robert E. Pendley, and Charles K. Ebinger (Boulder: Westview Press, 1985), pp. 156–157.

76. For a detailed account see Richard G. Hewlett and Jack M. Holl, *Atoms for Peace and War 1953–1961: Eisenhower and the Atomic Energy Commission* (Berkeley: University of California Press, 1989), pp. 432–435.

77. David Shea Teeple, "Atoms for Peace—or War?" *National Review*, 12 January 1957, pp. 35–37.

78. Glenn T. Seaborg, *Stemming the Tide: Arms Control in the Johnson Years* (Lexington: Lexington Books, 1987), p. 300.

79. Christian Joppke, *Mobilizing Against Nuclear Energy: A Comparison of Germany and the United States* (Berkeley: University of California Press, 1993), pp. 169–171.

80. Brenner, *Nuclear Power and Non-Proliferation*, p. 125.

81. For a detailed account by a participant in the congressional struggle over Tarapur see Edward Markey, *Nuclear Peril: The Politics of Proliferation* (Cambridge, Mass.: Ballinger 1982).

82. U.S. Congress, Senate Committee on Governmental Affairs, *Nuclear Nonproliferation and U.S. National Security*, 100th Cong., 1st sess., 1987, p. 183.

83. *Congressional Quarterly (CQ) Almanac* 1989, pp. 501–503; *CQ Almanac* 1990, pp. 198–201; *CQ Weekly Report* 1991, pp. 2185–2186, 2805–2806, 2886, 2964–2965, 3467, 3540, 3599–3600.

84. Herbert P. Kitschelt, "Political Opportunity Structures and Political Protest: Anti-Nuclear Movements in Four Democracies," *British Journal of Political Science* 16 (January 1986): 66.

85. Ibid.

5

Faded Nuclear Dreams: German and U.S. Exports to Argentina and the Philippines

In this chapter I will present the two nuclear export cases involving a German reactor export to Argentina and the export of a Westinghouse reactor to the Philippines. The political decisions sanctioning the exports were reached at roughly the same time in 1980. Beyond that, the two cases suffered a similar fate. Originally it had been expected that the German-supplied Atucha II plant would begin producing electricity in June 1987 but at the end of 1988 the plant was only half-finished.[1] The Philippine plant had been ordered and built under the Marcos regime. From the outset it had been mired in controversy and by the time it was completed in 1985 it cost $2.2 billion rather than the original estimate of $1.1 billion. After the fall of Marcos Corazon Aquino mothballed the plant in 1986, and in 1988 the Philippine government filed suit against the supplier Westinghouse and the engineering firm Burns & Roe. In May 1993 a federal jury in New Jersey ruled against the Philippine government and cleared Westinghouse of bribery charges.[2] However, the primary emphasis of the two case studies will not be on the internal dynamics of the Argentine and Philippine nuclear programs but on the domestic decision-making processes leading to U.S. and German authorizations of the exports. In more concrete terms, the case studies will address the question of whether the differences between U.S. and German nuclear export policies are related to differences in the centralization of state institutions and in the relationship between state institutions and industry. Furthermore, this chapter will analyze the interaction between U.S. diplomatic pressure on Germany and the domestic German politics of nuclear exports.

THE GERMAN CASE

Before discussing the details of the contract between the German reactor manufacturer *Kraftwerk Union* and the Argentine government, though, it is important to gain a broad understanding of Argentina's nuclear power program and of the involvement of foreign suppliers in this program. The beginnings of nuclear power in Argentina date back as far as 1949.[3] As early as 1958 Argentina used U.S. plans to build a research reactor.[4] What is distinctive about Argentina's nuclear program, in contrast to that of its regional rival Brazil, is that Argentina placed heavy emphasis on self-sufficiency, and that Argentina demonstrated a "commitment to integrate national private firms into nuclear industrial activity," and a technological preference for heavy water reactors fueled with natural uranium rather than the more widespread light water technology.[5] Solingen argues that the Argentine emphasis on the participation of private domestic firms and preference of heavy water natural uranium technology, in distinction to Brazil's strategy of importing light water technology and building a state-run nuclear sector, reflects the impact of state institutions. At the time when Argentina initiated and implemented its ambitious nuclear program the governing regime did not enjoy a broad macropolitical consensus, rather the state apparatus was divided up among the three military services with the navy supervising the *Comisión Nacional de Energía Atómica* (CNEA), which enjoyed a high degree of lateral autonomy. In other words, the Argentine navy ran the nuclear program without much outside interference. As a consequence, the program reflected the navy's preferences that were partly shaped by institutional rivalries with other service branches. According to Solingen, "[t]he possibility of a greater role for national firms and technical resources enabled CNEA to create legitimating constituencies and clientilistic networks among industrial entrepreneurs and scientific elites. This strategy fit naturally with the navy's traditional penchant for technical excellence, often held as an advantage over the army."[6] This discussion of technological choice is quite different from the arguments usually made in nonproliferation circles. The U.S. government, for example, regards light water reactors as more proliferation resistant than heavy water technology, and recently U.S. officials apparently held out the prospect of assisting North Korea in redirecting its nuclear power program from heavy water to light water reactors.[7] In the domestic German debate on nuclear export policy the Social Democrats and Greens pointed out that outside of Europe Argentina's preferred reactor line had been chosen only by countries that had not signed the NPT, such as India.[8]

In 1968 the West German company Siemens won the contract to build Argentina's first power reactor Atucha I. Despite the fact that apparently the design of the Canadian bid was better, the German bid was successful, according to Daniel Poneman, because of "its superior financing terms, delivery time, and local participation. The better Canadian design was outweighed by the convenience of buying from a traditional trading partner, the reliability of Siemens (which had long had a branch in Argentina), and the full support for the sale by the German government."[9] After Siemens had won the contract the government-owned *Kreditanstalt für Wiederaufbau* provided loans for the construction, operation and maintenance of Atucha I totaling 175 million DM.[10] This sale was a mixed blessing for Siemens, however, since cost overruns came close to 100 percent, which Siemens absorbed by itself.[11]

In July 1971 the West German nuclear research center at Karlsruhe and CNEA signed a cooperation agreement focusing primarily on the fabrication, irradiation and testing of fuel elements.[12] In the 1970s the German company *Reaktor-Brennelement Union GmbH* (RBU), a subsidiary of NUKEM and Kraftwerk-Union AG (KWU), worked on a fuel fabrication plant in Argentina with an annual capacity of 400 tons.[13] Furthermore, West Germany supplied a research reactor to Argentina which started up in 1972. However, German companies were not the only foreign suppliers involved in Argentina's nuclear program. In 1973 Argentina signed a contract with the Canadian reactor manufacturer AECL to build Argentina's second power reactor at Embalse.[14] Thus, when Argentina invited bids for a third reactor in 1978 it was generally assumed that either KWU or Atomic Energy of Canada Ltd (AECL) would win the contract. In 1978 Argentina was not only interested in a power reactor, though, but it also wanted a heavy water production plant. Until then Argentina had depended on foreign suppliers to run its reactors. A heavy water plant of its own would have taken Argentina one step closer to nuclear self-sufficiency. In the following section I will provide a summary of the key dates in the German decision-making process to approve this export deal.

Outline of German Decision-Making Process

During the summer of 1978 KWU submitted its bid for the reactor to the Argentine atomic energy commission CNEA.[15] Within the same time frame the German company Friedrich Uhde and the Swiss firm Sulzer followed with their bids for the heavy water plant. In February 1979 CNEA asked the bidders for information on the conditions their home governments would require before issuing export licenses. Both the nuclear council (*Nuklearrat*) and the nuclear cabinet committee (*Nuklearkabinett*) planned to discuss the Argentina project and possible West German participation in it in mid-February 1979.[16] The meeting of the cabinet committee was postponed twice, however, and in March 1979 the cabinet decided not to reach a substantive decision at that time but to consult first with the United States and Argentina.[17]

On May 15, 1979, following another cabinet meeting on this matter, State Secretary Haunschild of the ministry for research and technology met with Carlos Castro Madero, the head of the CNEA, to discuss the German position on safeguards. On July 24, 1979, the German government presented the Argentine ambassador with a document (a so-called "non-paper"), which had been personally approved by German Chancellor Schmidt and which explained under what conditions German authorities would approve the export of a reactor and/or a heavy water plant. Later that summer the economics minister Count Lambsdorff traveled to Argentina and personally supported the German bid in a conversation with Castro Madero. These efforts met with success, and on October 1, 1979, the CNEA announced that KWU had won the contract for the reactor, whereas the Swiss company Sulzer secured the order for a heavy water plant.

Kraftwerk Union wasted no time and applied for an export license on October 2. In November 1979 the nuclear council and the nuclear cabinet committee both discussed the issue, and German officials continued their talks with their Argentine counterparts at a variety of places, including the general conference meeting of the IAEA in New Delhi in December 1979. Several months later, on March 19, 1980, the West German government decided at a cabinet meeting that an export license would be granted under the condition that Argentina complied with a number of nonproliferation requirements that had also been decided upon at that meeting. On the basis of these guidelines a German government delegation negotiated a diplomatic note exchange on March 24 and 25, 1980, in Buenos Aires. This exchange of notes was signed by representatives of the two governments on May 8, 1980.[18] The West German *Bundesamt für Wirtschaft* granted an export license in June 1980.[19]

This export proved to be one of Germany's most controversial nuclear export deals. First of all, the sale led to diplomatic tensions between West Germany and Canada whose bid had lost. According to a Canadian newspaper account, "[d]iplomatic sources in Ottawa describe relations with West Germany as 'seriously impaired' and 'at the lowest point we can recall.'"[20] U.S. diplomats expressed their concerns and held Germany responsible for providing Argentina with the opportunity to close its nuclear fuel cycle and consequently to acquire a nuclear weapons capability.[21] On April 19, 1982, just when the conflict between Great Britain and Argentina over the Falkland Islands (Malvinas) escalated, a BBC program with the title "Germany and the Argentine Bomb" tried to show how the Germans, and some old Nazis in particular, "had provided Argentina with the technology to make an atomic bomb."[22]   In order to understand this controversy we need to take a closer look at the diplomatic negotiations that accompanied this sale.

Commercial Competition and Safeguards

When Germany's KWU and Canada's AECL submitted their bids for the Atucha II reactor the price tag of the German offer was $1.579 billion, whereas AECL asked for $1.075 billion. This raises the question of why Argentina was willing to spend $500 million more by ordering from Germany rather than Canada. According to Carlos Castro Madero, an important reason why CNEA preferred the KWU offer over the Canadian bid was the previous experience CNEA had with the two suppliers. KWU had built Argentina's first reactor Atucha I for the price set forth in the contract. Atucha I had an excellent operating record, and KWU had been willing to fulfill further Argentine wishes even when its was not obliged by contract to do so. In 1973 CNEA had signed a contract with AECL for the construction of a second reactor, which was to be finished in January 1980 for an estimated price of $320 million. In the fall of 1979 this estimate was changed such that the reactor would finally come on stream in March 1982 for a price of $1 billion.[23] The president of CNEA also maintained that the bids were not fully comparable, and if one took into consideration not only the cost of building the plant but also the "costs of the nuclear fuel cycle, the operation and maintenance" of the plant, the overall price difference between the two bids narrowed considerably.[24]

However, critics of the deal contended that the real reason why German and Swiss companies rather than a Canadian firm had been awarded the contracts was that Germany and Switzerland had attached fewer political restrictions to the sale and had undercut the Canadians in that way. Thus, this case was part of a larger dispute among the principal nuclear suppliers in the 1970s. The United States had criticized Germany's willingness to sell an entire nuclear fuel cycle to Brazil a few years earlier, and from the 1970s through the 1980s the United States, with strong support from Canada, pushed for "full-scope safeguards" as a condition for nuclear exports to non-NPT members.

Turning to the details of the case at hand, at the end of February 1979 the U.S. government urged the German economics minister, Count Lambsdorff, to sell heavy water technology to Argentina only under the condition that Argentina renounce reprocessing.[25] In April 1979 the Canadian government informed the Argentine authorities that Canada would be willing to supply heavy water technology only under the condition of full-scope safeguards. Canada did not insist on a link with Argentine reprocessing efforts, though. The following month German State Secretary Haunschild told the president of CNEA that Germany would demand full-scope safeguards if a German company won the contract for the heavy water plant. When asked repeatedly by Carlos Castro Madero what would happen if Germany won the reactor contract but the Swiss company Sulzer were to build the heavy water plant, Haunschild replied that Germany would follow the London Supplier Guidelines. These guidelines did not require full-scope safeguards, but Haunschild expressed strong doubts that Switzerland would withstand diplomatic pressure from the United States to require full-scope safeguards. At roughly the same time State Secretary Günther van Well of the German foreign office held talks in Canada. He told his Canadian hosts that it would be desirable if Canada and West Germany insisted on the same safeguards conditions.

The charges that Germany undercut Canadian nonproliferation efforts to clinch the sale for a German company are largely based on what happened during the following three months. On July 24, 1979, the Argentine ambassador in Bonn received a document that stated that Germany would require full-scope safeguards for the export of a heavy water production plant. If Germany were to export only a nuclear reactor Germany would reach an export licensing decision in accordance with paragraphs 4 and 14 of the Nuclear Suppliers' Group guidelines. Paragraph 4 states that "[s]uppliers should transfer trigger list items only when covered by IAEA safeguards," whereas paragraph 14 refers to consultations among suppliers on particularly sensitive cases.[26] A brief prepared by the economics ministry explained that this essentially meant Germany would not require full-scope safeguards, but if diplomatic pressure (from the United States) became too strong Germany could change its position after consultations with other suppliers. A German foreign office memorandum on the same matter stated that Argentina wanted to buy the reactor from Germany under facility-specific safeguards and the heavy water plant from Switzerland, also without full-scope safeguards.[27] According to the foreign office memo, this would imply undercutting the Canadian safeguards conditions.

At the end of August 1979 Count Lambsdorff traveled to Argentina and expressed a strong interest in securing the reactor contract for a German company. He further told his Argentine host that Germany would not require full-scope safeguards for the reactor and he asked Carlos Castro Madero not to mention safeguards if KWU won the contract but to justify such a decision on technical and commercial grounds. On August 31, 1979, the Canadian ambassador in Bonn inquired about rumors that Germany was demanding less stringent safeguards than Canada. German foreign office representatives told the Canadian ambassador that Germany would require full-scope safeguards if German companies received the contracts for both the reactor and the heavy water plant. If the contracts were split, however, between Germany and a third party the situation would change.

On October 1, 1979, Carlos Castro Madero announced the contract awards. His twenty-six-page press statement did not refer to safeguards as a decisive factor. A few days later the German embassy in Buenos Aires sent a report to Bonn that stated that although the CNEA had not alluded to safeguards in its public announcements, safeguards provisions had been important for internal Argentine deliberations. On October 15, 1979, a meeting took place between the German and Swiss foreign ministers. At this meeting the Swiss government firmly declared that Switzerland would not insist on full-scope safeguards. A few months later the West German government reached a final decision along the same lines. Nevertheless, the safeguards provisions that Germany negotiated with Argentina went beyond Germany's legal obligations. In fact, German safeguards demands were disliked by the Argentines to the extent that they "threatened to . . . arrest the Atucha-2 deal."[28] In the note exchange of May 8, 1980, Argentina was called upon to change its 1972 safeguards agreement for Atucha I and delete a clause in that agreement limiting the duration of safeguards. Argentina committed itself to support the goals of the Non-Proliferation treaty and assured that it would not contribute to the spread of nuclear weapons. Nuclear material and facilities of German origin shall not be used for the manufacture of nuclear weapons nor for other military purposes, such as nuclear submarines or other nuclear explosives. Argentina also declared its willingness to place all special fissile material and nuclear facilities in Argentina at the time of the issuance of the export license under IAEA controls (de facto full-scope safeguards). The retransfer provisions of the note exchange corresponded to the London supplier guidelines.[29]

The content of the safeguards agreement still did not please the Canadian government but German officials were more concerned about the U.S. reaction. There were a number of different ways in which the United States and U.S. companies were involved in the export of the Atucha II reactor and the heavy water plant, and the United States had a few levers at its disposal. First of all, the United States put pressure on Germany through regular diplomatic channels. At the end of October 1979, for example, President Carter sent his special presidential representative on nonproliferation matters Gerard C. Smith to Germany to express U.S. disappointment at how Germany had obtained the deal with Argentina.[30] In the months before West German and Swiss authorities issued licenses for the reactor and heavy water plant U.S. pressure lessened, however.[31] Another indication of diminishing U.S. pressure can be seen in the approval by the Carter administration of a small shipment of low enriched uranium to Argentina in June 1980.[32]

U.S. companies had a stake in the German reactor export since the U.S. firm Combustion Engineering had been selected to receive a subcontract for part of the reactor vessel. Opponents of this subcontract in the U.S. Arms Control and Disarmament Agency and the State Department succeeded in delaying the export licensing process, though, and the contract was then awarded to the German-Brazilian joint venture NUCLEP.[33] The United States also had a more powerful instrument at its disposal, however, since West Germany faced the "possibility that . . . [it] might need to buy substantial quantities of U.S. heavy water for the first charge of the Atucha II reactor."[34] According to the *New York Times*, before Argentina had awarded the reactor contract to KWU, "the West German . . . government approached the United States to seek a guarantee of heavy water for the plant if it . . . [won] the bid."[35] In 1981 West Germany in fact asked for U.S. approval to sell 143 tons of U.S. origin heavy water to Argentina.[36] The Reagan administration granted this approval in a controversial decision in 1983.[37] In 1981 the Reagan administration had already approved the sale of a process control computer for the Swiss-supplied heavy water plant in Argentina.[38] Thus, to understand this case recognizing the relationships and trade-offs between commercial considerations and political objectives is crucial. From a West German perspective, though, it was not only the maximization of export sales as such that mattered. Rather, some German politicians perceived a clear link between nuclear exports and the health of the domestic nuclear energy program.

Exports and German Nuclear Energy Policy

When the former economics minister Count Lambsdorff testified at a *Bundestag* hearing on December 7, 1989, he argued that at the end of the 1970s the government was making strong efforts to save the German nuclear energy program. In this context he had become worried about the ability of KWU to maintain its technical and engineering capabilities. The company faced the prospect of losing key personnel due to a lack of orders.[39] To illustrate what was behind those arguments, in the domestic market KWU had not received an order for a nuclear power plant since 1975. This dry spell finally ended in August 1980 with the contract award for the power station Isar-2.[40] In the international arena KWU had been quite successful in the mid-1970s. At the end of 1975 KWU received an order from Spain to supply much of the equipment for the first unit of the nuclear power station at Trillo.[41] The major event in 1975, however, was the treaty between West Germany and Brazil, which was to lead to the construction of eight nuclear power plants and a number of other facilities in Brazil. In July 1975 KWU received the "letter of intent" from NUCLEBRAS for the first two 1300 megawatt units.[42] In

July 1976 KWU signed a contract for the construction of two nuclear power plants at Busher in Iran.[43]

By 1978, however, the picture had begun to change. That year, the date when Angra II, the first German-supplied nuclear power plant in Brazil, was expected to come on stream was changed from 1983 to 1984.[44] At the end of 1979 it looked more like it would take until 1987 to finish the plant.[45] Brazilian officials became skeptical about the wisdom of the 1975 treaty: "A senior government official recently said that electricity of nuclear origin was costing US $1,500–1,700 per installed KW, against US $500–600 for hydroelectric power (including long distance transmission cost). Nuclebras is already talking about building six rather than eight reactors over the next 12 years."[46] In Iran KWU had not received any more payments after November 1978, and the company terminated the contract in the summer of 1979.[47] To make matters worse, the nuclear industry feared that these domestic and international problems would reinforce each other. The *Frankfurter Allgemeine Zeitung* quoted the head of KWU as saying that "competitors in the international market were already using the sales argument that since 1975 no nuclear power plant had been ordered in Germany."[48] In 1980/81 the capacity utilization rate of KWU's manufacturing plants was 52 percent.[49] But, in one way at least the prospects looked brighter at the international front than at home. Although the German nuclear industry faced a very vocal and radicalized anti-nuclear movement at home, opposition to nuclear exports was limited.

Nuclear Exports and Political Protest

The internal West German decision-making process in the Argentine case was characterized by the fact that the important decisions were made almost exclusively within the executive branch, the level of parliamentary involvement was low, and domestic opposition to the export by parties and interest groups remained ineffective. There are a few indications of internal conflict within the executive branch. On March 4, 1979, the *New York Times* reported that "[t]he potential contract has already created sharp divisions within the Bonn government."[50] In an editorial for the *Süddeutsche Zeitung* Udo Bergdoll wrote that Chancellor Schmidt, fearing the international ramifications of the deal, was holding back economics minister Lambsdorff who wanted to secure the sale for economic reasons.[51] The deal also encountered opposition from within the Social Democratic party, as the Young Socialists (*Jungsozialisten*) spoke out against a commitment to grant an export license if the contract was awarded to a German company.[52] Social Democratic critics of the nuclear power program planned to submit a resolution at a party convention in December 1979, which, among other things, opposed further nuclear exports in the interest of a worldwide peace policy.[53] The resolution was defeated, however.

The Green party also opposed nuclear exports. Its 1980 party platform said that the export of nuclear facilities was creating new military risks and undermined international efforts to contain the spread of nuclear weapons. Therefore, the Greens demanded an immediate stop to all exports of nuclear power plants and other dangerous nuclear facilities.[54] However, at the time when the important decisions on the Atucha II sale were made, the Greens had just begun to emerge on the political scene and were not yet represented in the *Bundestag*.

Parliamentary involvement consisted primarily of the use of oral and written questions directed at government ministers. Most of these questions came from Social Democratic deputies who were concerned about safeguards and possible adverse foreign reactions to the West German sale.[55] Protest activities against the sale of a reactor to Argentina were mainly organized by the *Forschungs- und Dokumentationszentrum Chile-Lateinamerika* (research and documentation center Chile-Latin America), which was part of the German *Dritte Welt-Bewegung* (Third World movement). On the 1980 deal with Argentina it published a special report.[56] Furthermore, on March 19, 1980, members of this group gained access to the annual Siemens shareholders convention in Berlin and through a sit-in, distributing pamphlets, a speech to the shareholders, and so on, attempted to disrupt the convention.[57] A resolution that was also distributed at the convention demanded the cancellation of the contract with the Argentine military government and an end to the nuclear cooperation with Argentina.[58]

The most thorough public examination of German-Argentine cooperation occurred almost a decade after the Atucha II sale, however. In January 1988 the rumor mills in Germany were running wild with unsubstantiated speculations that German company *Transnuklear* had illegally shipped plutonium to Libya or Pakistan.[59] The questionable dealings of this company resulted in the appointment of a special parliamentary committee that conducted a wide-ranging investigation covering, among other things, German nuclear cooperation with Argentina.[60]

THE AMERICAN CASE

First discussions concerning the Philippine nuclear project began as far back as 1972.[61] In 1974 the Philippine government committed itself to order two 626 MW nuclear power plants from Westinghouse.[62] In June 1975 the U.S. government-owned Eximbank decided to finance only one Philippine nuclear plant.[63] The actual contract for the supply of the first Philippine nuclear plant was signed by Philippine President Ferdinand

Marcos and Westinghouse Power Systems President Gordon Hurlbert in 1976.[64]   On November 18, 1976, Westinghouse applied for an export license for the reactor.[65] About a year later, in December 1977, the State Department issued a recommendation on behalf of the executive branch to approve the license.[66] On January 25, 1978, the State Department reversed its position and asked the Nuclear Regulatory Commission "to defer action on the application."[67] This change resulted from mounting criticism of the project on grounds that Westinghouse had bribed Philippine officials and that the project was unsafe and uneconomical. On May 6, 1980, the NRC in a split decision authorized the issuance of two export licenses to Westinghouse covering the Philippine reactor and components.

From then on the fate of the Philippine nuclear power project increasingly depended on the outcome of the various economic and political crises that the Philippines faced in the 1980s. In the early 1980s the Philippines experienced an economic crisis, and as the global and Philippine energy situation changed, any economic justification for the project collapsed.[68] When the Philippines decided to embark on this project, "the Philippines got 96 percent of its energy from imported oil. . . Meanwhile, largely because of its successful geothermal program, the nation's dependence on imported oil . . . [fell] to 57 percent" in 1984.[69] On top of that came cost overruns, interest rates rose worldwide in the early 1980s, and the trend in oil prices became less predictable.

If this was not enough, the Philippine plant became a focal point of opposition to the Marcos regime "and a target of guerrilla insurgents, who . . . [in 1985] blew up transmission line pylons connecting the plant to the capital city of Manila."[70] In the 1986 presidential election campaign in the Philippines Corazon Aquino also spoke out against the project, while the plant itself was essentially being completed.[71] By the time Corazon Aquino came to power the cost of the plant had increased from $1.1 billion in 1976 to $2.1 billion.[72] The problem that the Aquino government faced was that, despite its opposition to the plant, it was legally committed to pay back loans incurred for the plant, and the interest charges on these loans came to about $355,000 a day.[73]

U.S. authorities became involved in this export in two ways. First, the Export-Import Bank put together a financing package for the project in the early and mid-1970s, and then the executive branch took almost four years to decide on an export license. Although the initial decision of the Eximbank to provide financing for the plant aroused little controversy, this changed during the licensing process, and then Eximbank's decision received greater scrutiny as well.

Eximbank Financing

Before discussing the specifics of the Philippine loans we should note that in the mid-1970s U.S. nuclear export policy became a hotly debated issue in Congress, and one point of discussion focused on the role of the Eximbank in supporting U.S. nuclear power exports.[74] In these debates Representative Clarence Long, who later became one of the most vocal congressional opponents of the Philippine project, took a strong position against Eximbank loans for nuclear power plants in the Third World.[75]

In this particular case discussions of the project among the Philippine government, Eximbank, and Westinghouse started in 1972. In June 1975 Eximbank decided to finance only one nuclear plant instead of two, as originally planned.[76] The decision to finance only one reactor has to be seen in light of the fact that in June 1974 the cost of two plants was estimated at $500 million, but by September 1975 it had increased to $1.1 billion for one plant.[77] In November 1975 the Bank referred the financing request to Congress, which raised no objections, so that "the Bank authorized the credit on December 18, 1975."[78] The financial commitments of the Eximbank for the Philippine project totaled $644 million, making it Eximbank's largest loan package. $277 million were a direct loan, and $367 million a financial guarantee for Philippine bond sales in the U.S.[79] A group of private banks led by Citicorp, Amex Bank, and Manufactures Hanover raised $256.6 million in the private market.[80]

In late 1977 and early 1978 the story broke that corruption had been involved in the Philippine contract award to Westinghouse. Several articles in the *New York Times* raised the suspicion that Westinghouse had won the contract over its competitor General Electric because of improper or illegal payments by Westinghouse to a close friend of Philippine President Marcos. These corruption charges centered around Herminio T. Desini who was married to a cousin of Imelda Marcos. Westinghouse confirmed that it had paid a fee to one of Desini's companies "for assistance in obtaining the contract and for implementation services." In addition to this fee, which at that time was estimated to be several million, another Desini company sold a $668 million insurance policy for the Westinghouse reactor, and a construction company owned by Desini headed a group of contractors for the civil works part of the project. In October 1975 Desini also bought Asia Industries, the local distributor for Westinghouse.[81] Since these charges became public after the Export-Import Bank had already committed its funds to the project, this controversy did not affect U.S. financing of the plant. However, opponents of the project used corruption charges as one more argument in their fight against an export license for the plant.

The Licensing Process

The controversy over the export license for the Philippine plant did not only involve questions specific to this particular export but should be seen as part of a larger struggle. In more general terms this export raised questions of whether the NRC or the executive branch should consider the safety and environmental impact of exports in export licensing proceedings, and if yes, how extensive such safety and environmental reviews should be. Furthermore, what was the proper format for such reviews, and to what extent should the public be allowed to participate in them?[82] Although the NRC had already decided a couple of times not to consider such factors, environmentalists had reason to believe that change was waiting in the wings. In 1977 the Council on Environmental Quality (CEQ) had drafted regulations that would have required environmental impact statements for nuclear exports. The State Department was vehemently opposed to this proposal.[83] On January 4, 1979, President Carter issued executive order 12114 "Environmental Effects Abroad of Major Federal Actions." The State Department, in cooperation with other executive agencies, then developed procedures for implementing the order.[84] These procedures provided that the State Department, with the input of other agencies such as the Department of Energy or the Export-Import Bank, prepare concise environmental reviews of proposed nuclear exports, not including exports of nuclear fuel.

The specific environmental issues raised by this particular export relate to the seismic and volcanic characteristics of the plant site. The Natural Resources Defense Council (NRDC), the Union of Concerned Scientists (UCS), and the Sierra Club noted that the site was located in "an area of high seismic activity with severe risks of earthquakes and resulting tidal waves. Within 90 miles of the site there are three active volcanoes. The nearest volcano, Mt. Natib, is only 5 miles away."[85] On top of that came the fact that the plant site was very close to Subic Bay Naval Base and not very far from Clark Air Force Base.

It is against this background that Westinghouse applied for an export license on November 18, 1976. About a year later, on December 12, 1977, the State Department recommended that NRC issue the license. Until then the project had attracted relatively little public attention. In January 1978 this started to change. On January 4, 1978, Clarence D. Long, chairman of the Subcommittee on Foreign Operations of the House Appropriations Committee, wrote two letters to Secretary of State Vance and NRC chairman Hendrie.[86] In his letter to Cyrus Vance, Long argued that

As Chairman of the Appropriations subcommittee with the responsibility for seeing that economic development of poor nations is pursued effectively and economically, I strongly oppose this project as uneconomic, a threat to human safety and the environment, ineffective in obtaining energy relative to alternative means and immeshed in possibilities of corruption and conflicts of interest.[87]

Long also challenged NRC export licensing policies, specifically the refusal of the NRC to consider environmental impacts of proposed nuclear exports that might occur within the territory of foreign nations.[88] Around the same time the *New York Times* published several articles on the corruption issue. The Union of Concerned Scientists charged that "the design for the 620 megawatt, $1.1 billion plant 45 miles northwest of Manila is unreliable and probably unsafe."[89] All these activities helped to bring about a change in the position of the State Department, which asked the NRC on January 25, 1978, not to take any further action on the export license application. Meanwhile, work on the plant had started, and on August 3, 1978, Westinghouse filed for an export license for reactor components that were "needed to permit continued construction of the reactor."[90]

Events during the following year, however, proved to be ominous for the nuclear industry and brought construction at the Philippine site to a temporary halt. The most important event of 1979 concerning nuclear power was the accident at the Three Mile Island nuclear plant at Harrisburg, Pennsylvania. In the Philippines President Marcos suspended construction of the plant and appointed a three-member special commission to examine the safety of the nuclear power project.[91] There are reasons to believe, though, that the establishment of the commission was a mere public relations maneuver.[92] Nevertheless, on September 28, 1979, the Department of State recommended the issuance of an export license for the Westinghouse reactor and, in addition to its usual submission, included a concise environmental review of the Philippine reactor project. The Department of Energy, however, was not fully satisfied with the environmental review and commented that "we feel that certain areas of this environmental report require additional information in order to provide an adequate summary of the pertinent environmental issues to a decision-maker."[93]

The September 28, 1979, recommendation of the State Department had come about as a result of a lawsuit that Westinghouse had initiated against the NRC and the State Department during the summer of 1979. U.S. District Court Judge June Green denied Westinghouse's claim that "the NRC and the State Department were guilty of 'arbitrary and capricious conduct in excess of their authority under the Atomic Energy Act' when they decided to check health and safety aspects of the proposed reactor."[94] Although Westinghouse had lost the lawsuit, it had been successful in getting the State Department to agree to come to a decision by September 28, 1979.[95]

With the recommendation of the State Department in hand, the NRC finally had to consider its own position on the export and the larger policy questions at hand. Thus, on October 19, 1979, the NRC invited the interested public to submit their views on whether the NRC in fact had the legal authority to consider the health, safety, and environmental impacts of exported nuclear facilities in export licensing decisions.[96]

The Arguments of the Participants. On the basis of the responses to the NRC's requests for comments we can outline the coalitions that formed for and against this export and their views. Most of the various environmental and other participating interest groups, but obviously not the nuclear industry, opposed the export and favored environmental reviews of nuclear exports. This list of interest groups included not only such large and well-known groups as the Sierra Club, the Natural Resources Defense Council, and the Union of Concerned Scientists but a variety of other quite diverse groups, such as the Interfaith Center on Corporate Responsibility, the Center for Development Policy, and the Seattle chapter of the National Lawyers Guild. They were joined by most of the members of Congress who took an active interest in this case, including Representatives Dellums and Long and Senator Claiborne Pell. Within the executive branch, the Council on Environmental Quality also favored environmental reviews of nuclear exports.[97] The NRDC, the Union of Concerned Scientists, and the Sierra Club argued that the Atomic Energy Act, the National Environmental Policy Act, and the Nuclear Non-Proliferation Act, taken together, required the NRC to consider health, safety, and environmental impacts of an exported nuclear facility when ruling on an export application.[98] More specifically, these groups asserted that any major accident at the Philippine plant could endanger the common defense and security of the United States because of the plant's location near two very important U.S. military bases.[99]

Diametrically opposed to the views of the above-mentioned groups were representatives of the nuclear industry. They also found a congressional supporter, in this case at least, in Senator Frank Church, the former chairman of the Senate Foreign Relations Committee.[100] The consulting firm Ebasco took the position that the NRC should leave foreign policy, an area in which it lacked authority and competence, to the State Department.[101] Westinghouse dismissed arguments that the presence of American military bases near the Philippine plant site demanded an NRC health, safety, and environmental review and found it ridiculous to "make the determination of the Commission's jurisdiction turn on the location of a proposed power plant vis-à-vis the happenstance of an American military base near the facility."[102] The Philippine

Nuclear Power Corporation granted that the NRC could consider generic safety questions posed by U.S. manufactured nuclear power plants, but all other health, safety and environmental impacts of an exported facility fell solely into the jurisdiction of the authorities of the importing country.[103]

The State Department was essentially on the same side as the nuclear industry, but the department conceded that under certain circumstances the NRC could conduct limited environmental reviews. In general, the State Department favored the approach the NRC had taken in earlier decisions, such as the Babcock & Wilcox case, and thus denied that the NRC had the legal authority to consider health, safety, and environmental impacts. The Atomic Energy Act requires the NRC to consider in its review of export license applications whether a proposed export would be inimical to the common defense and security of the United States or to the health and safety of the American public. According to the State Department, this meant that the NRC was authorized to consider the impact of an exported facility on the global commons since such impacts could also affect the health and safety of the U.S. public. However, the NRC should limit its reviews by referring to the generic impact statement of "U.S. Nuclear Power Export Activities" prepared by the ERDA in 1976.[104]

The State Department also established a link between environmental reviews and U.S. nonproliferation policy. According to the State Department, the United States needed to be perceived as a reliable nuclear supplier because through its participation in nuclear commerce the United States gained leverage over customers to further the goal of nonproliferation.[105] To the extent that environmental reviews undercut the image of the United States as a reliable supplier, they undermined U.S. nonproliferation policy as well. To flesh out this line of thinking, environmental reviews would be regarded as an intrusion into the responsibilities of sovereign states, they would increase the unpredictability of U.S. nuclear export decisions and the length of the licensing process and possibly make export licenses the subject of a growing number of lawsuits by antinuclear groups. At least, these were the fears of the nuclear industry.[106] Senator Church argued that any further delays in the licensing process or a denial of an export license for the Philippine reactor would hurt U.S. interests in the region.[107] His colleague Senator Pell, on the other hand, feared that in the case of a serious accident the U.S. would be criticized for exporting a dangerous facility and "[s]uch reactions would exacerbate U.S. foreign relations and might well be seized upon by hostile nations in an effort to embarrass and discredit this country and thereby to weaken our influence abroad."[108]

The Final Decision. From the end of 1979 on, the process began to speed up. On December 18, 1979, the Subcommittee on International Economic Policy and Trade of the House Foreign Affairs Committee started hearings on "Nuclear Exports: International Safety and Environmental Issues." On January 29, 1980, the NRC met in public session to determine the scope of its jurisdiction, and, following that decision, on February 8, 1980, it requested interested members of the public to submit comments on: "(a) the health, safety, or environmental effects the proposed exports would have upon the global commons or the territory of the United States, and (b) the relationship of these effects to the common defense and security of the United States."[109]

On May 8, 1980, the NRC finally authorized the issuance of two export licenses to Westinghouse. In their majority opinion, Commissioners Hendrie and Kennedy reviewed the relevant legislation and came to the conclusion that the NRC did not have the legal authority "to evaluate impacts that do not bear on U.S. interests or the global commons." As far as the "NRC authority to evaluate the health, safety and environmental effects of exported facilities upon U.S. interests abroad" was concerned, the NRC majority asserted that legally it was neither required nor precluded from considering such effects. In this case it meant what effects an accident would have upon two U.S. military bases and about 30,000 U.S. citizens living there. However, on policy grounds the NRC decided not to take these effects into consideration because

no matter how thorough the NRC review, the Commission still would not be in a position to determine that the reactor could be operated safely. We reach this conclusion because the NRC review would inherently have to be less complete than its review of domestic reactor applications. . . .
    A partial review could in fact have adverse results because it would give the misleading impression that the NRC is assuring the safety of the facility as eventually constructed and is assuming some responsibility for its safety. This could lead recipient nations to place undue reliance upon the NRC review and to reduce their own efforts and expenditures to develop an indigenous capability to construct, operate and maintain the plant safely.[110]

In addition, the NRC feared that such a review could be seen as an intrusion into the exclusive responsibilities of the recipient country.[111]

In declining to assess the possible health and safety risks that an exported facility might pose to U.S. interests abroad, the NRC rejected the position of one of its own staff offices, the Office of Policy Evaluation (OPE), which had argued for a limited health, safety, and environmental review.[112] Chairman Ahearne and Commissioner Bradford agreed with OPE, but whereas Ahearne merely abstained, Bradford voted against issuance of the licenses and wrote a dissenting opinion that was highly critical of the majority. He found it particularly strange that the majority evaluated "the impact on fish no closer than twelve miles to the Philippine coast while ignoring the impact of an accident on the 30,000 U.S. citizens stationed at the Subic Bay Naval Base and the Clark Air Force Base within 10 and 30 miles of the plant."[113] Commissioner Gilinsky concurred with the majority.

The NRC also denied requests for a stay of commission orders until petitioners could seek judicial review of the NRC decision.[114] The NRDC then went to court to seek an overturn of the NRC decision. On March 30, 1981, the federal appeals court for the District of Columbia circuit upheld the decision by the NRC.[115] At that point all legal obstacles against the export were removed.

ANALYSIS

These two cases clearly show differences in the factors that are critical for shaping U.S. and German export control policy. To understand the German case one must grasp the subtleties of the diplomatic negotiations among the governments of Germany, Argentina, the United States, Canada, and Switzerland. Although the German government did not give in to diplomatic pressure on full-scope safeguards, Chancellor Schmidt was concerned about avoiding another diplomatic conflict with the United States over nuclear exports. Schmidt had less to fear from domestic opposition. In practice the economics ministry, the ministry for research and technology, and the foreign office handled nuclear export deals. Other domestic actors found few opportunities to challenge German export control policy.

International pressure also provides the key to understanding change in German export control policy. Beginning in 1989 the German government began an intensive review of its export control policy that, among other things, resulted in a policy shift on full-scope safeguards. In 1990 the government announced that in the future it would require full-scope safeguards. The initial impetus for the change in German export control policy had been the harsh criticism from abroad. A few months before the German decision on full-scope safeguards and in anticipation of the fourth NPT review conference, U.S. Secretary of State James Baker had written letters to the German ministers of foreign affairs and the economy. In these letters Baker had made the urgent request that Germany join the United States, Japan, and other suppliers in tightening conditions for nuclear exports.[116]

What happened was that international pressure "reverberated" in domestic German politics.[117] After the exposure of German export control scandals from the Rabta affair to German participation in Iraq's ballistic missile, chemical, and nuclear weapons programs not just the opposition parties but also leading politicians in the governing coalition recognized the need for change. However, this still leaves us with the question of why diplomatic pressure contributed to a policy change at the end of the 1980s, whereas similar pressure had been ineffective in the mid-1970s and during the negotiations on the Atucha II deal. Here it is crucial to recognize that in the 1970s German nuclear export policy rested on a solid consensus that included the relevant actors in the executive branch and the leadership of all major political parties. In the 1980s this consensus broke down as the foreign office moved in a different direction than the economics ministry, some Greens challenged the export orientation of the German economy, and the Social Democrats changed their position on safeguards policy as well.[118] This then set the stage for international pressure to tip the balance in favor of policy change at the end of the 1980s.

Decision making in the German case took place almost exclusively within the executive branch which, according to state structure arguments, should have insulated the German state from societal demands and enhanced the German state's autonomy. Such arguments fail to recognize differences among various societal actors and in their relationship to state institutions. The effect of state centralization is not so much to insulate the state, or a particular state institution, from society, but centralization of state agencies handicaps some societal actors more than others in their efforts to gain access to the state. Nuclear power provides a perfect example. Lönnroth and Walker, among others, have found that states with centralized and closed policy-making structures have had fewer difficulties in pushing forward with nuclear power programs than states with decentralized and open structures, such as the United States.[119]

Antinuclear movements have had to rely on such strategies as demonstrations, interventions in regulatory and court proceedings, where the opportunity for that existed, referendums or to organize in a political party. Nuclear industries, on the other hand, did not have to solve the same problems of access to state institutions. In West Germany the industry could rely on the ministry of atomic affairs and later its successor, the ministry for research and technology, while in the United States the industry had a natural ally in the Atomic Energy Commission (AEC). Krasner recognizes that some executive institutions have close ties to their clienteles in society. However, there is more to it than that. The decision to grant an export license for Atucha II was not reached in an obscure industry-dominated regulatory agency but at the cabinet level. One does not have to subscribe to any elite conspiracy theory to realize that KWU's parent company, the largest private employer in Germany at the time, could rely on a few more informal channels to make its voice heard than antinuclear activists fighting with Molotov cocktails and sling shots against tear gas and water cannons. In the United States the old nuclear "subgovernment," consisting of the AEC and the Joint Committee on Atomic Energy, was dismantled in the mid-1970s and replaced with a more decentralized decision making structure for nuclear policy.[120] This did not make the American state less autonomous as a whole, however, but some of these changes put opponents of nuclear power on a somewhat more equal footing with the industry and its supporters.

In the American case a discussion of domestic politics is crucial for understanding the case. Here we also see a good example of the tendency to use export controls for a variety of purposes beyond the more traditional national security goals, which had been behind the establishment of peacetime export controls in the 1940s. In this case environmentalists inside and outside of the Carter administration attempted to use export control policy to further their own agenda. The distinguishing characteristic of this case lies in the importance of the judicial and quasi-judicial decision making of the courts and the NRC. In contrast to the German case, regular executive branch departments and the nuclear industry were not the only relevant domestic actors, but the decisions of the State Department could be challenged through the NRC and the courts. The NRC and the courts thus became potential "veto points" to executive decisions. This also distinguishes this case from export licensing decisions, which fall under the jurisdiction of the Commerce Department, which administers the Export Administration Act. Under the EAA companies did not have recourse to the courts if licensing requests had been denied. Industry has fought for expanded judicial review of Commerce Department rulings, although presumably industry would not want to open the process so widely that any group, for example, antinuclear activists, could challenge licensing decisions.

NOTES

1. *Nuclear Engineering International*, February 1989, p. 52; *Atomwirtschaft-Atomtechnik*, April 1983, p. 166.
2. "Philippines Expected to File Suit Against Westinghouse," *New York Times*, 1 December 1988, p. 29; "Westinghouse, Jersey Firm Are Sued by the Philippines," *New York Times*, 2 December 1988, p. 30; "Jury Clears Westinghouse," *New York Times*, 19 May 1993, p. D9; Robin Broad with John Cavanagh, *Plundering Paradise: The Struggle for the Environment in the Philippines* (Berkeley: University of California Press, 1993), p. 123.
3. For more information on the Argentine nuclear power program see Carlos Castro Madero, "Planning for Nuclear Self-Sufficiency in Argentina," *Nuclear Engineering International*, September 1982, pp. 30–32; Daniel Poneman, "Nuclear Proliferation Prospects for Argentina," *Orbis* 27 (Winter 1984): 853–880; Leonard S. Spector, *Nuclear Proliferation Today* (New York: Vintage Books, 1984),

pp. 199–204; Ruth Stanley, "Co-operation and Control: The New Approach to Nuclear Non-proliferation in Argentina and Brazil," *Arms Control* 13 (September 1992): 191–213; Etel Solingen, "Macropolitical Consensus and Lateral Autonomy in Industrial Policy: The Nuclear Sector in Brazil and Argentina," *International Organization* 47 (Spring 1993): 263–298.

4. Spector, *Nuclear Proliferation Today*, p. 200.

5. Solingen, "Macropolitical Consensus and Lateral Autonomy," pp. 269, 289–290.

6. Ibid., p. 290.

7. "U.S.-North Korea Meeting Yields Some Gains on Arms," *New York Times*, 20 July 1993, p. A2.

8. Germany, Deutscher Bundestag, *Drucksache* 11/7800, p. 730.

9. Daniel Poneman, *Nuclear Power in the Developing World* (London: George Allen & Unwin, 1982), p. 73.

10. *Energiewirtschaftliche Tagesfragen*, January/February 1969, p. 37.

11. Poneman, *Nuclear Power*, pp. 73–74.

12. West Germany, Deutscher Bundestag, *Drucksache* 9/1657, p. 33.

13. *KWU-report*, no. 19 (1975), p. 20; *KWU-report*, no. 32 (1980), p. 8; IAEA document INFCIRC/250.

14. Stanley, "Co-operation," p. 196.

15. The following chronology is largely based on the findings of a German parliamentary investigative committee that in the late 1980s studied a variety of nuclear policy issues, including German nuclear exports to and cooperation with Argentina, Brazil, India, Pakistan, and South Africa. See Germany, Deutscher Bundestag, *Drucksache* 11/7800.

16. *Frankfurter Allgemeine Zeitung*, 8 February 1979, p. 2.

17. Klaus Broichhausen, "Bonn vor schwierigen Entscheidungen in der Nuklearpolitik," *Frankfurter Allgemeine Zeitung*, 16 February 1979, p. 3; "Sitzung des Nuklear-Kabinetts erst Anfang März," *Frankfurter Allgemeine Zeitung*, 22 February 1979, p. 6; "Argentinien-Export noch unentschieden," *Süddeutsche Zeitung*, 9 March 1979, p. 6.

18. Personal communication from an official in the ministry for research and technology, July 13, 1982.

19. Forschungs- und Dokumentationszentrum Chile-Lateinamerika, ed., *Der Griff nach der Bombe: Das deutsch-argentinische Atomgeschäft* (Berlin: Forschungs- und Dokumentationszentrum Chile-Lateinamerika, 1981), p. 5; Arbeitsgemeinschaft gegen Atomexporte, *Sulzers Bombengeschäft mit Argentinien: Schweizer Beihilfe zum Atomkrieg* (Zurich and Berne, Arbeitsgemeinschaft gegen Atomexporte, 1980), p. 13.

20. "Possible sale of reactor hurts Bonn-Ottawa links," *Globe and Mail*, 6 November 1979, p. 14.

21. Germany, Deutscher Bundestag, *Drucksache* 11/7800, p. 954.

22. "Bonn Criticizes BBC for Bomb Allegations," *New York Times*, 22 April 1982, p. A12.

23. Carlos Castro Madero, press statement of 1 October 1979 supplementing Decree 2441 of 28 September 1979, p. 10.

24. Ibid., pp. 12–13.

25. The following account of the diplomatic negotiations is based on Germany, Deutscher Bundestag, *Drucksache* 11/7800, pp. 193–199, except where indicated through separate footnotes.

26. For a text of the guidelines see Brenner, *Nuclear Power and Non-Proliferation*, pp. 296–299.

27. The relevant IAEA model safeguards agreements are INFCIRC/66 for safeguards limited to a specific facility and INFCIRC/153 for full-scope safeguards.

28. Poneman, "Nuclear Proliferation Prospects," p. 875.

29. Interviews with officials in the German foreign office and the ministry for research and technology, July 13 and 23, 1982.

30. *Der Spiegel*, 19 November 1979, p. 47; *Nuclear Engineering International*, January 1980, p. 10.

31. John M. Gedden, "Swiss, Germans Ignore U.S. Objections, Sell Nuclear Technology to Argentina," *Wall Street Journal*, 16 June 1980, p. 17.

32. John Redick, "Nuclear Trends in Latin America," in *Governance in the Western Hemisphere*, ed. Viron P. Vaky (New York: Praeger, 1983), p. 223.

33. Redick, "Nuclear Trends," pp. 222–223; Spector, *Nuclear Proliferation Today*, p. 212.

34. Spector, *Nuclear Proliferation Today*, p. 209.

35. "Argentina May Accept Inspection of Atom Projects," *New York Times*, 25 March 1979, p. 3.

36. Milton Benjamin, "U.S. to Allow Argentina Nuclear Aid," *Washington Post*, 18 August 1983, pp. A1, 13.

37. Ibid.; Spector, *Nuclear Proliferation Today*, pp. 215–217.

38. Spector, *Nuclear Proliferation Today*, p. 211.

39. Germany, Deutscher Bundestag, *Drucksache* 11/7800, pp. 200–201.

40. Häckel, "The Politics of Nuclear Exports," p. 76, footnote 4.

41. Hans Michaelis, *Handbuch der Kernenergie* (Munich: Deutscher Taschenbuch Verlag, 1982), vol. 1, p. 450.

42. Ibid., p. 451.

43. Ibid.

44. *Latin America Political Report*, 3 March 1978, p. 70.

45. *Nuclear Engineering International*, November 1979, p. 6.

46. *Latin America Political Report*, 3 March 1978, p. 70.

47. *Atomwirtschaft-Atomtechnik*, July 1979, p. 345; Michaelis, *Handbuch*, vol. 1, p. 450.

48. "Kernkraftindustrie befürchtet Technologielücke," *Frankfurter Allgemeine Zeitung*, 4 September 1979, p. 13.

49. *Atomwirtschaft-Atomtechnik*, April 1983, p. 176.

50. "Bonn Is Hesitating on Atom-Plant Deal," *New York Times*, 4 March 1979, p. 4.

51. Udo Bergdoll, "Bonns Nuklearpolitik in der Klemme," *Süddeutsche Zeitung*, 12 March 1979, p. 4.

52. "Reaktor-Export nach Argentinien umstritten," *Frankfurter Allgemeine Zeitung*, 8 February 1979, p. 2.

53. "'Gegenantrag' in der SPD zur Kernenergie," *Frankfurter Allgemeine Zeitung*, 13 November 1979, p. 4.

54. Die Grünen, *Das Bundesprogramm*, p. 11.

55. See West Germany, Deutscher Bundestag, *Drucksachen* 8/1050, p. 23; 8/3552, pp. 13–14; 9/1618; 9/1657; 9/1700; 9/1856; 9/1989; 10/569, p. 2.

56. FDCL, *Der Griff nach der Bombe*.

57. Ibid., pp. 126–127.

58. Ibid., p. 128.

59. Hoppe and Koch, *Bomben-Geschäfte*, pp. 17–20.

60. Germany, Deutscher Bundestag, *Drucksache* 11/7800.

61. John L. Moore, answers to written questions from Representative Long, appearing in U.S. Congress, House Committee on Appropriations, *Foreign Assistance and Related Agencies Appropriations for 1979: Hearings Before a Subcommittee of the House Committee on Appropriations*, 95th Cong., 2d sess., 1978, part I, p. 116.

62. *New York Times*, 18 June 1974, p. 64.

63. John Moore, answers, p. 116.

64. *Nuclear Engineering International*, March 1976, p. 11.

65. Westinghouse Electric Corporation, 11 N.R.C. 631, 632 (1980).

66. Ibid.

67. Ibid.

68. For more information on economic problems in the Philippines under Ferdinand Marcos see "Die Philippinen im Sumpf der Krise," *Neue Zürcher Zeitung*, Fernausgabe, 22 June 1983, p. 15; "Manilas Industrialisierungspolitik im Schleudern," *Neue Zürcher Zeitung*, Fernausgabe, 26/27 June 1983, p. 10.

69. "Manila's Nuclear Plans Spur Ire and Reflection," *New York Times*, 22 October 1984, p. 27; see also "Fission Frission," *The Economist*, 27 October 1984, p. 70.

70. *Nuclear News*, March 1986, p. 79.

71. Ibid.

72. "Manila Cabinet Considers Scrapping Atomic Plant," *New York Times*, 10 April 1986, p. 6.

73. "Manila Labors to Pay for Unused Atomic Plant," *New York Times*, 25 May 1986, p. A16.

74. See, for example, some of the testimony in U.S. Congress, House Committee on International Relations, *Nuclear Proliferation: Future U.S. Foreign Policy Implications*, 94th Cong., 1st sess.; U.S. Congress, House Committee on Banking, Currency and Housing, *Oversight Hearings on the Export-Import Bank*, 94th Cong., 2d sess.; U.S. Congress, House Committee on Banking, Finance and Urban Affairs, *To Extend and Amend the Export-Import Bank Act of 1945*, 95th Cong., 1st sess.

75. See his testimony in U.S. Congress, *To Extend and Amend*, pp. 261–282.

76. *New York Times*, 12 February 1978; John Moore, answers, p. 116.

77. John Moore, answers, p. 117.

78. Ibid., p. 116.

79. John L. Moore, Testimony Before U.S. Congress, House Committee on Appropriations, *Foreign Assistance*, pp. 118–119.

80. John Moore, answers, pp. 118–119.

81. *New York Times*, 14 January 1978, p. 6.

82. The Philippine case was not the first time that these questions had been considered by the NRC. On May 7, 1976, the NRC decided in response to petitions by the Natural Resources Defense Council and the Sierra Club that the NRC would not take into account safety procedures of foreign nuclear facilities before issuing export licenses for nuclear fuel shipments. See Edlow International Company, 3 N.R.C. 563, 564 (1976). The following year a similar question came up, this time concerning the export of a Babcock & Wilcox reactor to Germany. On February 16, 1977, a West German citizens' initiative, the *Bürgeraktion Atomschutz Mittelrhein e.V.* (Citizen Action Group for the Nuclear Protection of the Middle Rhine) filed a petition with the NRC and asserted that the NRC had to prepare an environmental impact statement for the plant site in Germany. The NRC denied that it had such a responsibility. See Babcock & Wilcox, 5 N.R.C. 1332 (1977).

83. Constance Holden, "Environmental Assessment Sought for Federal Actions Abroad," *Science* 201 (18 August 1978): 599–600.

84. These procedures were published in 44 *Federal Register* 65560 (13 November 1979).

85. Natural Resources Defense Council, Sierra Club, and Union of Concerned Scientists, Statements of Views on Further Public Proceedings, comments submitted to the Nuclear Regulatory Commission, in U.S. Congress, House Committee on Foreign Affairs, *Nuclear Exports: International Safety and Environmental Issues*, 96th Cong., 2d sess., p. 124.

86. Clarence D. Long, letters to Cyrus Vance and Joseph Hendrie, in U.S. Congress, House Committee on Appropriations, *Foreign Assistance*, pp. 68–73.

87. Ibid., p. 68.

88. Ibid., p. 73.

89. *Washington Post*, 15 February 1978.

90. 11 N.R.C. 631, 633.

91. "Philippines Suspends Construction on Controversial Nuclear Reactor," *Washington Post*, 16 June 1979, p. A9.

92. "Manila's Nuclear Debate," *New York Times*, 9 July 1979, p. D5; "Manila Rushing Study of A-Plant, Expert Says," *Washington Post*, 20 July 1979, p. A7.

93. Robert J. Stern, U.S. Department of Energy, "Review of Environmental Report on the Philippine Nuclear Power Plant Unit I" (Memorandum for Harold D. Bengelsdorf).

94. "Westinghouse Rebuffed on A-Plant," *Washington Post*, 31 August 1979, p. A4.

95. Ibid.

96. 44 *Federal Register* 61476 (25 October 1979).

97. Council on Environmental Quality, to John Ahearne, Chairman, Nuclear Regulatory Commission, 25 January 1980, p. 2.

98. NRDC, Sierra Club, and Union of Concerned Scientists, "Statement of Views on Further Public Proceedings," p. 86.

99. Ibid., pp. 96–97.

100. Frank Church, U.S. Senator, to Jimmy Carter, U.S. President, 21 December 1979.

101. Ebasco Services Incorporated, Comments in Response to Commission Order Issued, 19 October 1979, p. 13.

102. Westinghouse Electric Corporation, comments submitted to Nuclear Regulatory Commission, quoted in Leonard Bickwit and Edward J. Hanrahan, Memorandum for the Commissioners (SECY-80-20), appendix, p. 6.

103. National Power Corporation (Philippines), comments on Nuclear Regulatory Commission's scope of jurisdiction, p. 8.

104. U.S. State Department, Views of the Department of State on Procedural and Jurisdictional Issues," in U.S. Congress, House Committee on Foreign Affairs, *Nuclear Exports*, pp. 215–216.

105. Louis Nozenzo, Testimony Before U.S. Congress, House Committee on Appropriations, *Foreign Assistance*, p. 46.

106. Ebasco, Comments, pp. 13–14.

107. Frank Church, U.S. Senator, to Jimmy Carter, U.S. President, 21 December 1979.

108. Claiborne Pell, U.S. Senator, to Carlton Kammerer, Nuclear Regulatory Commission, 9 November 1979.

109. 11 N.R.C. 631, 649.

110. Ibid.

111. Ibid.

112. Bickwit and Hanrahan, Memorandum (SECY-80-20), p. 27.

113. 11 N.R.C. 631, 666 (Commissioner Bradford dissenting).

114. 11 N.R.C. 631, 662.

115. *Natural Resources Defense Council v. Nuclear Regulatory Commission*, 647 F.2d 1345, 1348 (D.C. Cir. 1981).

116. Preisinger, *Deutschland und die nukleare Nichtverbreitung*, p. 161.

117. Putnam, "Diplomacy and Domestic Politics," pp. 454–456.

118. In fact, officials in the foreign office with responsibility for non-proliferation issues had come to regard German nuclear policies of the 1970s as dubious achievements. See Preisinger, *Deutschland und die nukleare Nicht-verbreitung*, pp. 157–158.

119. Lönnroth and Walker, *The Viability*, pp. 47–48.

120. James R. Temples, "The Politics of Nuclear Power: A Subgovernment in Transition," *Political Science Quarterly* 95 (Summer 1980): 239–260.

6

Guns and Oil, Natural Gas, and Energy Security

In this chapter I will present and analyze the remaining four cases dealing with German and U.S. arms exports and trade with the former Soviet Union. These four cases have substantial common elements. All four cases are part of long-term political controversies. The intra-Western conflict over the Urengoi-Uzhgorod pipeline project was not the first time East-West energy trade had resulted in a considerable level of tension not only between the West and the Soviet Union, but between the United States and its Western European allies as well. Back in 1962/63 the United States had attempted to impose an embargo on wide-diameter pipes for the Friendship oil pipeline. Similarly, arms sales proposals to Saudi Arabia almost always generate political controversy.

ARMS EXPORTS TO SAUDI ARABIA

The domestic politics of U.S. and German arms exports to Saudi Arabia can be analyzed from two different, although interrelated, angles, or perspectives. First of all, we may analyze the struggle between competing domestic groups and interests over the sale of radar surveillance aircraft, tanks, fighter jets, and the like. In the United States this primarily involves the Arab and Israeli lobbies and companies with business interests in the Middle East, whereas in Germany political parties, party factions, and business interests represent the major actors. Secondly, and this is particularly important for the American case, the political fights over the approval of arms sales to Saudi Arabia form part of an institutional struggle between the executive and legislative branches of government. In Germany we find a weaker version of this conflict. Because of structural differences between the United States and

Germany these institutional struggles take different forms and have different political consequences in the two countries.

German Arms Exports to Saudi Arabia

The beginnings of West German negotiations with Saudi Arabia over the sale of *Leopard II* tanks go back to 1980. In June 1980 King Chalid of Saudi Arabia visited West Germany and, as was revealed later, expressed an interest in acquiring West German weapons.[1] On March 2, 1981, the German news magazine *Der Spiegel* published an interview with the Saudi Crown Prince Fahd.[2] In this interview Fahd acknowledged that the Saudis wanted to buy arms from West Germany but denied that they had made any formal requests. The following month Chancellor Schmidt went to Saudi Arabia and other Middle Eastern countries. He unsuccessfully attempted to downplay the significance of the arms export issue and instead stressed the good economic and political relations between the two countries. Schmidt apparently told his hosts that West Germany was unable at the time to supply Saudi Arabia with arms, but he held out hope for the future by pointing out that the West German government was working on a revision of its arms export guidelines.[3] As a further note of caution Schmidt added that such revised guidelines required the support of parliament.[4] Although we do not know precisely what Chancellor Schmidt did or did not promise the Saudis at those and other meetings, it is clear that the Saudi government came away with the impression that it would eventually get the *Leopard II* tank.[5]

Whatever promises Schmidt had made, his government eventually recognized its inability to overcome the opposition, particularly within the governing parties, against the export of West German tanks to Saudi Arabia. Thus, in June 1982 the West German ambassador to Saudi Arabia informed the Saudi government that its arms request would not be fulfilled.[6] In the fall of 1982 Schmidt's government fell, and the new Christian Democratic Chancellor Kohl visited Saudi Arabia in October 1983. For the new government the dilemma was that no matter what it decided, it would either offend the Israelis or the Saudis. Kohl attempted to get out of this situation by persuading the Saudis to drop their request for *Leopard II* tanks, and instead he agreed to a more general cooperation in the security field between West Germany and Saudi Arabia.[7] Beyond the general security cooperation agreement, the two governments arranged for a Saudi group of experts to visit Germany by the end of the year. These experts were to decide which German weapons Saudi Arabia might need for defensive purposes.[8]

Although the question of West German tank exports appeared settled at that time, Kohl had opened the door for other Saudi purchases.

In June 1985 Horst Ehmke, a leading Social Democratic member of parliament, charged that the West German government had made important decisions concerning arms exports to Saudi Arabia. Kurt Schäuble, then head of the chancellor's office, denied this and accused Ehmke of lying. A government spokesman then declared that the export only involved police equipment.[9] In October 1985 the government admitted that on May 4, 1985, the federal security council had cleared the export of technical documents for an ammunition plant to Saudi Arabia, and shortly thereafter the *Bundesamt für gewerbliche Wirtschaft* issued the necessary export license.[10]

In September 1985 Great Britain and Saudi Arabia reached an agreement on the sale of the ground attack version of the *Tornado* jet, which is jointly manufactured by Great Britain, Germany, and Italy.[11] This deal had been under discussion for several years, and in May 1983 West Germany had waived its right to object to exports of this plane and of any other weapon coproduced by Great Britain and West Germany in the future.[12] In November 1986 the leader of the CSU and premier of Bavaria Franz-Josef Strauß visited Saudi Arabia and publicly advocated a change in West German arms export policy that would allow more arms exports to Saudi Arabia.[13] At a meeting between Saudi officials and West German defense industry executives the West German ambassador felt obliged, however, to explain the principles of West German arms export policy and to stress that any exports would require licenses.[14] Shortly thereafter it was revealed that Saudi Arabia had for some time expressed an interest in West German submarines.[15]

As a general rule, German politics on arms exports is fairly easy to follow. The German left opposes arms exports or at least favors tight restrictions while the right wants German policies to be normal like those of the United States, Great Britain, or France. When it comes to highly visible arms sales to the Middle East, however, we see a different pattern. In this case both the Schmidt and Kohl governments favored arms sales to Saudi Arabia for economic reasons. They received support from business interests and politicians who favored closer ties to the Arab world, such as the Social Democrat and Middle East expert Hans-Jürgen Wischnewski and the Free Democrat Jürgen Möllemann who was the president of the German-Arab society.[16] The opposition to such sales included not only left-wing Social Democrats and Greens, who opposed arms exports out of principle, but also more conservative politicians who emphasized Germany's moral obligations toward Israel. Contrary to what one might expect, the leadership of the German metalworkers union opposed the sale.[17]

The economic arguments in favor of West German arms exports to Saudi Arabia included the fact that in 1980 Saudi Arabia was not only the largest but also the cheapest supplier of oil to West Germany. In

September 1980 the average price of a ton of Saudi crude oil was about 100 DM lower than the average price of oil from all other suppliers.[18] By 1981 Saudi Arabia had become the second largest non-European trading partner of West Germany after the United States.[19] There were hopes that the Saudi five-year plan for 1981–1985 would translate into annual orders for West German companies of around 20 billion DM.[20] Hermann Becker, chief executive officer (CEO) of West Germany's largest construction company, wrote in 1981 that Saudi Arabia had become the most important customer of West Germany's construction industry.[21] Furthermore, in the early 1980s West Germany, partly as a result of rising oil prices, faced the problem of how to finance current account deficits. In 1980 the West German government reached a long-term financial agreement with Saudi Arabia.[22] In 1981 Saudi Arabia lent the West German government about 11 billion DM in direct credits. The following year a similar agreement was reached but for a lower amount.[23]

Opponents argued that the proposed exports would not achieve their goals. On the economic front, Norbert Gansel, the most outspoken Social Democratic critic of arms exports, wrote in 1981 that tank manufacturers already had plenty of orders on the books. He denied that oil supplies could be secured through arms exports to Saudi Arabia. Such a link could be achieved only by combining an arms export deal with a governmental agreement on oil supplies. In fact, Arab oil-producing countries had offered such governmental agreements before to bypass oil multinationals, and West Germany had rejected those offers. In any case, West Germany had received oil in the past not because it supplied other countries with weapons but because it was willing and able to pay for oil imports. Gansel also asserted that Saudi Arabia was willing to lend money to West Germany because this was a sound investment, not because of expected favors in the form of arms supplies. Finally, he doubted that Saudi capital investment plans and German expectations of profiting from such investments were realistic.[24] Eugen Loderer, then leader of the German metal workers union (*IG Metall*), took the position in an interview in 1981 that the German export industry had been highly successful without high levels of arms exports and that there was no reason to fear that this would change in the future.[25] Four years later his successor Mayr denied that arms exports had a significant impact on the job situation in West Germany.[26]

In reality, the relative significance of Saudi oil imports decreased rather dramatically in the 1980s, as shown in table 19. Furthermore, after peaking in 1982, the relative importance of German exports to Saudi Arabia declined as well.[27] On the other hand, however, as major domestic procurement programs began to run out in the 1980s, the de-

TABLE 19
Saudi Arabia's Significance as a Trading Partner of West Germany

	West German Exports to Saudi Arabia as a Percentage of Total West German Exports	West German Imports of Saudi Petroleum, Petroleum Products and Related Material (SITC 33) as a Percentage of All West German SITC 33 Imports
1980	1.2	-
1981	1.5	19.8
1982	2.0	15.1
1983	1.7	6.0
1984	1.3	3.8
1985	1.0	2.6
1986	0.6	4.8
1988	0.5	3.7
1990	0.5	4.7

Source: Calculations based on OECD data.

fense industry faced increasingly rougher times and clearly would have benefited from increased exports.

Proponents of arms sales to Saudi Arabia also stressed West German foreign policy interests in the region. Jürgen Möllemann argued that the West had to find means to stabilize the vital Persian Gulf region militarily and to secure peace in the region. He regarded arms transfers as the most promising instrument in general and for West Germany in particular.[28] Erwin Horn, a Social Democratic member of parliament, argued that it was in Western Europe's interest to play a more active role in the Middle East and not to leave this area to the superpowers. Thus, West German arms exports could increase the European presence in the region.[29]

On the opposing side Annemarie Renger, a prominent right-wing Social Democrat, acknowledged that the West should help Saudi Arabia against the increasing threat of the Soviet Union, but the West German contribution to this effort should not be of a military nature. According to her, the legacy of Germany's past demanded a different treatment of German than of American arms exports to Saudi Arabia.[30] Norbert Gansel was very skeptical about new expanded international roles for West Germany. He questioned whether West Germany, which he characterized as half a nation with limited sovereignty, was a state like any other state. The world had never benefited but suffered from German overconfidence, and the Jews had to suffer the most. According to Gansel, the historical and political consequences of this experience represented the real national interest.[31]

Finally, the conflict over arms exports to Saudi Arabia also involved a controversy over the role of parliament in arms export decisions. One reason why the Saudi arms request initially aroused so much opposition was that it had come soon after the West German federal security council had agreed to sell submarines to Pinochet's Chile without informing parliament first. This had outraged left-wing members of the SPD. When the SPD/FDP government revised the arms export guidelines in 1982 chancellor Schmidt resolved the issue of parliamentary involvement by writing letters to the leaders of the three party delegations in the *Bundestag*. In these letters Schmidt notified the party leaders that in the future he would inform them of specific arms export decisions pending in the federal security council. He also invited two members of each of the governing parties' parliamentary delegations to attend meetings of the council.

After the Christian Democrat Kohl had come to power, the Social Democrats accused him of not honoring the promises of his predecessor, specifically concerning arms exports to Saudi Arabia.[32] The Christian Democrats had a different view of the relationship between the executive and parliament in this issue area, however. In a radio interview in April 1983 Werner Marx, a Christian Democratic foreign policy expert, argued that the government needed as much flexibility as possible for reaching sound arms export decisions. He did not oppose informing parliament but stressed that decisions should be made by the executive, not by parliament.[33]

Some themes in this debate, specifically those concerning the balance between securing influence in the Persian Gulf and Israel's security needs may appear to be similar to the conflict over U.S. arms sales to Saudi Arabia. However, as we will see in the following case study, there are quite significant differences between the two cases as well.

U.S. Arms Exports to Saudi Arabia

On October 28, 1981, the U.S. Senate approved an arms sales package to Saudi Arabia which included five E-3A Airborne Warning and Control System (AWACS) aircraft, 101 ship sets of conformal fuel tanks for F-15 aircraft, 1177 AIM-9L Sidewinder air-to-air missiles, and eight KC-707 aerial tanker aircraft. On July 2, 1986, the U.S. Air Force turned the first AWACS over to Saudi Arabia.[34] This particular deal was the most spectacular arms sale to Saudi Arabia yet, but it is important to realize that this sale is only part of a larger arms relationship between the two countries. As table 20 shows, deliveries of U.S. arms to Saudi Arabia grew quite rapidly, both in absolute and relative terms, in the early to mid-1980s but declined toward the end of the decade. At the beginning of the 1990s, though, Saudi Arabia again embarked on a major shopping spree for arms. The data provided in table 20 also indicate that the U.S. foreign military construction sales program has almost exclusively been a program to build up Saudi military infrastructure. According to a congressional staff report, up to 1980 U.S. defense programs for Saudi Arabia consisted largely of military construction. The provision of training amounted to 20 percent and the supply of hardware took up the remaining 20 percent.[35] Among different types of hardware, "[t]he largest single category of Saudi spending on U.S. weapons and ammunition has been for combat aircraft."[36]

Chronology of Events. Although the main fight over the AWACS/F-15 enhancement package occurred during the Reagan administration, the origins of this sale go back to the Carter administration. In 1978 the United States sold $2.5 billion worth of F-15 fighter aircraft to Saudi Arabia. To secure congressional approval of the sale, the administration assured Congress in letters by Secretary of Defense Brown and Assistant Secretary Bennett and in congressional testimony that the F-15 would not be equipped with conformal fuel tanks, which extend the range of the jets, or multiple ejection bomb racks. Furthermore, Congress was told that the Saudis would not receive an aerial refueling capacity for the F-15s, AIM-9L Sidewinder missiles or EC-2 or E-3A radar surveillance aircraft.[37]

In 1979 two U.S. AWACS planes were deployed in Saudi Arabia for two months after a conflict had erupted between North and South Yemen. In 1980, following the outbreak of the Iran-Iraq war, the Saudi government requested the deployment of U.S. AWACS planes in Saudi Arabia again to counter threats to its Eastern oil provinces. This time, though, U.S. aircraft remained stationed in the area. Besides allaying Saudi security fears, this deployment wetted the appetite of the Saudis to buy their own AWACS system. As a Senate committee report noted, "[i]t is not clear from the record precisely how far the Carter administration had gone prior to the election toward deciding to provide" AWACS and equipment to enhance Saudi F-15s.[38] Nevertheless, former Secretary of State Alexander Haig wrote in his memoirs that

a study of Saudi air defense needs had been carried out by the U.S. Air Force. On the basis of this study, the Pentagon bureaucracy had decided that the more sophisticated E-3A, or simply AWACS as it came to be called, was what the Saudis needed. The Saudis knew this. I did not know it, and I do not believe that Muskie or Brown knew it, either. The judgment had been made by men deep in the American bureaucracy talking to counterparts in the Saudi defense establishment on the basis of technical needs rather than political considerations.[39]

In any case, after Carter had left office, the new Reagan administration had to decide on the issue. In February 1981 Secretary of State Haig told the Saudi ambassador in Washington that the administration would seek congressional approval of the bulk of the arms package with the exception of bomb racks.[40] The crucial decision within the administration on the arms sale took place on April 1, 1981, at a meeting of the National Security Council. Alexander Haig and Secretary of Defense Weinberger did not fully agree on the merits of this sale. As Haig later put it in his memoirs, he "supported the sale of an airborne warning and surveillance system in principle. . . . But the Pentagon had gone too far too fast."[41] However, after his blunders following the assassination attempt on President Reagan, Haig was not in the position to be able to forcefully press his views, and the NSC approved the sale of AWACS aircraft, aerial tankers, and F-15 enhancement equipment.[42] On April 21, 1981, the White House formally announced its intention to go ahead with the proposed sale.[43]

Not surprisingly, however, this arms sales proposal encountered very heavy opposition in Congress. Even before the formal White House announcement of the sale, twenty senators declared their opposition to the sale of F-15 enhancement equipment in speeches on March 24, 1981.[44] In June 1981 54 senators signed a letter to President Reagan urging him to cancel the sale of AWACS planes to Saudi Arabia.[45]

Although the administration had announced the sale in April, it had not taken the steps to set in motion the formal legislative review process. On August 24, 1981, Under Secretary of State James L. Buckley presented the deal to Congress and set out the timetable for congressional action. According to this schedule, the twenty-day informal review period was to start on September 9, and Congress would receive formal notification of the sale on October 1. If Congress wanted to block the sale, it then had thirty days to pass concurrent resolutions disapproving the sale.[46] On October 14, 1981, the House of Representatives passed such a resolution to block the deal by a wide margin of 301–111.[47] This action had been anticipated, however, and the administration had already decided to focus most of its lobbying efforts on the Senate. The fight was quite intense, and on October 28 the Senate voted 48–52 to reject a resolution disapproving the sale.[48]

One factor, which helped the administration in turning around skeptical senators, involved a letter by President Reagan to Senator Baker, which did not receive its final form until the day of the Senate vote on October 28. In this letter President Reagan promised that the United States would deliver the AWACS planes to Saudi Arabia only after a presidential certification to Congress that Saudi Arabia had met

TABLE 20
U.S. Arms Sales to Saudi Arabia in Thousands of Dollars and as a Percentage
of Worldwide U.S. Arms Sales

	FY 1981	FY 1983	FY 1985	FY 1987	FY 1989	FY 1990
Foreign Military Sales Deliveries	1,429,586.0 18.8	3,835,596.0 35.6	1,369,056.0 18.1	3,229,207.0 29.0	634,734.0 9.2	895,376.0 12.5
Foreign Military Construction Sales Deliveries	1,491,597.0 100.0	2,153,170.0 99.7	901,117.0 97.7	242,546.0 91.5	346,602.0 88.9	263,093.0 75.7
Commercial Arms Sales	71,540.0 3.3	126,529.0 13.8	308,186.0 5.9	138,589.0 2.6	161,934.0 3.7	11,992.0 0.4

Source: U.S. Defense Security Assistance Agency, *Foreign Military Sales, Foreign Military Construction Sales and Military Assistance Facts* (Washington, D.C.: DSAA, 1991); percentage figures computed by the author.

certain conditions. These conditions dealt with the security of AWACS technology, U.S. access to information acquired from Saudi AWACS missions, limitations on third-country participation in the Saudi AWACS program, restrictions on AWACS flight operations, and Saudi contributions to the peaceful settlement of conflict in the Middle East.[49] In February 1982 Defense Secretary Weinberger flew to Saudi Arabia to negotiate agreements with Saudi Arabia that would meet the conditions set forth in President Reagan's letter to Senator Baker. However, Weinberger's mission met at best with mixed success. After his talks with Saudi officials "Weinberger . . . said arrangements for the [AWACS] sale to the Saudis . . . [had] been completed, but he . . . declined to say whether the arrangements . . . had been signed."[50] Weinberger's Saudi counterpart, on the other hand, denied having signed such an agreement.[51]

This last incident showed that the fight over AWACS was not over yet. In 1985 President Reagan signed a foreign aid bill, the International Security and Development Cooperation Act, which transformed President Reagan's certification promises into a legal requirement.[52] In the spring of 1986 the Reagan administration proposed a new arms sales package for Saudi Arabia, which consisted of Sidewinder, Stinger, and Harpoon missiles.[53] Both the House and the Senate passed resolutions disapproving the sale, but the Senate upheld President Reagan's veto after the administration had removed Stinger missiles from the package.[54] The missile sale had encountered very strong congressional opposition despite the fact that the main Jewish lobby group, the American Israel Public Affairs Committee (AIPAC), had decided not to actively fight against it. A possible reason for this decision could have been to concentrate instead on defeating the delivery of AWACS, which was expected later in the year.[55]

On June 18, 1986, President Reagan wrote a letter to the speaker of the House Tip O'Neill and certified that all conditions necessary for the transfer of AWACS to Saudi Arabia had been met.[56] After the grueling fight over the missile sale, however, congressional opponents were not interested in another battle, and "AIPAC signaled that it would not actively fight to block the transfer . . . largely because of the requirement to reimburse the Saudis for the $3 billion they . . . already paid for the planes."[57] This removed all political obstacles to the delivery of the AWACS planes.

Israel, Moderate Arabs, and U.S. Interests in the Middle East. This case pitted the Reagan administration, business interests that stood to gain from the sale, and the Arab American lobby against the pro-Israel lobby both inside and outside of Congress.[58] The Reagan administration did not regard this sale simply as a discrete event in U.S.-Saudi relations but put it into a broader context of U.S. goals toward other countries in the Middle East and toward the Soviet Union. On August 24, 1981, the State Department released a background paper which argued that the sale had to "be measured against four primary U.S. objectives for the region:

- Continuation of stable and secure access to regional oil;
- Prevention of the spread of Soviet influence;
- Security of friendly states in the region, including Israel; and
- Demonstration of our constancy and resolve in supporting overall regional security."[59]

In regard to Saudi Arabia, the most concrete purpose was to strengthen the Saudi air defense system and specifically to help defend oil installations in Saudi Arabia's Eastern provinces. Due to the relatively flat terrain, ground-based radar stations could not provide warning of an impending attack in time for Saudi F-15s to scramble and engage enemy aircraft before the enemy had a chance to hit Saudi targets. An airborne radar system helped to solve that problem. AIM-9L Sidewinder missiles further contributed to decreasing time pressure for Saudi F-15s because these missiles could be fired head-on against enemy aircraft instead of having to maneuver to the rear of the enemy first.[60]

Besides helping the Saudis defend themselves, and thereby reducing the likelihood that the United States would have to intervene itself, the State Department also argued that the sale of U.S. equipment would strengthen U.S. forces if direct U.S. intervention became necessary.[61]

More broadly, the United States and Saudi Arabia viewed this sale as a sign of U.S. commitment to Saudi Arabia and, in Secretary of State Haig's words, as important for "restoring confidence in the United States as a reliable partner."[62]   The goal of demonstrating U.S. commitment and reliability as a security partner was not only directed at Saudi Arabia, however.   Targets of this political signal included the other countries in the region as well.   Friendly nations should feel reassured, whereas opponents of U.S. policies in the Middle East, such as revolutionary Iran, had to be deterred from attacks on U.S. allies.   Last but not least, the Reagan administration consistently emphasized the Soviet threat in the Middle East.   Thus, particularly in the post-Afghanistan environment, arms sales to conservative Arab states represented one way of countering Soviet expansionism.   Under Alexander Haig's tenure as Secretary of State this policy carried the label of "strategic consensus."   Haig wanted to transcend the bitter Arab-Israeli conflict by uniting Israel and moderate Arab nations behind a consensus that the Soviet Union constituted the primary security threat to the region.   Although his concept of "strategic consensus" did not survive Haig's tenure in office, the State Department continued to emphasize that U.S. arms supplies to Saudi Arabia served broad strategic interests and should not be examined solely from the perspective of the Arab-Israeli conflict. Undersecretary of State and former ambassador to Saudi Arabia Richard Murphy told members of Congress in 1986 that he was

disturbed by assertions circulating that would attempt to tie a formal and direct linkage between our routine arms supply to Saudi Arabia and peaceful resolution of the Arab-Israeli dispute.   This is a narrow approach to a complex set of issues. . . . We, Israel, and the moderate Arabs would lose.   In the final analysis, the Soviets would be the winners.[63]

With the end of the Cold War such arguments are passé, but one factor that has increased in importance since the early 1980s is the issue of jobs for American defense workers.[64]   In his memoirs Haig recalled "that the argument that American workers and manufacturers should benefit from the sale in terms of wages and profits played a persuasive role in our deliberations."[65]   One of the key members of the Reagan administration, Defense Secretary Caspar Weinberger, had previously been a vice-president of Bechtel, a construction company with extensive contracts in Saudi Arabia, and Haig's successor George Shultz had ties to Bechtel as well.   The company that had the most to gain from the AWACS sale was Boeing.   To bolster political support for the deal Boeing asked its suppliers to write their representatives in Congress on behalf of the sale.[66]   Westinghouse, another commercial beneficiary of the sale, joined the fray and "hired a Washington public relations consultant to help out."[67]   The Mobil oil company placed advertisements in

newspapers that told Americans that Saudi Arabia had more to offer to
the U.S. economy than oil supplies. Good relations with Saudi Arabia
meant "trade for America, jobs for Americans, and strength for the
dollar."[68]

Pro-Israel groups perceived the AWACS/F-15 enhancement package
as a threat to the security of Israel and questioned the supposedly
moderate policies of Saudi Arabia and the stability and trustworthiness
of the Saudi regime. Israel's supporters in the United States feared that
Saudi Arabia could use AWACS and enhanced F-15s to monitor Israeli
military activities deep inside Israel and execute an Arab air attack on
Israel. Others, such as Senate minority leader Robert Byrd did not
consider the sale as a major security threat to Israel but were concerned
about a possible loss of highly complex U.S. technology to the Soviets.[69]

As the fight over AWACS moved into high gear in the fall of 1981,
some of the substantive controversies began to recede, and the debate
was couched more in terms of who makes or ought to make foreign
policy. More specifically, President Reagan charged Israel, and Prime
Minister Begin in particular, with interference in U.S. affairs when he
stated at a news conference that "[i]t is not the business of other nations
to make American foreign policy."[70] In the following case studies,
though, we will see European governments charging the Reagan
administration with violation of their sovereignty.

THE URENGOI-UZHGOROD PIPELINE

In 1981 and 1982 a controversy shook the Western alliance with the
United States facing a solid front of its major Western European allies.
The conflict centered around a pipeline that was to carry natural gas
from the Soviet gas fields at Urengoi to Uzhgorod on the Soviet-Czech
border. The Reagan administration wanted to block the building of this
pipeline and used economic sanctions, including the denial of export
licenses, for that purpose. European governments vigorously protested
this move and eventually forced the Reagan administration to back
down.

This was not the first time that East-West energy trade had become a
divisive issue within the Western alliance, nor was it the first major
natural gas pipeline deal between Western Europe and the Soviet Union.
In the late 1950s the Soviet Union had started an export drive to sell oil to
Western Europe, and at the same time it began to import increasing
amounts of large-diameter pipes from Western suppliers. The Soviets
needed Western pipe imports to build an oil pipeline from the Urals-
Volga oil fields to Eastern European countries. The Kennedy administration and American oil companies became increasingly concerned about
Western European imports of oil and also wanted to block or at least

delay the completion of the so-called Friendship oil pipeline. On November 21, 1962, the United States secured the passage of a secret NATO resolution, which asked NATO members to stop deliveries of large-diameter pipe to Soviet bloc countries. In the course of enforcing this embargo the West German government had to weather a storm of protest from the opposition and affected companies, but it decided to cooperate with the United States.[71]

East-West energy trade entered a new phase with the conclusion of large-scale natural gas pipeline deals in the 1970s. On February 1, 1970, West German companies signed three spectacular contracts. The pipe manufacturer Mannesmann received a Soviet order for 1.2 million tons of large-diameter steel pipes to be used for a natural gas pipeline from Siberia to the German-Czech border. Ruhrgas and Sojusneftexport signed a contract for the supply of 52 billion cubic meters natural gas, and West German banks provided a credit to the Soviet Union valued at 1.2 billion DM.[72] Additional natural gas contracts between Ruhrgas and the Soviet Union followed in 1972 and 1974. Thus, from a commercial perspective the 1981 deal was neither unique, except for its size, nor a novum.

As Axel Lebahn has pointed out, one of the historical ironies of the 1982 pipeline controversy lies in the fact that originally American natural gas companies had explored the idea of importing Soviet natural gas from the Urengoi region.[73] In 1971 the American company Tenneco decided that it would be unable to satisfy the growing demand for natural gas in the United States and began to explore the possibility of importing natural gas from the Soviet Union. These discussions led to the so-called North Star project. Under the terms of this project natural gas would flow from the gas field at Urengoi through a pipeline to a facility near Murmansk where the gas would have been liquefied and transported by LNG (liquefied natural gas) tankers to the United States.[74] The inability to secure most-favored-nation status for the Soviet Union and Export-Import Bank financing effectively killed the project.[75] This sketch of the historical context has illustrated that the 1982 pipeline controversy should not be examined as an isolated incident but has to be viewed in the larger context of East-West relations.

Chronology of Events

The Soviet Union began concrete discussions with Western companies on increased Soviet natural gas deliveries at the end of 1979.[76] In May 1980 the West German cabinet discussed the problem of an increased dependency on Soviet natural gas and reaffirmed an earlier assessment dating from 1978 that a Soviet market share of 30 percent would be acceptable.[77] Also in May 1980 a meeting of the German-

Soviet economic commission took place, which had originally been scheduled for January but had been postponed because of the Afghanistan invasion.[78] On June 24, 1980, Chancellor Schmidt met with the chairmen of the pipe manufacturer Mannesmann and of Deutsche Bank, the leading West German bank, and, among other topics, touched on the new natural gas pipeline deal.[79] Shortly thereafter, Schmidt and Foreign Minister Genscher traveled to Moscow, and during that visit the two governments approved negotiations for a new natural gas project.[80] According to Axel Lebahn, the chief negotiator for Deutsche Bank, this declaration gave the green light for the ensuing negotiations not only between Soviet and West German companies but the other Western European firms as well.[81]

The course of the negotiations between the Soviet Union and Western companies deviated significantly from previous gas-pipeline deals.[82] In the past the Soviet Union had designated a single company as general contractor and relied on one bank consortium to put together a credit package. This time the Soviet Union negotiated with separate national bank consortia and individual Western suppliers for the various subcontracts. As a result, Soviet negotiators played off different Western suppliers against each other and achieved very favorable terms in the credit and equipment contracts.

Politically, the pipeline project aroused relatively little controversy in 1980. The Carter administration did not oppose the project or at least did not make a major issue of it. Within West Germany conservative members of parliament criticized the proposed project, but this criticism remained limited.[83]

Both the pace of the negotiations and the controversy surrounding the pipeline deal picked up in 1981. The leaders of the major advanced industrial nations discussed the pipeline issue at the Ottawa economic summit in July 1981. President Reagan was not successful, however, in persuading the Western Europeans to drop the pipeline project.[84] On the domestic West German front the West German central bank on July 2, 1981, raised the ceiling for AKA line B credits from 3 to 5 billion DM in order to facilitate the financing of the West German part of the pipeline deal.[85] Later that month Soviet negotiators made the necessary concessions to overcome an almost yearlong deadlock in the credit negotiations with the West Germans and the French.[86] German banks then announced an agreement on the outline of a credit package to finance West German equipment exports to the Soviet Union.[87] In this context the *Frankfurter Allgemeine Zeitung* reported that other West German exporters were angered by the fact that most of the below market-rate AKA line B funds were to be used for the highly politicized pipeline credits.[88] F. Wilhelm Christians, co-chairman of Deutsche Bank's managing board, recalled that his "bank, as leader of the syndicate, was viewed more and more critically, and so was I. One or two banks even withdrew from the syndicate."[89]

In the fall of 1981 a U.S. delegation led by Under Secretary of State Myer Rashish attempted to convince Western European governments of the advantages of forgoing Soviet natural gas imports and instead relying on increased shipments of U.S. coal and on Norwegian natural gas. For a number of reasons, however, this "offer" was quite unrealistic.[90] Even former Secretary of State Haig later admitted in his memoirs that "[i]n the final analysis, Washington had no alternatives to offer."[91] Around the same time the Soviet Union reached agreements with Western natural gas importers. In November 1981 Ruhrgas and Sojusgasexport signed a contract on Soviet natural gas exports to West Germany two days before a visit by Leonid Brezhnev to Bonn.[92]

In the fall of 1981 the political and economic situation in Poland continued to deteriorate, and on December 13, 1981, the Polish government declared martial law. Shortly thereafter President Reagan announced economic sanctions against Poland.[93] Since the Reagan administration regarded the Soviet Union as the mastermind behind the repression in Poland and since the U.S.S.R. took an uncompromising stand on the situation in Poland, President Reagan extended sanctions against the Soviet Union on December 29, 1981, including licensing requirements "for export to the Soviet Union . . . [of] an expanded list of oil and gas equipment."[94] Technically these sanctions meant that oil and gas equipment, which previously could be exported to the Soviet Union under a general license, now required a validated export license. Furthermore, the Commerce Department stopped issuing such licenses.[95] Thus, on January 8, 1982, the U.S. government blocked the sale of equipment by General Electric to European companies that needed these components to build gas turbine compressor stations for the Siberian pipeline.[96]

Members of the Reagan administration recognized the importance of allied cooperation with American sanctions. In January 1982 the foreign ministers of the NATO alliance met in Brussels to discuss the situation in Poland and the Western response to it. Instead of endorsing President Reagan's sanctions, however, the West Europeans only pledged not to undermine them.[97] Meanwhile, the Soviet Union and its Western European negotiating partners made further progress on the pipeline deal. On January 23, 1982, Gaz de France and Sojusgasexport signed a twenty-five-year gas supply contract.[98] The following month the West German cabinet formally approved the gas contract between Ruhrgas and Sojusgasexport, which was required by West Germany's foreign trade act.[99]

Although the pipeline deal provided the most dramatic example of differences between U.S. and Western European East-West trade policies, the Reagan administration pressured its Western European allies on a number of other related issues as well. Prominent among them was the question of Western credits to the Soviet bloc. In March 1982 an American delegation led by Under Secretary of State James Buckley traveled around Europe and primarily discussed the credit issue. For a while it appeared that a resolution of the intra-alliance conflict was in sight with the United States moderating its opposition to the pipeline and the Western Europeans accepting some limitations on credits to the Soviet bloc.[100] However, hopes for a compromise proved to be an illusion, and soon after the economic summit at Versailles in early June 1982 the Reagan administration extended its sanctions related to the pipeline. President Reagan announced the hardening of the U.S. position on June 18, and on June 22, 1982, the Commerce Department issued new regulations which extended the pipeline sanctions and "prohibited unaffiliated foreign companies from exporting foreign-origin products that were manufactured with technology acquired through licensing agreements with U.S. companies, whether or not the U.S. technology had been subject to controls at the time of export from the United States."[101]

From the perspective of Western European governments, this changed the meaning of the pipeline controversy. It no longer involved only a debate over Western European energy dependence on the Soviet Union, differences over East-West trade in general, or Western responses to the situation in Poland.   Rather, the United States in a very provocative way had claimed the extraterritorial applicability of its laws and had challenged the sovereignty of its Western European allies. Not surprisingly, France took the lead in picking up this challenge and defied American attempts to hinder Western European participation in the pipeline.   In August 1982 French President Mitterrand ordered the French subsidiary of the Dallas-based energy equipment company Dresser Industries to fulfill its contracts with the Soviet Union and ship compressors for the Siberian pipeline to its Soviet customer. The United States promptly responded by imposing penalties on the French company.[102] In the following weeks the game repeated itself for British, German, and Italian companies. European companies would defy the U.S. embargo and ship pipeline equipment to the Soviet Union, and the United States imposed sanctions on these companies.[103]

Even while the United States took steps to penalize European companies that had defied American sanctions, members of the Reagan administration searched for ways to drop the pipeline sanctions and put economic pressure on the Soviet Union through other means. According to George Shultz, the United States and its European NATO allies reached a preliminary agreement on ending the sanctions during a meeting of NATO foreign ministers at La Sapinière, Canada, in early October.[104] On November 13, 1982, President Reagan announced that the allies had reached an agreement to take a variety of steps to reevaluate East-West trade. Therefore, there was "no further need" for the pipeline sanctions.[105] However, hours before Reagan gave the speech lifting the sanctions Jacques Attali had asked Washington to reconsider the text of the agreement, and following President Reagan's speech the French government immediately denied being part of any such agreement.[106]

The intra-alliance conflict and consultations over the Siberian pipeline represent one important aspect of this issue, but equally important for our purposes here are the domestic decision processes and controversies behind U.S. and West German actions. Although in the past U.S. presidents could count on considerable domestic support for restrictions on trade with the Soviet Union, President Reagan encountered considerable domestic opposition to the pipeline sanctions. In Congress, for example, Representative Paul Findley (R.-Ill.) introduced a bill that would have repealed the sanctions. On August 10, 1982, the House Foreign Affairs Committee approved this bill by a vote of 22–12. The twenty-two representatives favoring the bill included seven Republicans.[107] Even supporters of the bill, though, did not expect it to become law, and on September 29, 1982 the House of Representatives only passed an amended version of the bill which effectively defeated its original purpose.[108] Nevertheless, the episode showed that President Reagan not only faced international but domestic constraints as well.

Meanwhile, on the other side of the Atlantic, the West German Deutsche Bank AG and the Soviet foreign trade bank initialed a credit agreement for German pipeline equipment supplies in June 1982. On July 13, 1982, a West German bank consortium and its Soviet business partner signed the agreement in Leningrad.[109] At this point the important agreements concerning the West German participation in the pipeline had been reached. The one outstanding issue remained the building of a separate pipeline that was to branch off the main pipeline in Czechoslovakia and supply West Berlin with Siberian natural gas. For most of its length, this pipeline was to go through East German territory. On March 30, 1983, the involved parties signed the necessary agreements for the delivery of Soviet natural gas to West Berlin.[110] On October 1, 1984, the Soviet Union began its deliveries of natural gas on the basis of the fourth contract between Ruhrgas and Sojusgasexport.[111] A year later Berlin started receiving Soviet natural gas.[112]

West German Objectives and Decision Processes

In providing the political support for and following through on the pipeline deal, the West German government pursued four main objectives. First of all, the West German government saw the natural gas contract as a way to further diversify its energy supplies and decrease West German dependence on Middle Eastern energy sources. Thus, although the Reagan administration argued that additional Soviet natural gas exports to Western Europe would make West Germany and other Western importers dependent on the Soviet Union, West German officials essentially asserted that the deal would make Germany less vulnerable to turmoil in energy markets.[113]

Second, initially there were high hopes that the pipeline deal would translate into several billion dollars worth of Soviet equipment orders for West German companies. West German expectations reached as far as 10 billion DM.[114] For some of the West German bidders, large Soviet orders were particularly important because, at the time of the equipment negotiations, they faced deep economic problems. This was especially true for AEG-Kanis, which had received a contract to supply forty-seven turbines for gas compressor stations worth 600 million DM. At that time its parent company AEG-Telefunken experienced a severe financial crisis that eventually led it to declare bankruptcy, constituting the largest corporate failure in West Germany since World War II.

Before the start of the equipment negotiations, but soon after the Afghanistan crisis, then Chancellor Schmidt declared in a speech to the West German parliament on February 28, 1980, that West Germany's economic relations with the Soviet Union had been built up over a long period of time, initially for mainly political reasons. By 1980, however, these relations, and specifically the export of West German machinery, had come to play a significant economic role as well, much more so than the East-West trade of certain other countries, by which Schmidt alluded to the United States.[115] In 1982 he emphatically stated that his government would not be drawn into economic warfare against the Soviet Union.[116]

Third, the West German government credited East-West economic relations, and cooperative projects, such as the pipeline deal, with performing a stabilizing function for East-West relations overall. Foreign Minister Genscher argued in a speech in 1982, which specifically addressed the pipeline issue and American sanctions, that common economic interests could prevent a change in international relations detrimental to European interests.[117] Whereas détente had died in the United States under President Carter, the West German government of Social and Free Democrats wanted to preserve the benefits of détente even after, or possibly especially after, Afghanistan and martial law in Poland.

Finally, after President Reagan had raised the stakes in the controversy with the extraterritorial application of U.S. export control laws, West Germany's sovereignty and its ability to fulfill its commitments to its trading partners became an issue. Foreign Minister

Genscher, for example, argued that by following through on its pipeline contracts West Germany affirmed its contractual fidelity to all its economic partners.[118] Thus, in the West German case economic and political motives were clearly intertwined. This leads us to the question of how state and private economic actors cooperated or conflicted with each other.

There are a number of facets to the interactions between state and private economic actors in this case. First of all, West German officials repeatedly stressed that the West German state was not a party to any of the actual contracts that constitute the pipeline deal.[119] In contrast to some of the French and Italian firms involved, the major West German companies participating in this deal were privately owned. This was true of Ruhrgas, the main gas importer, Deutsche Bank as the head of the West German bank consortium, and the equipment suppliers AEG-Kanis, Liebherr, and Mannesmann.

Nevertheless, the conclusion and implementation of the pipeline deal also required cooperation between the state and private actors in a variety of different ways. First, the Soviet and West German governments approved the start of negotiations during Chancellor Schmidt's visit to Moscow in 1980. On February 17, 1982, the West German cabinet approved the natural gas contract between Ruhrgas and Sojusgasexport as part of the outcome of these negotiations.

A number of state agencies also became at least indirectly involved in the credit negotiations. Part of the credit package consisted of supplier credits, which were refinanced through AKA line B funds. As noted earlier, in view of demands for AKA line B funds resulting from the pipeline deal, the West German central bank on July 2, 1981, raised the ceiling for line B credits from 3 to 5 billion DM. Furthermore, 95 percent of the credit was covered by the Hermes credit insurance company against political and economic risks.[120] This required approval by the cabinet because the limit for the coverage of credits to the Soviet Union had been reached, and it was necessary to go above that ceiling.[121]

Another highly political aspect of the West German part of the pipeline deal involved the inclusion of West Berlin. Compared to the scale and complexity of the Urengoi-Uzhgorod project as a whole, it may appear trivial to build a relatively short branch pipeline through East German territory to supply West Berlin. The problems here were not of an economic nature but involved high politics. Despite deténte, the status of West Berlin continued to cause friction between West Germany and the Soviet Union.[122] From a technical and legal perspective these negotiations were complicated by the large number of parties involved and legal requirements about who could and could not enter into a contract with whom. In this case the Soviet Union delivered the natural gas to Ruhrgas, which in turn delivered it to an East German company.

The ultimate customer was the Berlin company GASAG, but because this company was not allowed to enter into contracts with East German companies, Ruhrgas bought the gas back at the Berlin border and then sold it to GASAG.[123]

Finally, West German government officials could no longer maintain that the pipeline deal was a primarily commercial affair when the Reagan administration challenged the sovereignty of its Western European allies. In contrast to the British and the French, the West German state did not possess the legal instruments to order West German companies to fulfill their contracts with the Soviet Union. Instead, the West German companies received letters urging them to honor their contracts.[124]

Although state-industry interactions in this case raise a complex set of issues, domestic opposition to the pipeline deal remained limited. Conservative Christian Democratic deputies in parliament put forward a number of questions that indicated opposition to the pipeline deal or some of its terms and that also showed sympathy for the position of the Reagan administration.[125] However, any hopes the Reagan administration may have had that a Christian Democratic government would prove to be more accommodating turned out to be unfounded. After the Social and Free Democratic government had fallen during the fall of 1982, the new Christian Democratic–led government continued its support for the pipeline project.[126]

U.S. Objectives and Decision Processes

Although West German objectives were fairly clear, the American case presents a much more complicated and muddled picture. As Baldwin observed, "the goals and targets of the Reagan administration are nearly impossible to determine."[127] When President Reagan announced the imposition of sanctions on the Soviet Union on December 29, 1981, he stated that "[b]y our actions we expect to put powerful doubts in the minds of the Soviet and Polish leaders about this continued repression. The whole purpose of our actions is to speak for those who have been silenced and to help those who have been rendered helpless."[128] However, even writers who vehemently disagree on the lessons to be drawn from this case agree that linking the pipeline sanctions to the declaration of martial law and the suppression of Solidarity in Poland obscures rather than illuminates the real meaning of this case. According to Jentleson,

Events in Poland ... were more precipitating than causal. In fact, the objectives to be served by blocking the Siberian pipeline not only were more complex than a mere response to the Polish situation, but in a more fundamental way were part and parcel of an overarching strategy to purge from American policy all remnants of economic inducement and revert to Cold War-style economic coercion.[129]

Although academic analysts of this case nevertheless came up with fairly neat distinctions among different objectives pursued by the Reagan administration, the actual public record of what various administration officials said at different times yields a far more confusing picture. An analysis of congressional testimony by administration officials clearly shows that the Reagan administration was involved in a review of its policy on export controls covering oil and gas equipment several months before the imposition of martial law in Poland. Consider, for example, the following exchange between Congressman Lagomarsino and Deputy Assistant Secretary of State Johnston at a Congressional hearing on May 25, 1982:

Mr. Lagomarsino. I am somewhat confused here as to whether we are talking about one thing or two things. Are we saying that because of the Polish martial law declaration that we have imposed pipeline controls on the Soviet Union or is it something that stands on its own?
Mr. Johnston. It was one of the measures being considered in the U.S. Government for a series of months before the Polish martial law, and when martial law was declared in Poland, it was one of the series of actions put into effect at the same time we terminated the rights of the Polish airline to come into the United States, terminated their fishing rights in U.S. coastal waters.
Mr. Lagomarsino. It was put into effect at that time, but if the Polish martial law were lifted, would that change our position on the pipeline?
Mr. Johnston. I would not make that connection that closely. I think if the Polish martial law were lifted, we would have to make a general assessment about what the United States was going to do.[130]

Other representatives of the State Department, however, claimed a closer link between the situation in Poland and the pipeline sanctions. Representative Solarz was as confused about the real purpose of the sanctions as Congressman Lagomarsino, and he sought clarification from Under Secretary of State James L. Buckley at a hearing on August 4, 1982:

Mr. Solarz. I am not clear exactly what the purpose of the pipeline decision was. At various times I have heard it said that the purpose was to deny the Soviet Union scarce foreign exchange. At other times I have heard the purpose was to reduce the dependence of our European allies on natural gas from the Soviet Union. On still other occasions, I have heard the purpose described as one designed to put additional pressure on the Soviet Union to bring about a lifting of martial law in Poland. Could you tell me which of these various objectives is our major concern, or are all of them the purpose of this endeavor?
Mr. Buckley. I think we have to separate the fact that not only this administration, but the prior administration has urged the Europeans not to contract for Soviet gas for the two reasons you first stipulated. We lost that argument in part

because we did not come up with a plausible, immediately available alternative. But if you are talking about the purpose of these sanctions, let me quote from the man who enacted them: "The objective of the United States in imposing the sanctions has been and continues to be to advance reconciliation in Poland."
Mr. Solarz. So in other words, if reconciliation in Poland is advanced, we would be prepared to rescind the pipeline decision?
Mr. Buckley. It depends on how far they are advanced.[131]

Although these remarks by Johnston and Buckley did not provide full clarification either, we can conclude that there was more involved in the pipeline sanctions than an attempt to end martial law in Poland. Nevertheless, as Henry Nau, who worked for the National Security Council at the time, summarized the controversy, "[t]he pipeline . . . might never have become a major allied controversy if the Soviet-inspired coup in Poland had not occurred in December 1981 to alter radically the psychological environment."[132] Some of the confusion also reflects the fact that the Reagan administration was itself divided on the pipeline issue with the State Department taking a different position than the Pentagon.

Conflict within the administration reached its peak over the extension of the pipeline sanctions in June 1982. According to Alexander Haig, National Security Advisor Clark scheduled a NSC meeting in June 1982 at a time when, as Clark knew, Haig could not attend.[133] At that meeting the NSC decided to extend the reach of the sanctions against the strong opposition of the State Department, and shortly thereafter Haig resigned. Haig's resignation cannot be attributed entirely to the pipeline affair, but it was a contributing factor.

The hard-line pro-sanctions group led by Defense Secretary Caspar Weinberger, National Security Advisor William Clark, and other relatively high-ranking officials, including Richard Perle of the Defense Department and Lawrence Brady from Commerce, did not only face opposition from within the administration but from Congress as well. As should be expected, however, Congress itself showed internal divisions. The most vehement opponents of the sanctions came from the state of Illinois where two companies hit especially hard by the sanctions, Caterpillar and Fiat-Allis, had important plants.[134] Other members of Congress, though, favored a very tough stand on the pipeline. Senator Garn, for example, did not accuse the Reagan administration of going too far in its opposition to the pipeline but faulted it for not taking decisive actions sooner.[135] When the House Foreign Affairs Committee voted on a bill to repeal the pipeline sanctions, Committee Chairman Zablocki opposed this measure not only for substantive policy reasons but also because it would unduly interfere with the administration's right to conduct foreign policy.[136]

One way in which this conflict over East-West energy trade differed from previous controversies is that in the 1980s business interests became increasingly vocal in voicing their opposition to export controls which put them at a disadvantage to their foreign competitors. Opposition came, first of all, from the companies directly affected by the sanctions. Caterpillar, for example, had contracts to sell the Soviet Union some of the pipe layers needed to build the pipeline. On December 3, 1981, Caterpillar had gained presidential approval to export 200 pipe layers. Within the same month, however, the president reversed his decision. Although this sale by itself may not have been very important, Caterpillar had seen its market position in the Soviet Union erode because of sanctions that had been imposed by President Carter in 1978. From 1970 until mid-1978 Caterpillar had sold the Soviet Union 1,943 large track-type tractors and pipe layers compared to 341 sold by its main competitor Komatsu of Japan. After the imposition of President Carter's human rights sanctions, from mid-1978 to 1981, Komatsu's sales rose to 1,988, whereas sales by Caterpillar dropped to 336 units.[137] Then President Reagan announced the pipeline sanctions, which came at a time when the country already faced a severe recession.

But in this case not only individual companies but national business organizations also actively lobbied for the repeal of the sanctions. After the extension of the pipeline sanctions in June 1982 the president of the American Chamber of Commerce, Richard Lesher, openly criticized the administration in a letter to Ronald Reagan on July 14, 1982:

Over the last year and one-half, the Chamber has repeatedly cautioned he Administration with regard to both the effectiveness and the domestic economic costs of unilateral foreign policy export controls. In building overseas markets vital to our economic security, U.S. export performance relies heavily on both quality and dependability. In this regard, the Chamber is concerned that the new controls will only aggravate further our international reputation for commercial reliability.[138]

Alexander Trowbridge, president of the National Association of Manufacturers, joined this chorus of criticism leveled against Reagan's sanctions policy.[139] Thus, overall the Reagan administration faced a situation not only of Western European defiance but of considerable domestic opposition as well.[140]

CONCLUSION

These four cases illustrate some of the differences between U.S. and German export control policy and foreign policy more generally. In the German cases we saw the consensus-oriented German foreign policy-making process at work. When consensus could not be achieved, as in the Saudi arms deal, two German governments vacillated and irritated their foreign partners. The German East-West trade case showed the close cooperation between government and industry in that area. In the two U.S. cases we found pitched battles over both turf and policy content between Congress and the executive and among different executive departments. The arms export cases also demonstrated the limited utility of institutional arguments about the effect of state centralization. Even though the American state is usually depicted as a weak and decentralized state and despite the fact that the German arms export approval process is less fragmented and generally less open to outside intervention than in the United States, the American state was able to implement its preferences, whereas the German state was not.

All four cases are set in the 1980s, but they contain valuable lessons for export control policy in the post–Cold War world as well. Export control policy involves trade-offs between export promotion and national security interests. Such trade-offs did not disappear with the end of the Cold War but may turn out to be even more difficult in the future than in the past. What appears to have changed, though, is how these trade-offs are resolved. Whereas the United States has begun to put greater emphasis on "economic security," Germany has taken steps to curtail irresponsible behavior by some German exporters. To use the example of arms exports, during the 1992 election campaign President Bush announced the sale of 72 F-15 fighter aircraft to Saudi Arabia and told McDonnell Douglas workers that "[i]n this time of economic transition, I want to do everything to keep Americans at work."[141] At the same time the United States conducted negotiations with China, France, Great Britain, and Russia on arms transfers to the Middle East, and the Bush administration pushed China to abide by the rules of the MTCR and to stop selling ballistic missile technology. However, preserving the jobs of American defense workers through lavish Middle Eastern arms deals does not fit well with asking other countries to show restraint in their export sales.

A more promising way to use economic incentives in export control policy is to offer countries economic compensation if they follow responsible export control policies. In September 1993 the United States and Russia announced plans to cooperate more closely in their space programs. As part of the deal Russia agreed to export controls on missile technology and in return gained access to the international market for commercial satellite launching.[142] However, the Siberian gas pipeline case showed the limits of America's ability to offer economic compensation for cooperation on export controls and related trade issues. In the early 1960s the United States had been able to thwart a Soviet "oil offensive" by offering Italy, which had begun to increase its imports of Soviet oil, alternative supplies at low prices.[143] In the early

1980s the United States could not offer the Western Europeans either alternative energy supplies or compensation for pipeline equipment exports. The U.S.-Russian agreements on space cooperation and missile technology controls show that economic compensation can still be a useful tool, but it appears unlikely that the United States would be able or willing to offer such deals to Russia and a number of other Soviet successor states on a sustained basis until these countries have mastered their economic problems at some point in the relatively distant future.

Turning to Germany's role, under Chancellor Schmidt, West German foreign policy began to show an assertiveness that had been absent earlier. Yet, the failed Saudi arms deal illustrated the limits of an independent German foreign policy beyond the confines of Europe. In the wake of German reunification analysts again speculated about the future directions of the country's foreign policy after Germany had regained its full sovereignty. However, Germany's actions and inaction during the Gulf War of 1991 and the debate over out-of-area missions for German troops show that the past still casts a long shadow, particularly when it comes to arms exports and German policy toward the Middle East.

NOTES

1. "Bonn and Saudi Arabia to Strengthen Ties," *Financial Times*, 20 June 1980; *Der Spiegel*, 5 January 1981, pp. 19–22.

2. *Der Spiegel*, 2 March 1981, pp. 28–32.

3. "Keine Waffen für Saudi Arabien," *Frankfurter Rundschau*, 29 April 1981, p. 1.

4. "Kanzler gab bereits Zusage," *Frankfurter Rundschau*, 30 April 1981, p. 1.

5. West Germany, *Verhandlungen des Deutschen Bundestages*, 10. Wahl-periode, Stenographische Berichte 10/53, pp. 3739–3740.

6. Ibid., p. 3733.

7. "Eine Versteifung auf die 'Leo-Frage' könnte die Verständigung beeinträchtigen," *Frankfurter Allgemeine Zeitung*, 8 October 1983, p. 2.

8. "Waffenlieferungen an die Saudis in der Schwebe—Kohl heimgekehrt von der Nah-Ost Reise," *Frankfurter Allgemeine Zeitung*, 12 October 1983, p. 2.

9. "Streit über Waffenexport," *Badische Zeitung*, 21 June 1985, p. 2.

10. "Ehmke wurde Anfang Juli von den Rüstungsvorhaben informiert," *Frankfurter Allgemeine Zeitung*, 12 October 1985, p. 1.

11. "Saudis Say Reagan Cleared Purchase of British Planes," *New York Times*, 16 September 1985, p. 1.

12. "Tornado-Deal: 'Da wurde Bonn geleimt,'" *Der Spiegel*, 3 December 1984, p. 153.

13. "Strauß für mehr Waffenexport," *Badische Zeitung*, 25 November 1986, p. 5; "Strauß: Saudis wünschen Waffen aus Bonn," *Süddeutsche Zeitung*, 27 November 1986, p. 9.

14. "Nach der Wahl eine neue Grundlage," *Der Spiegel*, 1 December 1986, pp. 17–18.

15. "U-Boot-Geschäft mit den Saudis," *Frankfurter Allgemeine Zeitung*, 2 December 1986, p. 1.

16. Wischnewski's nickname was "Ben Wisch."

17. This may be partly explained by the close relations between German unions and Israel's Histradut. See Thomas Risse-Kappen, "Muddling Through Mined Territory: German Foreign Policy-Making and the Middle East," in *Germany and the Middle East: Patterns and Prospects*, ed. Shahram Chubin (New York: St. Martin's Press, 1992), p. 184.

18. Herbert Wilkens and Hans-Joachim Ziesing, "Die wirtschaftliche Bedeutung des Mittleren Ostens für die Bundesrepublik Deutschland," *Der Bürger im Staat* 31 (March 1981): 27.

19. "Facetten der Bonner Mittelostpolitik," *Neue Zürcher Zeitung*, 27 April 1981, p. 3.

20. Rochus-Ernst Freiherr von Lüttwitz, "Deutsch-saudiarabische Zusammenarbeit—worum es in Wirklichkeit geht," in *Saudi Arabien: Partner für die Bundesrepublik Deutschland* (Hamburg: Nah- und Mittelost Verein, 1981), p. 20.

21. Hermann Becker, "Saudi-Arabiens Bedeutung für die deutsche Bauindustrie," in *Saudi-Arabien: Partner für die Bundesrepublik Deutschland* (Hamburg: Nah- und Mittelost Verein, 1981), p. 25.

22. Hans Matthöfer, "Saudi-Arabiens finanzpolitische Bedeutung für die Bundesrepublik Deutschland," in *Saudi-Arabien: Partner für die Bundesrepublik Deutschland* (Hamburg: Nah- und Mittelost Verein, 1981), p. 20.

23. "Erneut saudische Kredite für den Bonner Haushalt," *Neue Zürcher Zeitung*, 11 February 1982, p. 17.

24. Norbert Gansel, "Waffengeschäfte: Eine politische Weichenstellung," *Der Überblick* 1/1981.

25. *Wirtschaftswoche*, 2 February 1981, p. 43.

26. "IG Metall gegen Panzer-Export nach Saudi Arabien," *Frankfurter Allgemeine Zeitung*, 27 February 1985, p. 3.

27. For a more detailed discussion of German economic interests in the Middle East see Hans Maull, "Economic Relations with the Middle East: Weight and Dimensions," in *Germany and the Middle East: Patterns and Prospects*, ed. Shahram Chubin (New York: St. Martin's Press, 1992), pp. 113–135.

28. Jürgen Möllemann, "Frieden und Stabilität am Golf," in *Saudi-Arabien: Partner für die Bundesrepublik Deutschland* (Hamburg: Nah- und Mittelost-Verein, 1981), pp. 42–43.

29. Erwin Horn, "Veränderte Herausforderungen für die westliche Sicherheitspolitik," in *Saudi-Arabien: Partner für die Bundesrepublik Deutschland* (Hamburg: Nah- und Mittelost-Verein, 1981), p. 54.

30. *Der Spiegel*, 12 January 1981, pp. 26–27.

31. Gansel, "Waffengeschäfte," p. 18.

32. Transcript of an interview by Radio Bremen with Horst Ehmke, *SPD-Pressedienst*, 29 June 1985; "Ehmke: Keine Informationen über Munitionsfabrik erhalten," *Frankfurter Allgemeine Zeitung*, 14 October 1985, p. 5.

33. Transcript of an interview by Deutschlandfunk with Dr. Werner Marx, *Wehrtechnik*, June 1985, p. 115.

34. U.S. Congress, House Committee on Foreign Affairs, *Presidential Certification on the Delivery of AWACS to Saudi Arabia*, 99th Cong., 2d sess., p. 18.

35. U.S. Congress, House Committee on Foreign Affairs, *Saudi Arabia and the United States: The New Context in an Evolving "Special Relationship*," 97th Cong., 1st sess., pp. 47–48.

36. U.S. Congress, Senate Committee on Foreign Relations, *The Proposed AWACS/F-15 Enhancement Sale to Saudi Arabia*, 97th Cong., 1st sess., p. 2.

37. Ibid., p. 3.

38. Ibid., p. 4.

39. Alexander M. Haig, Jr., *Caveat: Realism, Reagan and Foreign Policy* (New York: Macmillan, 1984), p. 175.

40. Ibid., p. 176.

41. Ibid., p. 178.

42. Ibid., p. 179; Laurance I. Barrett, *Gambling with History: Ronald Reagan in the White House* (New York: Penguin Books, 1984), p. 268.

43. "U.S. Will Go Ahead on Deal with Saudis for 5 Radar Planes," *New York Times*, 22 April 1981, p. 1.

44. "20 Senators Criticize Providing Equipment for F-15 to the Saudis," *New York Times*, 25 March 1981, p. 11.

45. "Majority in Congress Urge Reagan Not to Sell Awacs to Saudi Arabia," *New York Times*, 25 June 1981, p. 1.

46. "Saudi Air Deal Is Formally Sent to the Congress," *New York Times*, 25 August 1981, pp. 1, 4.

47. "Senate Nears Crucial Vote on AWACS Sale," *Congressional Quarterly Weekly Report*, 24 October 1981, p. 2054.

48. "Senate Supports Reagan on AWACS Sale," *Congressional Quarterly Weekly Report*, 31 October 1981, p. 2095.

49. U.S. Congress, *Presidential Certification*, pp. 73–77.

50. "Saudi Is Reported to Agree to Terms on Use of AWACS," *New York Times*, 26 February 1982, p. 1.

51. "AWACS Accord Is Denied by Saudi," *New York Times*, 2 March 1982, p. 3.

52. "Congress Clears Foreign Aid Authorization Bill," *Congressional Quarterly Weekly Report*, 3 August 1985, p. 1542.

53. "Big Missile Sale to Saudi Arabia Opposed by Key Congress Panels," *New York Times*, 24 April 1986, p. 1.

54. "Reagan Finally Carries the Day on Saudi Arms," *Congressional Quarterly Weekly Report*, 7 June 1986, p. 1262.

55. "Senate Rejects Saudi Arms Sale, 73–22," *New York Times*, 7 May 1986, p. 3.

56. U.S. Congress, *Presidential Certification*, pp. 67–72.

57. "It's Official: Saudis to Get AWACS Planes," *Congressional Quarterly Weekly Report*, 21 June 1986, p. 1390.

58. Steven L. Spiegel, *The Other Arab-Israeli Conflict: Making America's Middle East Policy from Truman to Reagan* (Chicago: University of Chicago Press, 1985), p. 398.

59. *Department of State Bulletin* 81 (October 1981): 53.

60.   For more in-depth descriptions of the military justifications of the Saudi air defense enhancement package see U.S. Congress, *The Proposed AWACS/F-15 Enhancement Sale*, pp. 14–26; Anthony H. Cordesman, *The Gulf and the Search for Strategic Stability: Saudi Arabia, the Military Balance in the Gulf, and Trends in the Arab-Israeli Military Balance* (Boulder: Westview Press, 1984), pp. 305–323.

61.   *Department of State Bulletin* 81 (October 1981): 55.

62.   *Department of State Bulletin* 81 (November 1981): 60.

63.   *Department of State Bulletin* 86 (June 1986): 72.

64.   For a more general discussion of the likely economic impact of restrictions on U.S. arms sales to the Middle East see William D. Bajusz and David J. Louscher, *Arms Sales and the U.S. Economy: The Impact of Restricting Military Exports* (Boulder: Westview Press, 1988).

65.   Haig, *Caveat*, p. 178.

66.   "Boeing Lobbying for AWACS Sale," *New York Times*, 1 October 1981, p. 30.

67.   "The Great Divide, 1981: Taking Sides on AWACS," *New York Times*, 1 October 1981, p. A28.

68.   *New York Times*, 8 October 1981, p. 27.

69.   "Excerpts from Senator Byrd's Speech Opposing AWACS Sale to the Saudis," *New York Times*, 22 October 1981, p. A16.

70.   "Reagan Says U.S. Would Bar a Takeover in Saudi Arabia That Imperiled Flow of Oil," *New York Times*, 2 October 1981, p. 1.

71.   For a more detailed description of the Soviet oil offensive and of the 1962/63 pipe embargo see Jentleson, *Pipeline Politics*, chapters 3 and 4.

72.   Wörmann, *Der Osthandel*, pp. 115–116.

73.   Axel Lebahn, "Die 'Jamal-Erdgasleitung': UdSSR-Westeuropa im Ost-West Konflikt," *Aussenpolitik* 34 (1983): 256–280.

74.   For a more detailed description see statement by Jack H. Ray, executive vice president of Tenneco, in U.S. Congress, Senate Committee on Foreign Relations, *Multinational Corporations and United States Foreign Policy*, 93d Cong., 2d sess., pp. 40–61.

75.   Jentleson, *Pipeline Politics*, p. 142.

76.   Lebahn, "Die 'Jamal-Erdgasleitung,'" p. 265; F. Wilhelm Christians, *Paths to Russia: From War to Peace*, trans. Joachim Neugroschel (New York: Macmillan, 1990), pp. 51–52.

77.   Claudia Wörmann, *Osthandel als Problem der Atlantischen Allianz: Erfahrungen aus dem Erdgas-Röhren-Geschäft mit der UdSSR*, Arbeitspapiere zur Internationalen Politik, no. 38 (Bonn: Europa Union Verlag, 1986), p. 97; "Moskau will mit Schmidt über Geschäfte reden," *Frankfurter Allgemeine Zeitung*, 26 June 1980, p. 11.

78.   Wörmann, *Osthandel als Problem*, p. 97.

79.   *Frankfurter Allgemeine Zeitung*, 26 June 1980, p. 11.

80.   *Europa-Archiv*, 1980, p. D435.

81.   Lebahn, "Die 'Jamal-Erdgasleitung,'" p. 267.

82.   For detailed discussions of the negotiations and the resulting contracts see Antony J. Blinken, *Ally Versus Ally: America, Europe, and the Siberian Pipeline Crisis* (New York: Praeger, 1987), chapters 2 and 3; Thane Gustafson, *Soviet Negotiating Strategy: The East-West Gas Pipeline Deal 1980–1984* (Santa Monica:

Rand, 1985); Lebahn, "Die 'Jamal-Erdgasleitung'"; Wörmann, *Osthandel als Problem*, pp. 93–107.

83. *Frankfurter Allgemeine Zeitung*, 20 November 1980, p. 13.

84. For an insider account of the Ottawa and subsequent summits that addressed East-West trade issues see Nau, *The Myth of America's Decline*, chapter 10.

85. "Verärgerung über Zinsvorteile für die Sowjets," *Frankfurter Allgemeine Zeitung*, 27 July 1981, p. 9. AKA is a syndicate of over fifty German banks that pooled some of their resources to provide export financing. AKA can use three lines of credit. Funds from lines A and C are given out at market rates. Line B credits, however, involve preferential financing terms; it is a special rediscount facility at the *Deutsche Bundesbank*. The interest rate for line B credits is set at 1.5 percent above the official discount rate. On top of that comes a 0.6 percent exchange tax. See Wolfgang Arendt, "25 Jahre AKA Ausfuhrkredit-Gesellschaft mbH," *Die Bank* 17 (April 1977): 21–24.

86. Gustafson, *Soviet Negotiating Strategy*, pp. 20–21.

87. "Das Röhren-Erdgas-Geschäft wird gestreckt," *Frankfurter Allgemeine Zeitung*, 27 July 1981, p. 9.

88. "Verärgerung über Zinsvorteile," *Frankfurter Allgemeine Zeitung*, 27 July 1981, p. 9.

89. Christians, *Paths to Russia*, p. 24.

90. Jentleson, *Pipeline Politics*, pp. 185–189; Blinken, *Ally Versus Ally*, pp. 95–96.

91. Haig, *Caveat*, p. 253.

92. Gustafson, *Soviet Negotiating Strategy*, pp. 30–31.

93. "Reagan Takes Economic Action Against Poland," *Washington Post*, 24 December 1981, p. 1.

94. *Washington Post*, 30 December 1981, p. A14.

95. Homer E. Moyer, Jr., and Linda A. Marby, "Export Controls as Instruments of Foreign Policy: The History, Legal Issues and Policy Lessons of Three Recent Cases," *Law & Policy in International Business* 15 (1983): 67–68.

96. "U.S. Asks Its Allies to Deny to Soviet Parts for Pipeline," *New York Times*, 11 January 1982, p. 1.

97. *Department of State Bulletin*, February 1982, pp. 19–20.

98. "France Agrees to 25-Year Deal For Soviet Gas," *Washington Post*, 24 January 1982, p. A1.

99. Wörmann, *Osthandel als Problem*, p. 101.

100. Blinken, *Ally Versus Ally*, pp. 99–101.

101. Moyer and Marby, "Export Controls," p. 70.

102. "U.S. to Blacklist Firm If It Defies Pipeline Embargo," *Washington Post*, 26 August 1982, p. A1.

103. "U.S. Imposes Sanctions on an Italian Firm for Violating Ban on Soviet Gas Pipeline," *Wall Street Journal*, 7 September 1982, p. 3; "U.S. Penalizes John Brown Over Pipeline As Judge Upholds Sanctions for Dresser," *Wall Street Journal*, 10 September 1982, p. 5; "U.S. Imposes Import Ban on 4 German Firms for Supplying Soviet Pipeline Material," *Washington Post*, 6 October 1982, p. A20.

104. Shultz, *Turmoil and Triumph*, pp. 140–141.

105. *New York Times*, 14 November 1982, p. 24.

106. Shultz, *Turmoil and Triumph*, p. 142.

107. *Congressional Quarterly Weekly Report*, 14 August 1982, p. 1961.

108. *Congressional Quarterly Weekly Report*, 2 October 1982, p. 2467.

109. "Das deutsch-sowjetische Erdgas-Röhren-Geschäft," *Neue Zürcher Zeitung*, 15 July 1982, p. 9; Deutsche Bank AG, press release, 13 July 1982.

110. Wörmann, *Osthandel als Problem*, p. 101.

111. Personal interview, 26 November 1986.

112. Ruhrgas AG, *Geschäftsbericht* 1985, p. 16.

113. See for example a speech by former chancellor Schmidt in the *Bundestag*: West Germany, *Verhandlungen des Deutschen Bundestages*, 9. Wahlperiode, Stenographische Berichte 9/108, p. 6573.

114. Lebahn, "Die 'Jamal-Erdgasleitung,'" p. 267.

115. West Germany, *Verhandlungen des Deutschen Bundestages*, 8. Wahlperiode, Stenographische Berichte 8/203, p. 16170.

116. West Germany, *Verhandlungen des Deutschen Bundestages*, 9. Wahlperiode, Stenographische Berichte 9/108, p. 6572.

117. Ibid., p. 6612.

118. Ibid.

119. See, for example, West Germany, *Verhandlungen des Deutschen Bundestages*, 9. Wahlperiode, Stenographische Berichte 9/91, p. 5486; 9/110, p. 6694; West Germany, Deutscher Bundestag, 9. Wahlperiode, *Drucksachen* 9/1891, p. 7.

120. Wörmann, *Osthandel als Problem*, p. 107.

121. Personal interview, Bonn, 2 December 1986.

122. To fully understand the political implications of Soviet natural gas supplies to West Berlin we have to consider the fate of another large Soviet-West German energy cooperation project in the 1970s, the plan to build a West German nuclear power plant at Kaliningrad. West Germany's Kraftwerk Union wanted to build a nuclear power plant at Kaliningrad, which in turn would supply West Germany with electricity. The West German government wanted to include West Berlin in this project. These plans ran into opposition from a variety of quarters, including West Germany's allies and domestic West German resistance. However, the negotiations finally broke down because the Soviet Union would not or could not impose its will on East Germany. As described by Angela Stent, "[t]he East Germans objected to being used by the USSR as a transit route for electricity supplies to West Berlin." See Stent, *From Embargo to Ostpolitik*, p. 229.

123. Personal interview, Essen, 26 November 1986.

124. "British Also Set to Violate Ban," *Washington Post*, 26 August 1982, p. A1.

125. West Germany, Deutscher Bundestag, 9. Wahlperiode, *Drucksachen* 9/1856, p. 1; 9/1870, pp. 5–6; 9/1891, p. 1; 9/1916, pp. 14–15; 9/1929, pp. 9–10; 9/1939, p. 1; 9/1949, pp. 1–2; 9/1972, p. 6.

126. West Germany, Deutscher Bundestag, 9. Wahlperiode, *Drucksache* 9/2105, p. 1.

127. David A. Baldwin, *Economic Statecraft* (Princeton: Princeton University Press, 1985), p. 282.

128. *Washington Post*, 30 December 1981, p. A14.

129. Jentleson, *Pipeline Politics*, p. 175.

130. U.S. Congress, House Committee on Foreign Affairs, *Export Controls on Oil and Gas Equipment*, 97th Cong., p. 73.

131. Ibid., p. 112.

132. Nau, *The Myth of America's Decline*, p. 301.

133. Haig, *Caveat*, p. 312. Additional details on conflicts within the administration over this issue are provided by Nau, *The Myth of America's Decline*, chapter 10, and Shultz, *Turmoil and Triumph*, chapter 10.

134. See, for example, the numerous letters by Illinois Congressman Paul Findley to various administration officials in U.S. Congress, *Export Controls on Oil and Gas Equipment*, pp. 174–190.

135. U.S. Congress, Senate Committee on Banking, Housing, and Urban Affairs, *Proposed Trans-Siberian Natural Gas Pipeline*, 97th Cong., 1st sess., p. 2.

136. U.S. Congress, *Export Controls on Oil and Gas Equipment*, pp. 149–150.

137. Ibid., p. 78.

138. Ibid., p. 230.

139. Jentleson, *Pipeline Politics*, p. 206.

140. Ibid., pp. 216–217.

141. *Arms Control Today*, October 1992, p. 31.

142. "U.S. and Russians Join in New Plan for Space Station," *New York Times*, 3 September 1993, p. A1.

143. Jentleson, *Pipeline Politics*, pp. 107–113.

7

The Future of Export Control Policy

This book has explained the differences between U.S. and German policies by analyzing differences in the positions of the two countries in the international system, state strategies, and the values that support these strategies, the domestic politics of export controls, and institutional constraints. After World War II West Germany pursued a trading state strategy in stark contrast to the autarkic policies of the Nazi regime. Export-driven economic growth assumed the status of a national goal that no one challenged until the 1980s. When export promotion clashed with security concerns, West Germany frequently found itself in diplomatic conflict with the United States. Nevertheless, this book has also shown that the differences between U.S. and German policies cannot be reduced to a simple contrast between commercially oriented German policies and politically motivated American restrictions. In the 1960s, for example, the United States fairly aggressively marketed American nuclear technology abroad, whereas West Germany maintained significant restrictions on the sale of major conventional weapons systems. One reason why the first Reagan administration did not return more vigorously to a policy of nuclear export promotion was not so much concern over the spread of nuclear technology but the simple fact that the market had collapsed.[1] In the area of East-West trade more has been at stake economically for Germany than for the United States. Yet, during the Cold War both advocates and opponents of closer economic ties between East and West frequently overestimated the utility of economic carrots and sticks for bringing about political change in Eastern Europe. In Germany politicians were often more enthusiastic about the prospects for increased trade than business leaders. For the future, the key question will be whether a German trading state strategy will be compatible with a sustained commitment to a responsible export control policy.[2] In the case of the United States the most important issue will be whether the United States will continue to exercise leadership in this area.

This book has also argued that variations in broad state strategies do not simply reflect interests but rest on values that inform the choices of policy makers. In chapter 4, I argued that the values that underpinned U.S. and German export control policies, and broader state strategies more generally, have weakened. This may provide an opportunity for a strategy shift in the future. However, in the German case the challenges to the trading state strategy have not been strong enough to support a drastic reorientation of German foreign policy. Although some of the legal restrictions regarding the use of German troops abroad, for example, have fallen, it is quite unlikely that any German government will return to traditional great power policies in the near or medium-term future. In the U.S. case the failed efforts to rewrite the Export Administration Act show the difficulty in bringing about change in a policy area as narrow as export controls. Furthermore, the United States and Germany have differed in the kind of political actors who have become most heavily involved in the policy-making process. In Germany the established political parties and major interest groups supported liberal policies. To the extent that there was conflict, political parties articulated the different positions largely following a left-right continuum. Such distinctions break down, however, when it comes to German arms and arms-related sales to the Middle East. In the United States, on the other hand, the key battles have taken place within the executive branch and between the executive branch and Congress. Beyond that, a variety of interest groups have intervened and attempted to block arms sales to Saudi Arabia or to stop trade with the Communist enemy at the time of the Cold War. Until the late 1980s at least, American business interests were relatively ineffective in pushing for a liberalization of national security export controls.

Institutional factors made a difference as well, although not always in the ways predicted by the statist and "new institutionalist" literature. Differences in state centralization do not account for differences in export control policies. The fragmentation of the American state, however, has made it rather difficult to implement a comprehensive reform of U.S. export control policy, as demonstrated by the failure to enact a successor to the Export Administration Act since 1990. In Germany differences between the coalition partners in government and German federalism delayed the reform efforts for several months in 1990, but the institutional obstacles to concerted policy change were less severe than in the United States. Another institutional difference between Germany and the United States involved policy networks. In Germany fairly close ties existed between government officials in the economics ministry and industry. The far-reaching changes in German export control policy became possible only when additional actors became involved. In the United States, on the other hand, throughout the 1980s business groups lamented their lack of access and influence, but this appears to have changed under President Clinton.

More broadly, this book has demonstrated the utility of using system-, society- and state-centered approaches to foreign and foreign economic policy making in a complementary fashion rather than stressing the primacy of one approach over the others. More work needs to be done on the ways in which domestic politics, international negotiations, and institutions interact to produce outcomes not predicted by analyses that utilize only one approach at the expense of the others. As mentioned in chapters 1 and 4, the United States pressured Germany to change its liberal nonproliferation export control policies in the 1970s and 1980s. In the 1970s U.S. efforts enjoyed only limited success. At the end of the following decade, however, the domestic consensus supporting the established German policies had broken down, which provided an opening for renewed U.S. pressure. The scandal that changed the domestic German politics on this issue was German involvement in Iraq's and Libya's chemical weapons programs. In the mid-1980s the U.S. government first held discussions with West German officials on chemical weapons in the Middle East. According to George Shultz, "[t]he West German government seemed singularly indifferent and incurious about what their private companies were shipping to Iraq."[3] Beginning in 1986 U.S. government agencies supplied their counterparts in West Germany with information on a chemical weapons facility in Libya. In November 1988 George Shultz, CIA Director Webster, and Colin Powell discussed this issue with Chancellor Kohl and Foreign Minister Genscher.[4] From the American perspective these discussions did not yield satisfactory results. This changed after the *New York Times* published a series of articles on this issue. The Rabta plant became a major scandal, and export control policy was no longer an obscure technical issue, but for a short time at least, it dominated the front pages of German newspapers and it gained the attention of additional political actors besides the economics ministry and its clients in industry. Thus, "expanded participation" contributed to the success of American pressure.

On other occasions, though, political divisions within Germany may have worked to strengthen the German bargaining position in negotiations with the United States. In the 1960s the NPT became a major bone of contention in German politics. Although this issue awaits further archival research, it appears quite plausible that Germany was able to achieve at least a few changes in the final treaty text because the treaty was so divisive in Germany. Similarly, in 1989/1990 domestic opposition to CoCom strengthened the German position in negotiations over the liberalization of East-West controls.

To put the central concerns of this book in stronger terms, arguments about the primacy of systemic constraints or domestic politics and related controversies are often not particularly fruitful. Differences between U.S. and German export control policies and changes in these policies cannot be reduced to differences in state interests. Domestic politics, ideas, and institutions play a role as well. The end of the Cold War has heightened the sense of uncertainty in U.S. and German foreign policy, and ideas may serve as "road maps" in such times. However, since 1989 cartographers have been quite busy bringing out new maps, and often part of the uncertainty consists of the difficulty in deciding which is the most appropriate one. Furthermore, changes in interests have an impact on ideas. The current reassessment of U.S. and German state strategies was triggered by changes in the international environment and specifically the end of the Cold War. This leaves institutions. Institutions may retard or facilitate policy change. Yet, institutions also reflect particular interests and ideas. An analysis of institutions that leaves out the interests and ideas embodied in them is not particularly interesting. In regard to future research, we need more work that recognizes that "ideas do not float freely," as Risse-Kappen put it. Rather, institutions at least partially determine which ideas have a lasting impact and which do not. Institutions are not simply passive forces of inertia but shape and channel the flow of interests and ideas.

THE FUTURE: ENDURING CONFLICT, TECHNOLOGY DIFFUSION, AND INCONSISTENT U.S. LEADERSHIP

Although this book has focused on the differences between U.S. and German export controls, it appears that in the early 1990s there has been a convergence of U.S. and German policies. Germany has tightened its nonproliferation controls, whereas the United States liberalized the old East-West controls and shifted resources to combating the spread of weapons of mass destruction. Such a partial convergence does not encompass only the United States and Germany but also includes the policies of France and possibly even former targets of Western controls, such as Russia, Poland, and the Czech Republic.[5] This would seem to suggest that the prospects for international cooperation on this issue have increased considerably in the 1990s when, as Bertsch and Cupitt argue, the distinctions between East and West, and North and South have become increasingly irrelevant.[6] A broad convergence of policies does not imply harmony, however. During the Cold War German observers of U.S. export control policy suspected that some U.S.

initiatives reflected U.S. commercial interests as well as security concerns. Such suspicions have surfaced again during the negotiations on a successor regime to CoCom in 1994.[7] Even if the United States did not manipulate CoCom to its advantage in the past, today Clinton administration officials consistently emphasize the need to consider the economic impact of export controls. Thus, German negotiators vowed that they would not accept a regime that placed German companies at a disadvantage relative to their American competitors.

Since the end of the Cold War, a variety of proposals have been made to restructure existing export control regimes and to create new organizations, such as a "Technology Disarmament and Transfer Agency" or an "International Export Control Organization."[8] Furthermore, some analysts have expressed cautious optimism for extending multilateral export controls to additional issue areas, particularly to the area of conventional arms exports.[9] Beyond that, however, there is disagreement on whether existing multilateral arrangements should be merged or continue to function separately.[10]

This book will not attempt to add to the variety of organizational blueprints currently in circulation. Rather, this book will conclude with a discussion of three factors that will limit the effectiveness of international cooperation on export controls in the 1990s and beyond. First of all, despite the partial convergence of U.S. and German policies, conflict over export controls will continue to erupt. Although it is true that in the future it will become increasingly important to ensure the cooperation of non-Western countries, if the world's two largest exporters disagree it will be an almost impossible task to bring new suppliers into the fold. Second, the process of technology diffusion will turn some but not all export control efforts into exercises of futility. Finally, in the past the United States was the driving force behind the creation of all of the existing export control agreements. Although the United States may well be "bound to lead," as Nye puts it, there is reason to expect that U.S. leadership will be strong on some issues but weak on others, or to state it more briefly, inconsistent.[11]

Disagreements between the United States and European suppliers have emerged both in regard to the treatment of specific countries and concerning the creation of new export control regimes. In the early 1990s both the Bush and the Clinton administrations asked America's Western European and Japanese allies to curb their trade with Iran. Bush's initiative was rejected and Clinton only received a commitment from the European Community to study the problem.[12] In February 1992 the former German Economics Minister Möllemann stated in an interview that Germany had denied Iranian requests for completing the nuclear reactor at Busher and the building of a pesticide factory at Gadwin. However, Möllemann also argued that trade relations could play a positive role in facilitating political change in nondemocratic countries, including Iran.[13] Here it is important to recognize that Germany has been Iran's largest supplier and in 1991 German exports to Iran rose by about 60 percent over the 1990 level to reach a value of 6.7 billion DM. Besides the maintenance of economic ties, Germany also pursued a political dialogue with Iran in the 1980s and attempted to mediate in the Iran-Iraq war. These German diplomatic efforts included two visits by foreign minister Genscher to Tehran in 1984 and 1988. One German analyst even claimed that "[w]hen the Iranian government finally accepted the cease-fire on 17 July 1988 it had to be attributed largely to German diplomacy."[14]   However, the extent of such ties can be exaggerated, and in relative terms German exports to Iran in the 1980s and early 1990s never regained their prerevolutionary significance. Furthermore, in the eyes of some German officials and journalists the United States has begun to lose its credibility on this issue. On March 2, 1994, the German daily *Frankfurter Allgemeine Zeitung* reported on its front page that in 1993 the United States had surpassed Germany as Iran's most significant trading partner in terms of trade volume, although Germany still exported more to Iran than the United States.[15] The imposition of a total trade embargo against Iran in 1995 may have ended the hypocrisy in U.S. policy, but even U.S. officials realized that Western Europe and Japan would not cooperate, and thus this embargo is doomed from the beginning.

Western European suppliers have also been reluctant to respond to U.S. initiatives on the creation of a multilateral export control agreement for supercomputers, which play an important role in the design of nuclear weapons. Due to nonproliferation concerns, the United States has controlled the export of supercomputers for a number of years. Until Japan emerged as a viable alternative supplier, unilateral U.S. controls were sufficient. In the 1980s this changed, however, and the United States concluded an export licensing agreement for supercomputers with Japan. In 1991 the United States and Japan decided to change their informal export control agreement and to initiate discussions with a few European countries that now have the capability to produce super-computers as well.[16] Thus, when the United States faced no competitors in the supercomputer market, it relied on unilateral actions to control the diffusion of the technology. Forming an export control regime would have been pointless at that time, because the United States was the only supplier. As the United States lost its monopoly position, it first entered a bilateral agreement with its major commercial competitor and then, unsuccessfully so far, attempted to gain the support of European governments for a supercomputer export control agreement.[17]

Even if European suppliers had become partners to a new supercomputer agreement this would not have saved efforts to control the spread of such technology. Since the first Cray machines entered the market supercomputer technology has changed significantly. The trend even in large computers appears to favor microprocessor-based technology which means "that it is increasingly simple for computer designers to hook together the fastest microprocessors into systems that have near-supercomputer performance levels."[18] Thus, the availability of hardware is becoming less of a constraint in producing such machines, although it may still be difficult to write the appropriate software. From an export control perspective this is not much of a consolation, though, because the spread of software is inherently more difficult to control than hardware components. More generally, the era in which civilian industries benefited from the "spin-off" generated by cutting-edge military technologies appears to have ended. Rather, today many technological innovations are developed first for civilian use and only later appear in new weapon systems.

Supercomputers may also be indicative of a broader pattern in which dominant powers, such as the United States, push for multilateral restraints on technology transfer precisely at those times when their own technological advantages are eroding. This may partially explain the renewed interest in constraints on the transfer of conventional arms. A recent study by the Office of Technology Assessment (OTA) argued that through extensive technology transfer the United States had created new centers of arms production around the world. An unfortunate side effect of this technology diffusion was "the gradual and collective loss of control over the destination and disposition of potent weapons emanating from many different parts of the world."[19] In more concrete terms, this has led to concerns about the wisdom of "arming our allies" and about transferring the most sophisticated U.S. technology to allies in Europe and elsewhere, which may be profitable for individual U.S. defense companies but run counter to broader U.S. interests.[20] Krause has claimed that although technology diffusion motivates top supplier countries to stem this process, it also makes it more difficult to achieve effective international cooperation on technology transfer.[21]

Even if the United States seeks to curb advanced weapons technology transfer, the United States may be unable or unwilling to exercise effective leadership in this issue area. The United States played a leading role in the creation of all current multilateral export control agreements. However, the United States has not always assumed a constructive role in maintaining CoCom or the nuclear nonproliferation regime. To be more specific, CoCom declined in the 1970s in part because the United States did not carry out its leadership responsibilities, and this undermined the commitment of its Western European allies to CoCom. During the Cold War CoCom maintained an embargo on strategic goods and technologies. CoCom rules also allowed for exceptions to this embargo. Participating governments could issue administrative exceptions in some cases, whereas exceptions for more sensitive products required the submission of a general exception request to CoCom headquarters in Paris. In the 1970s the number of general exception requests increased significantly, with the United States accounting for a substantial portion of these requests. At the same time the United States became notorious for holding up decisions on exception requests by European suppliers.[22] Cooperation became more difficult as European suppliers increasingly viewed changes in U.S. policies as attempts to alter the distribution of gains from international cooperation in favor of the United States.[23]

An explanation of why the United States failed to play a responsible leadership role has to consider domestic factors. As Mastanduno argued, "the ability of the United States to carry out its responsibilities has been affected most critically by distinctive features of America's own export control policy, in particular the tendency to politicize strategic export controls and, more recently, the rise of the DOD [Department of Defense] in the control process."[24] Similarly, in the nuclear nonproliferation area the United States not only played a leading role in constructing and maintaining the regime, but at other times the United States abandoned any leadership role due to domestic considerations. One of the most dramatic examples of such behavior took place in July 1974 when the U.S. Atomic Energy Commission closed its order books on foreign contracts for low-enriched uranium. This action resulted from the Nixon administration's push to privatize enrichment services. The consequences of this stunning reversal of U.S. policy included the undermining of U.S. credibility as a reliable nuclear supplier and the acceleration of European plans to build indigenous enrichment facilities.[25] Thus, the United States indirectly encouraged the spread of one of the most sensitive technologies in a nuclear weapons program. The Nixon administration's "unbending commitment to a free-enterprise philosophy" overrode its international responsibilities.[26] From the perspective of foreign observers such policies

implied that fuel supply could become tied to private commercial ambitions in the United States as well as to governmental international security interests. The U.S. dominance of reactor orders abroad only increased such concerns. While commercial motives may not have been dominant in U.S. decisions, attitudes abroad clearly reflected a growing concern about U.S. commercial dominance and revealed the difficulty of distinguishing between commercial and international security motivations in the new atmosphere of international competition.[27]

On the other hand, the United States led an effort to strengthen CoCom in the 1980s and convinced its closest allies to establish the MTCR.

Joseph Nye has argued that the United States has retained the resources necessary to lead the world in the 1990s. According to Nye, "[t]he critical question is whether it will have the political leadership and strategic vision to convert these power resources into real influence in a transitional period of world politics."[28] Similarly, Henry Nau questioned theories of American decline.[29] The quality of American leadership depended on the nature of the policies it pursued, and while the United States followed inefficient policies in the 1970s, this changed again under the more assertive Reagan administration in the early 1980s. Both authors emphasize that American leadership rests not only on America's military might and economic resources but on what Nye calls "soft power resources," such as the international appeal of American values.

Clearly, what role the United States will play in international export control efforts will depend on choices that are not predetermined by structural factors. However, the distinction between the inefficient policies of the 1970s, when America was plagued by self-doubts, and confident leadership in the 1980s does not hold for export control policy. Although CoCom weakened in the 1970s, the Carter administration made strong efforts to bolster the nuclear nonproliferation regime. Although some of these efforts met with fierce resistance, as Reagan's East-West trade policies did a few years later, at a minimum they raised the consciousness of the allies. Under Reagan CoCom recovered, but the Reagan administration did not accord nonproliferation and strict nuclear export controls a high priority.

In recent years there also has been a growing disillusionment among both academics and U.S. policy makers with export controls. One example is Ashton Carter who participated in a major National Academy of Sciences study of U.S. export controls in 1992 and then took a position as Assistant Secretary of Defense under President Clinton. At a congressional hearing in August 1993 Carter testified that "export controls should play . . . a much reduced role relative to the past."[30] Some of the reasons for this disillusionment we have already discussed, such as the process of technological diffusion and concerns about U.S. competitiveness in international markets. Advocates of cooperative security have criticized existing export control regimes because they are inherently discriminatory, whereas a cooperative security regime should be built around the principle of "inclusiveness and nondiscrimination."[31] To illustrate this point, in 1993 K. Subrahmanyam charged that "export controls divide the world into North and South," and he called the Australia Group a "white nations' club" that practiced "apartheid."[32] Furthermore, in the past the United States frequently imposed controls unilaterally, which does not fit well with cooperative security's emphasis on multilateralism. Rather than denying access to technology through trade sanctions, these critics assert, the United States in cooperation with other countries should encourage greater transparency in the arms and defense-related trade. The UN arms transfer registry represents a first step in that direction.[33] Whether or not a greater emphasis on transparency and end-use assurances will be more effective in addressing proliferation problems than traditional export controls remains to be seen, but to the extent that such ideas inform the policies of the Clinton administration and the views of members of Congress they will have an impact.

This suggests that what we might see in the future are significant efforts in some areas, such as nonproliferation where the United States has taken a tough stance against Iran, Iraq, and North Korea. But even on nonproliferation issues rhetoric may outstrip substance. Advocates of restraint in conventional arms transfers, however, will be disappointed. It may well be that nuclear proliferation is more important than the arms trade because of the immense destructive potential of nuclear weapons, but a cynic could argue that whereas nuclear export controls involve limited economic costs for the United States, arms exports bring billion dollar contracts to U.S. defense companies. Even if the quality of U.S. leadership does not rise to the occasion, no other power is likely to step in, at least in the foreseeable future. It appears as if the European Union (EU) has succeeded in at least a partial "harmonization" of national export control policies, but, given the rather mixed record of the EU, we should not expect bold new EU initiatives in this area. Thus, we may see greater cooperation on multilateral export controls among democratic and newly democratic nations, but discord, even among the closest allies of the United States, will continue to erupt. In those areas where political cooperation is possible, the continuing process of technological diffusion and the prospect of inconsistent U.S. leadership should caution us against unrealistic expectations for the future. But then again, a glass half empty is also half full.

NOTES

1. Peter Clausen, "The Reagan Nonproliferation Policy: A Critical Midterm Look," *Arms Control Today*, December 1982, p. 3.

2. Not everyone agrees that Germany will pursue a trading state strategy in the future. Mearsheimer expects that Germany eventually will acquire its own nuclear weapons. See John J. Mearsheimer, "Back to the Future: Instability in Europe After the Cold War," in *The Cold War and After: Prospects for Peace*, ed. Sean M. Lynn-Jones (Cambridge: MIT Press, 1991), pp. 141–192. Layne also expects Germany to seek the status of a traditional great power. As evidence for such a policy shift he points to Germany's policies in the former Soviet Union and former Yugoslavia, the German government's desire to gain a permanent seat on the UN Security Council etc. See Christopher Layne, "The Unipolar Illusion: Why New Great Powers Will Rise," *International Security* 17 (Spring

1993): 37–38. In contrast to Mearsheimer and Layne, who follow a rather narrow neorealist approach and almost completely neglect domestic politics, this book has argued that an analysis of domestic politics is critical for understanding U.S. and German export control policies.

3. Shultz, *Turmoil and Triumph*, p. 238.

4. Ibid., pp. 244–245; West Germany, Deutscher Bundestag, *Drucksache* 11/3995.

5. Gary K. Bertsch and Richard T. Cupitt, "Nonproliferation in the 1990s: Enhancing International Cooperation on Export Controls," *Washington Quarterly* 16 (Autumn 1993): 58.

6. Ibid., p. 53.

7. "Ein neues Exportkontrollsystem für Rüstungsgüter," *Frankfurter Allgemeine Zeitung*, 29 March 1994, p. 15.

8. Michael R. Lucas, "The Abolition of COCOM and the Establishment of a Technology Disarmament and Transfer Agency in the CSCE," *Bulletin of Peace Proposals* 21 (June 1990): 219–225; Reinhard Rode, "Improving Nonproliferation Export Controls," in *Proliferation and Export Controls*, eds. Kathleen Bailey and Robert Rudney (Lanham, Md.: University Press of America, 1993), p. 105.

9. Aaron Karp, "Controlling Weapons Proliferation: The Role of Export Controls," *Journal of Strategic Studies* 16 (March 1993): 18–45; Stephanie G. Neuman, "Controlling the Arms Trade: Idealistic Dream or Realpolitik?" *Washington Quarterly* 16 (Summer 1993): 53–75.

10. Bertsch and Cupitt, "Nonproliferation in the 1990s," pp. 68–69; Karp, "Controlling Weapons Proliferation," p. 27; Ashton B. Carter, William J. Perry, and John D. Steinbrunner, *A New Concept of Cooperative Security* (Washington, D.C.: Brookings Institution, 1992), p. 63.

11. Joseph S. Nye, *Bound to Lead: The Changing Nature of American Power* (New York: Basic Books, 1991).

12. "U.S. Hopes to Tighten Ban on Arms Sales to Iran," *New York Times*, 18 November 1992, p. A5; "U.S. Asks Europe to Ban Arms-Linked Sales to Iran," *New York Times*, 10 June 1993, p. A5.

13. *Die Zeit*, Canadian edition, 21 February 1992, p. 28.

14. Udo Steinbach. "Germany and the Gulf," in *Germany and the Middle East: Patterns and Prospects*, ed. Shahram Chubin (New York: St. Martin's Press, 1992), p. 217.

15. "Lebhafter Handelsaustausch zwischen Amerika und Iran," *Frankfurter Allgemeine Zeitung*, 2 March 1994, p. 1.

16. Keith Bradsher, "Computer Export Ban to Change," *New York Times*, 8 June 1991, p. 17.

17. John Markoff, "British Sell Computer to U.S. Lab," *New York Times*, 6 March 1993, p. 35.

18. "Shift Expected on Computer Exports," *New York Times*, 27 August 1993, p. D2.

19. OTA, *Global Arms Trade*, p. 15.

20. U.S. Congress, Office of Technology Assessment, *Arming Our Allies: Cooperation and Competition in Defense Technology*, OTA-ISC-449 (Washington, D.C.: Government Printing Office, 1990).

21. Krause, *Arms and the State*, p. 215.

22. See discussion in Mastanduno, *Economic Containment*, chapter 5.

23. Joseph M. Grieco, *Cooperation Among Nations: Europe, America, and Non-Tariff Barriers to Trade* (Ithaca: Cornell University Press, 1990).

24. Mastanduno, "The Management of Alliance Export Control Policy," p. 276.

25. Brenner, *Nuclear Power and Non-Proliferation*, chapter 2.

26. Ibid., p. 17.

27. Thomas L. Neff, *The International Uranium Market* (Cambridge, Mass.: Ballinger Publishing Company, 1984), p. 44.

28. Nye, *Bound to Lead*, p. 260.

29. Nau, *The Myth of America's Decline*.

30. U.S. Congress, House Committee on Science, Space, and Technology, *Export Control Reform in High Technology*, 103d Cong., 1st sess., p. 157.

31. Antonia Handler Chayes and Abram Chayes, "Regime Architecture and Principles," in *Global Engagement: Cooperation and Security in the 21st Century*, ed. Janne Nolan (Washington, D.C.: The Brookings Institution, 1994), p. 66.

32. K. Subrahmanyam, "Export Controls and the North-South Controversy," *Washington Quarterly* 16 (Spring 1993), pp. 135, 143.

33. For a quite ambitious proposal along those lines see Wolfgang H. Reinicke, "Cooperative Security and the Political Economy of Nonproliferation," in Nolan, *Global Engagement*.

Selected Bibliography

BOOKS, ARTICLES, AND PUBLIC DOCUMENTS

Abbott, Kenneth W. " Linking Trade to Political Goals: Foreign Policy Export Controls in the 1970s and 1980s." *Minnesota Law Review* 65 (1981): 731–889.

Aberbach, Joel D., Robert D. Putnam, and Bert Rockman. *Bureaucrats and Politicians in Western Democracies*. Cambridge: Harvard University Press, 1981.

Adenauer, Konrad. *Erinnerungen 1953–1955*. Stuttgart: Deutsche Verlags-Anstalt, 1966.

Adler-Karlsson, Gunnar. *Western Economic Warfare 1947 –1967: A Case Study in Foreign Economic Policy*. Stockholm: Almqvist & Wiksell, 1968.

Albrecht, Ulrich. "West Germany: New Strategies." *Journal of International Affairs* 40 (Summer 1986): 128–142.

Albrecht, Ulrich, Peter Lock, and Herbert Wulf. *Mit Rüstung gegen Arbeitlosigkeit?* Reinbek: Rowohlt Taschenbuch Verlag, 1982.

Allison, Graham T. *Essence of Decision: Explaining the Cuban Missile Crisis*. Boston: Little, Brown and Company, 1971.

Amerongen, Otto Wolff von. "Außenwirtschaft und Außenpolitik: Aus den Anfängen des deutschen Osthandels nach dem Zweiten Weltkrieg." *Osteuropa* 29 (May 1979): 419–424.

Anderson, Jeffrey J., and John B. Goodman. "Mars or Minerva? A United Germany in a Post-Cold War Europe." In *After the Cold War: International Institutions and State Strategies in Europe, 1989–1991*, eds. Robert O. Keohane, Joseph S. Nye, and Stanley Hoffmann, pp. 23–62. Cambridge: Harvard University Press, 1993.

Anthony, Ian. "Assessing the UN Register of Conventional Arms." *Survival* 35 (Winter 1993): 113–129.

Arbeitsgemeinschaft gegen Atomexporte. *Sulzers Bombengeschäft mit Argentinien: Schweizer Beihilfe zum Atomkrieg.* Zurich and Berne: Arbeitsgemeinschaft gegen Atomexporte, 1980.

Arendt, Wolfgang. "25 Jahre AKA Ausfuhrkredit-Gesellschaft mbH." *Die Bank* 17 (April 1977): 21–24.

Bailey, Kathleen. "Can Missile Proliferation Be Reversed." *Orbis* 35 (Winter 1991): 5–14.

Bajusz, William D., and David J. Louscher. *Arms Sales and the U.S. Economy: The Impact of Restricting Military Exports.* Boulder: Westview Press, 1988.

Baker, Russell, and Robert Bohlig. "The Control of Exports—A Comparison of the Laws of the United States, Canada, Japan, and the Federal Republic of Germany." *International Lawyer* 1 (January 1967): 163–191.

Baldwin, David A. *Economic Statecraft.* Princeton: Princeton University Press, 1985.

Baring, Arnulf. *Deutschland, was nun? Ein Gespräch mit Dirk Rumberg und Wolf Jobst Siedler.* Berlin: Siedler, 1991.

Barrett, Laurance I. *Gambling with History: Ronald Reagan in the White House.* New York: Penguin Books, 1984.

Becker, Hermann. "Saudi-Arabiens Bedeutung für die deutsche Bauindustrie." In *Saudi-Arabien: Partner für die Bundesrepublik Deutschland,* ed. Nah- und Mittelost-Verein, pp. 25–26. Hamburg: Nah- und Mittelost Verein, 1981.

Beckman, Robert L. *Nuclear Non-Proliferation: Congress and the Control of Peaceful Nuclear Activities.* Boulder: Westview Press, 1985.

Beitel, Werner, and Jürgen Nötzold. *Deutsch-sowjetische Wirtschaftsbeziehungen in der Zeit der Weimarer Republik.* Baden-Baden: Nomos, 1979.

Berman, Harold J., and John R. Garson. "United States Export Controls—Past, Present and Future." *Columbia Law Review* 67 (May 1967): 791–890.

Bertsch, Gary K. "U.S. Export Controls: The 1970s and Beyond." *Journal of World Trade Law* 15 (February 1981): 67–82.

Bertsch, Gary K., and Richard T. Cupitt. "Nonproliferation in the 1990s: Enhancing International Cooperation on Export Controls." *Washington Quarterly* 16 (Autumn 1993): 53–70.

Bertsch, Gary K., and Steve Elliott-Gower. "U.S. COCOM Policy: From Paranoia to Perestroika?" In *After the Revolutions: East-West Trade and Technology Transfer in the 1990s,* eds. Gary K. Bertsch, Heinrich Vogel, and Jan Zielonka, pp. 15–31. Boulder: Westview Press, 1991.

Besson, Waldemar. *Die Außenpolitik der Bundesrepublik: Erfahrungen und Maßstäbe.* Frankfurt: Ullstein, 1973.

Bethkenhagen, Jochen. "Soviet-West German Economic Relations: The West German Perspective." In *Economic Relations with the Soviet Union: American and West German Perspectives,* ed. Angela E. Stent, pp. 69–89. Boulder: Westview Press, 1985.

Bettauer, Ronald J. "The Nuclear Non-Proliferation Act of 1978." *Law and Policy in International Business* 10 (1978): 1105–1180.

Birrenbach, Kurt. *Meine Sondermissionen: Rückblick auf zwei Jahrzehnte bundes-deutscher Außenpolitik.* Dusseldorf: Econ Verlag, 1984.

Blinken, Antony J. *Ally Versus Ally: America, Europe, and the Siberian Pipeline Crisis.* New York: Praeger, 1987.

Braunthal, Gerard. *The Federation of German Industry in Politics*. Ithaca: Cornell University Press, 1965.

Brecht, Arnold, and Comstock Glaser. *The Art and Technique of Administration in German Ministries*. Cambridge: Harvard University Press, 1940; reprint ed., Westport, Conn.: Greenwood Press, 1971.

Bredow, Wilfried von, and Thomas Jäger. *Neue deutsche Außenpolitik: Nationale Interessen in internationalen Beziehungen*. Opladen: Leske und Budrich, 1993.

Brenner, Michael J. *Nuclear Power and Non-Proliferation: The Remaking of U.S. Policy*. Cambridge: Cambridge University Press, 1981.

Brittleson, Martyn. *Co-operation or Competition? Defence Procurement Options for the 1990s*. Adelphi Papers 250. London: International Institute for Strategic Studies, 1990.

Broad, Robin, with John Cavanagh. *Plundering Paradise: The Struggle for the Environment in the Philippines*. Berkeley: University of California Press, 1993.

Brzoska, Michael. "The Erosion of Restraint in West German Arms Transfer Policy." *Journal of Peace Research* 26 (May 1989): 165–177.

————. "Neue Richtlinien für den Waffenexport aus der Bundesrepublik Deutschland in die Dritte Welt." In *Jahrbuch Dritte Welt: Daten, Übersichten, Analysen 1*, eds. Joachim Betz and Volker Matthies, pp. 87–100. Munich: Verlag C.H. Beck, 1983.

————. "Arms Transfer Data Sources." *Journal of Conflict Resolution* 26 (March 1982): 77–108.

————. "Bundesdeutsche Rüstungsexporte in die Dritte Welt: Daten— Verfahren—Zusammenhänge." In *Militarismus und Rüstung: Beiträge zur ökumenischen Diskussion*, ed. Bernhard Moltmann, pp. 67–100. Heidelberg: Forschungsstätte der evangelischen Studiengemeinschaft, 1981.

Brzoska, Michael, and Peter Lock, eds. *Restructuring of Arms Production in Western Europe*. Oxford: Oxford University Press, 1992.

Bundesverband der Deutschen Industrie. *Bericht 1986–88 des Bundesverbandes der Deutschen Industrie e.V.* Cologne: BDI, 1988.

Carter, Ashton B., William J. Perry, and John D. Steinbrunner. *A New Concept of Cooperative Security*. Washington, D.C.: Brookings Institution, 1992.

Chayes, Antonia Handler, and Abram Chayes. "Regime Architecture and Principles." In *Global Engagement: Cooperation and Security in the 21st Century*, ed. Janne Nolan, pp. 65–130. Washington, D.C.: The Brookings Institution, 1994.

Checkel, Jeff. "Ideas, Institutions, and the Gorbachev Foreign Policy Revolution." *World Politics* 45 (January 1993): 271–300.

Christians, F. Wilhelm. *Paths to Russia: From War to Peace*. Translated by Joachim Neugroschel. New York: Macmillan, 1990.

Clausen, Peter A. *Nonproliferation and the National Interest: America's Response to the Spread of Nuclear Weapons*. New York: HarperCollins College, 1993.

Clemens, Clay. "Opportunity or Obligation? Redefining Germany's Military Role Outside of NATO." *Armed Forces & Society* 19 (Winter 1993): 231–251.

Cordell, Franklin D., for John L. Ellicott. "Judicial Review Under the Export Administration Act of 1979: Is It Time to Open the Courthouse Doors to U.S. Exporters?" In National Academy of Sciences. *Finding Common Ground: U.S. Export Controls in a Changed Global Environment*, pp. 321–335. Washington, D.C.: National Academy Press, 1991.

Cordesman, Anthony H. *The Gulf and the Search for Strategic Stability: Saudi Arabia, the Military Balance in the Gulf, and Trends in the Arab-Israeli Military Balance*. Boulder: Westview Press, 1984.

Crawford, Beverly. "Western Control of East-West Trade Finance: The Role of U.S. Power and International Regimes." In *Controlling East-West Trade and Technology Transfer: Power, Politics, and Policies*, ed. Gary K. Bertsch, pp. 280–312. Durham: Duke University Press, 1988.

Davis, Zachary S. *Non-Proliferation Regimes: A Comparative Analysis of Policies to Control the Spread of Nuclear, Chemical and Biological Weapons and Missiles*. Washington, D.C.: Congressional Research Service, 1991.

Dunn, Lewis A. *Controlling the Bomb: Nuclear Proliferation in the 1980s*. New Haven: Yale University Press, 1982.

Ehrenberg, Eckehart. *Der deutsche Rüstungsexport: Beurteilung und Perspektiven*. Munich: Bernard & Graefe Verlag, 1981.

Ellwein, Thomas. *Das Regierungssystem der Bundesrepublik Deutschland*, 5th ed. Opladen: Westdeutscher Verlag, 1983.

Epstein, William. *The Last Chance*. New York: The Free Press, 1976.

Erhard, Ludwig. *Deutschlands Rückkehr zum Weltmarkt*. Dusseldorf: Econ-Verlag, 1953.

Etheredge, Lloyd S. *Can Governments Learn? American Foreign Policy and Central American Revolutions*. New York: Pergamon Press, 1985.

Evans, Peter B., Harold K. Jacobson, and Robert D. Putnam, eds. *Double-Edged Diplomacy: International Bargaining and Domestic Politics*. Berkeley: University of California Press, 1993.

Fong, Glenn. "State Strength, Industry Structure and Industrial Policy: American and Japanese Experiences in Microelectronics." *Comparative Politics* 22 (April 1990): 273–299.

Forschungs- und Dokumentationszentrum Chile-Lateinamerika, ed. *Der Griff nach der Bombe: Das deutsch-argentinische Atomgeschäft*. Berlin: Forschungs- und Dokumentationszentrum Chile-Lateinamerika, 1981.

Frost, Ellen, and Angela Stent. "NATO's Troubles with East-West Trade." *International Security* 8 (Summer 1983): 179–200.

Funigiello, Philip J. *American Soviet Trade in the Cold War*. Chapel Hill: University of North Carolina Press, 1988.

Gansel, Norbert. "Waffengeschäfte: Eine politische Weichenstellung." *Der Überblick* 1/1981, pp. 16–18.

Garrett, Geoffrey, and Barry R. Weingast. "Ideas, Interests, and Institutions: Constructing the European Community's Internal Market." In *Ideas and Foreign Policy: Beliefs, Institutions, and Political Change*, eds. Judith Goldstein and Robert O. Keohane, pp. 173–206. Ithaca: Cornell University Press, 1993.

German Information Center. *Focus on Export Controls*. New York: German Information Center, 1992.

Germany. Deutscher Bundestag. *Drucksache* 11/7800.

Germany. Statistisches Bundesamt. *Statistisches Jahrbuch 1992 für die Bundesrepublik Deutschland*. Wiesbaden: Metzler & Poeschel, 1992.

Gibson, Martha Liebler. "Managing Conflict: The Role of the Legislative Veto in American Foreign Policy." *Polity* 26 (Spring 1994): 441–472.

Glotz, Peter. *Die falsche Normalisierung: Die unmerkliche Verwandlung der Deutschen 1989 bis 1994*. Frankfurt: Suhrkamp, 1994.

Goldmann, Kjell. *Change and Stablity in Foreign Policy: The Problems and Possibilities of Détente*. Princeton: Princeton University Press, 1988.

Goldstein, Judith. *Ideas, Interests, and American Trade Policy*. Ithaca: Cornell University Press, 1993.

Gourevitch, Peter. *Politics in Hard Times: Comparative Responses to International Economic Crises*. Ithaca: Cornell University Press, 1986.

_____. "The Second Image Reversed: The International Sources of Domestic Politics." *International Organization* 32 (Autumn 1978): 881–912.

Grewe, Wilhelm G. *Rückblenden 1976–1951*. Frankfurt: Propyläen, 1979.

Grieco, Joseph M. *Cooperation Among Nations: Europe, America, and Non-Tariff Barriers to Trade*. Ithaca: Cornell University Press, 1990.

Grimmett, Richard F. "The Role of Security Assistance in Historical Perspective." In *U.S. Security Assistance: The Political Process*, eds. Ernest Graves and Steven A. Hildreth, pp. 1–40. Lexington, Mass.: Lexington Books, 1985.

Gustafson, Thane. *Soviet Negotiating Strategy: The East-West Gas Pipeline Deal 1980–1984*. Santa Monica: Rand, 1985.

Haas, Ernst B. *When Knowledge is Power: Three Models of Organizational Change in International Organizations*. Berkeley: University of California Press, 1990.

Haas, Peter M. "Introduction: Epistemic Communities and International Policy Coordination." *International Organization* 46 (Winter 1992): 1–35.

Häckel, Erwin. *Die Bundesrepublik Deutschland und der Atomwaffensperrvertrag*. Arbeitspapiere zur Internationalen Politik, no. 53. Bonn: Europa Union Verlag, 1989.

_____. "The Domestic and International Context of West Germany's Nuclear Energy Policy." In *Nuclear Policy in Europe: France, Germany and the International Debate*, eds. Erwin Häckel et al., pp. 79–132. Arbeitspapiere zur Internationalen Politik, no. 12. Bonn: Europa Union Verlag, 1980.

Haftendorn, Helga. *Militärhilfe und Rüstungsexporte der BRD*. Dusseldorf: Bertelsmann Universitätsverlag, 1971.

Haig, Alexander M., Jr. *Caveat: Realism, Reagan and Foreign Policy*. New York: Macmillan, 1984.

Hall, Peter A. *Governing the Economy: The Politics of State Intervention in Britain and France*. New York: Oxford University Press, 1986.

Hammond, Paul Y., David J. Louscher, Michael D. Salomone, and Norman A. Graham. *The Reluctant Supplier: U.S. Decisionmaking for Arms Sales*. Cambridge, Mass.: Oelgeschlager, Gunn & Hain, 1983.

Hanrieder, Wolfram. *Germany, America, Europe: Forty Years of German Foreign Policy*. New Haven: Yale University Press, 1989.

Hartung, William D. "Curbing the Arms Trade: From Rhetoric to Restraint." *World Policy Journal* 9 (Spring 1992): 219–247.

Hausknecht, Johannes. *Das Bundesamt für gewerbliche Wirtschaft: Geschichte, Aufgaben, Organisation.* Eschborn: Bundesamt für gewerbliche Wirtschaft, 1975.

Heinz, John. *U.S. Strategic Trade: An Export Control System for the 1990s.* Boulder: Westview Press, 1991.

Hewlett, Richard G., and Jack M. Holl. *Atoms for Peace and War 1953–1961: Eisenhower and the Atomic Energy Commission.* Berkeley: University of California Press, 1989.

Hofhansel, Claus. "German Perspectives on Export Control Policy." In *International Cooperation on Nonproliferation Export Controls: Prospects for the 1990s and Beyond,* ed. Gary K. Bertsch, Richard T. Cupitt, and Steven Elliott-Gower, pp. 179–199. Ann Arbor: University of Michigan Press, 1994.

_____. "From Containment of Communism to Saddam Hussein: The Evolution of Export Control Regimes." *Arms Control* 14 (December 1993): 371–404.

_____. "Explaining Foreign Economic Policy: A Comparison of U.S. and West German Export Controls." *Journal of Public Policy* 10 (July–September 1990): 299–330.

Holl, Jack M. "The Peaceful Atom: Lore and Myth." In *Atoms for Peace: An Analysis After Thirty Years,* eds. Joseph F. Pilat, Robert E. Pendley, and Charles K. Ebinger, pp. 149–159. Boulder: Westview Press, 1985.

Horn, Erwin. "Veränderte Herausforderungen für die westliche Sicherheitspolitik." In *Saudi-Arabien: Partner für die Bundesrepublik Deutschland,* ed. Nah- und Mittelost-Verein, pp. 53–54. Hamburg: Nah- und Mittelost-Verein, 1981.

Husbands, Jo L. "How the United States Makes Foreign Military Sales." In *Arms Transfers in the Modern World,* eds. Stephanie G. Neuman and Robert E. Harkavy, pp. 155–172. New York: Praeger, 1979.

Ikenberry, G. John. "Conclusion: An Institutional Approach to American Foreign Economic Policy." *International Organization* 42 (Winter 1988): 219–243.

Ikenberry, G. John, David A. Lake, and Michael Mastanduno. "Introduction: Approaches to American Foreign Economic Policy." *International Organization* 42 (Winter 1988): 1–14.

Inman, Robert, Joseph Nye, William Perry, and Roger Smith, eds. *New Threats: Responding to the Proliferation of Nuclear, Chemical and Delivery Capabilities in the Third World.* Lanham, Md.: Aspen Strategy Group and University Press of America, 1990.

Inotai, András. "Economic Implications of German Unification for Central and Eastern Europe." In *The New Germany and the New Europe,* ed. Paul B. Stares, pp. 279–304. Washington, D.C.: Brookings Institution, 1992.

Jacobsen, Hanns-Dieter. "East-West Trade and Export Controls: The West German Perspective." In *Controlling East-West Trade and Technology Transfer: Power, Politics, and Policies,* ed. Gary K. Bertsch, pp. 159–182. Durham: Duke University Press, 1988.

_____. "Die amerikanischen Exportkontrollen als bündnispolitisches Problem." *Osteuropa-Wirtschaft* 31 (September 1986): 188–200.

_____. "Die Osthandelspolitik des Westens: Konsens und Konflikt." *Aus Politik und Zeitgeschichte*, 2 February 1985, p. 19–31.

_____. "High Technology in US Foreign Trade Relations." *Aussenpolitik* 36 (1985): 405–417.

Jacobsen, John Kurt, and Claus Hofhansel. "Safeguards and Profits: Civilian Nuclear Exports, Neo-Marxism, and the Statist Approach." *International Studies Quarterly* 28 (June 1984): 195–218.

Jentleson, Bruce W. "The Western Alliance and East-West Energy Trade." In *Controlling East-West Trade and Technology Transfer: Power, Politics, and Policies*, ed. Gary K. Bertsch, pp. 313–343. Durham: Duke University Press, 1988.

_____. *Pipeline Politics: the Complex Political Economy of East-West Energy Trade.* Ithaca: Cornell University Press, 1986.

Joppke, Christian. *Mobilizing Against Nuclear Energy: A Comparison of Germany and the United States.* Berkeley: University of California Press, 1993.

Kaiser, Karl, and Hanns W. Maull, eds. *Deutschlands neue Außenpolitik.* Vol. 1: *Grundlagen.* Munich: Oldenbourg, 1994.

Karl, Wolf-Dieter, and Joachim Krause. "Außenpolitischer Strukturwandel und parlamentarischer Entscheidungsprozess." In *Verwaltete Außenpolitik: Sicherheits- und entspannungspolitische Entscheidungsprozesse in Bonn*, eds. Helga Haftendorn, Wolf-Dieter Karl, Joachim Krause, and Lothar Wilker, pp. 55–82. Cologne: Verlag Wissenschaft und Politik, 1978.

Karp, Aaron. "Controlling Weapons Proliferation: The Role of Export Controls." *Journal of Strategic Studies* 16 (March 1993): 18–45.

Katzenstein, Peter J. "Coping with Terrorism: Norms and Internal Security in Germany and Japan." In *Ideas and Foreign Policy: Beliefs, Institutions, and Political Change*, eds. Judith Goldstein and Robert O. Keohane, pp. 265–295. Ithaca: Cornell University Press, 1993.

_____. "Stability and Change in the Emerging Third Republic." In *Industry and Politics in West Germany: Toward the Third Republic*, ed. Peter J. Katzenstein, pp. 307–353. Ithaca: Cornell University Press, 1989.

_____. *Policy and Politics in West Germany: The Growth of a Semisovereign State.* Philadelphia: Temple University Press, 1987.

Keeley, James F. "Containing the Blast: Some Problems of the Non-Proliferation Regime." In *Nuclear Exports and World Politics: Policy and Regime*, eds. Robert Boardman and James F. Keeley, pp. 194–232. New York: St. Martin's Press, 1983.

Kelleher, Catherine McArdle. *Germany & The Politics of Nuclear Weapons.* New York: Columbia University Press, 1975.

Kitschelt, Herbert P. "Political Opportunity Structures and Political Protest: Anti-Nuclear Movements in Four Democracies." *British Journal of Political Science* 16 (January 1986): 57–85.

Koppe, Holger, and Egmont R. Koch. *Bombengeschäfte: Tödliche Waffen für die Dritte Welt.* Munich: Knesebeck & Schuler, 1990.

Krasner, Stephen. "Approaches to the State: Alternative Conceptions and Historical Dynamics." *Comparative Politics* 16 (January 1984): 223–246.

_____. *Defending the National Interest: Raw Materials Investments and U.S. Foreign Policy.* Princeton: Princeton University Press, 1978.

Krause, Joachim, and Lothar Wilker. "Bureaucracy and Foreign Policy in the Federal Republic of Germany." In *The Foreign Policy of West Germany: Formation and Contents,* eds. Ekkehart Krippendorff and Volker Rittberger, pp. 147–170. Beverly Hills, CA: Sage, 1980.

Krause, Keith. *Arms and the State: Patterns of Military Production and Trade.* Cambridge: Cambridge University Press, 1992.

Kreile, Michael. *Osthandel und Ostpolitik.* Baden-Baden: Nomos, 1978.

Krüger, Peter. *Die Aussenpolitik der Republik von Weimar.* Darmstadt: Wissenschaftliche Buchgesellschaft, 1985.

Kubbig, Bernd W., and Harald Müller. *Nuklearexport und Aufrüstung: Neue Bedrohungen und Friedensperspektiven.* Frankfurt: Fischer Taschenbuch Verlag, 1993.

Kuczynski, Jürgen, and Grete Wittkowski. *Die deutsch-russischen Handelsbeziehungen.* 2nd ed. Berlin: Die Wirtschaft, 1948.

Kühnhardt, Ludger. "Wertgrundlagen der deutschen Außenpolitik." In *Deutschlands neue Außenpolitik,* eds. Karl Kaiser and Hanns W. Maull. Vol. 1: *Grundlagen,* pp. 99–127. Munich: Oldenbourg, 1994.

Küntzel, Matthias. *Bonn und die Bombe: Deutsche Atomwaffenpolitik von Adenauer bis Brandt.* Frankfurt: Campus, 1992.

Küsters, Hanns Jürgen. "Souveränität und ABC-Waffen-Verzicht: Deutsche Diplomatie auf der Londoner Neunmächte-Konferenz 1954." *Vierteljahresschrift für Zeitgeschichte* 42 (October 1994): 499–536.

Labrie, Roger P., John G. Hutchins, and Edwin W. A. Peura, with the assistance of Diana H. Richman. *U.S. Arms Sales Policy: Background and Issues.* Washington, D.C.: American Enterprise Institute for Public Policy Research, 1982.

Layne, Christopher. "The Unipolar Illusion: Why New Great Powers Will Rise." *International Security* 17 (Spring 1993): 5–51.

Lebahn, Axel. "Die 'Jamal-Erdgasleitung': UdSSR-Westeuropa im Ost-West Konflikt." *Aussenpolitik* 34 (1983): 256–280.

Lehman, Howard P., and Jennifer L. McCoy. "The Dynamics of the Two-Level Bargaining Game: The 1988 Brazilian Debt Negotiations." *World Politics* 44 (July 1992): 600–644.

Lellouche, Pierre. "Breaking the Rules Without Quite Stopping the Bomb: European Views." In *Nuclear Proliferation: Breaking the Chain,* ed. George H. Quester, pp. 39–58. Madison: The University of Wisconsin Press, 1981.

Levy, Jack S. "Learning and Foreign Policy: Sweeping a Conceptual Minefield." Paper presented at the 1992 Annual Meeting of the American Political Science Association, Chicago, September 3–6.

Lijphart, Arend. "Comparative Politics and the Comparative Method." *American Political Science Review* 65 (September 1971): 682–693.

Loeck, Christian. "Die Politik des Transfers konventioneller Rüstung: Strukturen und Einflußfaktoren im Entscheidungsprozess." In *Verwaltete Außenpolitik: Sicherheits- und entspannungspolitische Entscheidungsprozesse in Bonn,* eds. Helga Haftendorn, Wolf-Dieter Karl, Joachim Krause and Lothar Wilker, pp. 209–224. Cologne: Verlag Wissenschaft und Politik, 1978.

Long, William J. *U.S. Export Control Policy: Executive Autonomy vs. Congressional Reform.* New York: Columbia University Press, 1989.

Lönnroth, Måns, and William Walker. *The Viability of the Civil Nuclear Industry.* New York & London: International Consultative Group on Nuclear Energy, 1980.

Lucas, Michael R. "The Abolition of COCOM and the Establishment of a Technology Disarmament and Transfer Agency in the CSCE." *Bulletin of Peace Proposals* 21 (June 1990): 219–225.

Lüttwitz, Rochus-Ernst Freiherr von. "Deutsch-saudiarabische Zusammenarbeit—worum es in Wirklichkeit geht." In *Saudi Arabien: Partner für die Bundesrepublik Deutschland,* ed. Nah- und Mittelost Verein, pp. 9–11. Hamburg: Nah- und Mittelost Verein, 1981.

Mahoney Jr., Robert B., and David L. Wallace. "The Domestic Constituencies of the Security Assistance Program." In *U.S. Security Assistance: The Political Process,* eds. Ernest Graves and Steven A. Hildreth, pp. 125–162. Lexington, Mass.: D.C. Heath, 1985.

Maier, Charles S. *The Unmasterable Past: History, Holocaust, and German National Identity.* Cambridge: Harvard University Press, 1988.

Mann, Siegfried. *Macht und Ohnmacht der Verbände: Das Beispiel des Bundesverbandes der Deutschen Industrie e.V. (BDI) aus empirisch-analytischer Sicht.* Baden-Baden: Nomos, 1994.

Markey, Edward. *Nuclear Peril: The Politics of Proliferation.* Cambridge, Mass.: Ballinger 1982.

Markovits, Andrei S., and Simon Reich. "Should Europe Fear the Germans?" In *From Bundesrepublik to Deutschland: German Politics after Unification,* eds. Michael G. Huelshoff, Andrei S. Markovits, and Simon Reich, pp. 271–289. Ann Arbor: University of Michigan Press, 1993.

————. "The Latest Stage of the German Question: Pax Germanica in the New Europe." *Arms Control* 12 (September 1991): 60–76.

Mastanduno, Michael. *Economic Containment: CoCom and the Politics of East-West Trade.* Ithaca: Cornell University Press, 1992.

————. "Trade as a Strategic Weapon: American and Alliance Export Control Policy in the Early Postwar Period." *International Organization* 42 (Winter 1988): 121–150.

————. "Strategies of Economic Containment: U.S. Trade Relations with the Soviet Union." *World Politics* 37 (July 1985): 503–531.

Mastanduno, Michael, David A. Lake, and G. John Ikenberry, "Toward a Realist Theory of State Action." *International Studies Quarterly* 33 (December 1989): 457–474.

Matthöfer, Hans. "Saudi-Arabiens finanzpolitische Bedeutung für die Bundesrepublik Deutschland." In *Saudi-Arabien: Partner für die Bundesrepublik Deutschland,* ed. Nah- und Mittelost Verein, pp. 19–20. Hamburg: Nah- und Mittelost Verein, 1981.

Maull, Hanns W. "Economic Relations with the Middle East: Weight and Dimensions." In *Germany and the Middle East: Patterns and Prospects,* ed. Shahram Chubin, pp. 113–135. New York: St. Martin's Press, 1992.

————. "Zivilmacht Bundesrepublik Deutschland: Vierzehn Thesen für eine neue deutsche Außenpolitik." *Europa-Archiv* 47 (25 May 1992): 269–278.

_____. "Germany and Japan: The New Civilian Powers." *Foreign Affairs* 69 (Winter 1990/91): 91–106.

Mayntz, Renate, and Fritz W. Scharpf. *Policy-Making in the German Federal Bureaucracy.* Amsterdam: Elsevier, 1975.

McCain, John. "Controlling Arms Sales to the Third World." *Washington Quarterly* 14 (Spring 1991): 79–89.

McGhee, George. *At the Creation of a New Germany: An Ambassador's Account.* New Haven: Yale University Press, 1989.

McIntyre, John. "The Distribution of Power and the Interagency Politics of Licensing East-West High Technology Trade." In *Controlling East-West Trade and Technology Transfer: Power, Politics, and Policies,* ed. Gary K. Bertsch, pp. 97–133. Durham: Duke University Press, 1988.

Mearsheimer, John J. "Back to the Future: Instability in Europe After the Cold War." In *The Cold War and After: Prospects for Peace,* ed. Sean M. Lynn-Jones, pp. 141–192. Cambridge: MIT Press, 1991.

Mendelson, Sarah E. "Internal Battles and External Wars: Politics, Learning, and the Soviet Withdrawal from Afghanistan." *World Politics* 45 (April 1993): 327–360.

Merrill, Stephen A. "Operation and Effects of U.S. Export Licensing for National Security Purposes." In National Academy of Sciences, *Balancing the National Interest: U.S. National Security Export Controls and Global Economic Competition* , pp. 221–253. Washington, D.C.: National Academy Press, 1987.

Meyer-Wöbse, Gerhard. *Rechtsfragen des Exports von Kernanlagen in Nichtkernwaffenstaaten.* Studien zum Internationalen Wirtschaftsrecht und Atomenergierecht, vol. 62. Cologne: Carl Heymanns Verlag KG, 1979.

Michaelis, Hans. *Handbuch der Kernenergie.* 2 vols. Munich: Deutscher Taschenbuch Verlag, 1982.

Milner, Helen. "Resisting the Protectionist Temptation: Industry and the Making of Trade Policy in France and the United States During the 1970s." *International Organization* 41 (Autumn 1987): 639–665.

Möllemann, Jürgen. "Frieden und Stabilität am Golf." In *Saudi-Arabien: Partner für die Bundesrepublik Deutschland,* ed. Nah- und Mittelost Verein, pp. 41–44. Hamburg: Nah- und Mittelost-Verein, 1981.

Moyer, Homer E., Jr., and Linda A. Marby. "Export Controls as Instruments of Foreign Policy: The History, Legal Issues and Policy Lessons of Three Recent Cases." *Law & Policy in International Business* 15 (1983): 1–171.

Müller, Harald et al. *From Black Sheep to White Angel? The New German Export Control Policy.* PRIF Reports No. 32. Frankfurt: Hessische Stiftung Friedens- und Konfliktforschung, 1994.

_____. "German Foreign Policy after Unification." In *The New Germany and the New Europe,* ed. Paul B. Stares, pp. 126–173. Washington, D.C.: The Brookings Institution, 1992.

_____. *Nach den Skandalen: Deutsche Nichtverbreitungspolitik.* HSFK-Report 5/1989. Frankfurt: Hessische Stiftung Friedens- und Konfliktforschung, 1989.

National Academy of Sciences. *Finding Common Ground: U.S. Export Controls in a Changed Global Environment*. Washington, D.C.: National Academy Press, 1991.

_____. *Balancing the National Interest: U.S. National Security Export Controls and Global Economic Competition*. Washington, D.C.: National Academy Press, 1987.

Nau, Henry R. *The Myth of America's Decline: Leading the World Economy into the 1990s*. New York: Oxford University Press, 1990.

Naumann, Klaus. *Die Bundeswehr in einer Welt im Umbruch*. Berlin: Siedler, 1994.

Neff, Thomas L. *The International Uranium Market*. Cambridge, Mass.: Ballinger Publishing Company, 1984.

Neuman, Stephanie G. "Controlling the Arms Trade: Idealistic Dream or Realpolitik?" *Washington Quarterly* 16 (Summer 1993): 53–75.

Nolan, Janne E., ed. *Global Engagement: Cooperation and Security in the 21st Century*. Washington, D.C.: The Brookings Institution, 1994.

_____. "Cooperative Security in the United States." In *Global Engagement: Cooperation and Security in the 21st Century*, ed. Janne E. Nolan, pp. 507–542. Washington, D.C.: Brookings Institution, 1994.

Nolan, Janne E., and Albert D. Wheelon. "Third World Ballistic Missiles." *Scientific American* 263 (August 1990): 34–40.

Nollen, Stanley D. "Business Costs and Business Policy for Export Controls." *Journal of International Business Studies* 18 (Spring 1987): 1–18.

Nordlinger, Eric. "Taking the State Seriously." In *Understanding Political Development*, eds. Samuel P. Huntington and Myron Weiner, pp. 353–390. Boston: Little, Brown and Company, 1987.

_____. *On the Autonomy of the Democratic State*. Cambridge: Cambridge University Press, 1981.

Nötzold, Jürgen, and Hendrik Roodbeen. "The European Community and COCOM: The Exclusion of an Interested Party." In *After the Revolutions: East-West Trade and Technology Transfer in the 1990s*, eds. Gary K. Bertsch, Heinrich Vogel and Jan Zielonka, pp. 119–139. Boulder, Colo.: Westview Press, 1991.

Nye, Joseph S. *Bound to Lead: The Changing Nature of American Power*. New York: Basic Books, 1991.

Oerter, Stefan. "Neue Wege der Exportkontrolle im Bereich der Rüstungsgüter." *Zeitschrift für Rechtspolitik* 25 (February 1992): 49–55.

Ollig, Gerhard. "Rechtliche Grundlagen des Innerdeutschen Handels." In *Handelspartner DDR: Innerdeutsche Wirtschaftsbeziehungen*, eds. Claus-Dieter Ehlermann, Siegfried Kupper, Horst Lambrecht, and Gerhard Ollig, pp. 145–201. Baden-Baden: Nomos, 1975.

Organization for Economic Co-operation and Development. *OECD Economic Surveys: Germany*. Paris: OECD, 1986.

Pearson, Frederic S. "'Necessary Evil': Perspectives on West German Arms Transfer Policies." *Armed Forces & Society* 12 (Summer 1986): 525–552.

Pierre, Andrew J. *The Global Politics of Arms Sales*. Princeton: Princeton University Press, 1982.

Pisar, Samuel. *Coexistence and Commerce: Guidelines for Transactions Between East and West*. New York: McGraw-Hill, 1970.

Poneman, Daniel. "Nuclear Proliferation Prospects for Argentina." *Orbis* 27 (Winter 1984): 853–880.

————. *Nuclear Power in the Developing World*. London: George Allen & Unwin, 1982.

Pottmeyer, Klaus. *Kriegswaffenkontrollgesetz: Kommentar*. Cologne: Carl Heymanns, 1991.

Preisinger, Johannes. *Deutschland und die nukleare Nichtverbreitung: Zwischenbilanz und Ausblick*. Arbeitspapiere zur Internationalen Politik no. 76. Bonn: Europa Union Verlag, 1993.

Putnam, Robert. "Diplomacy and Domestic Politics: The Logic of Two-Level Games." *International Organization* 42 (Summer 1988): 427–460.

Radkau Joachim. *Aufstieg und Krise der deutschen Atomwirtschaft 1945–1975: Verdrängte Alternativen in der Kerntechnik und der Ursprung der nuklearen Kontroverse*. Reinbek: Rowohlt Taschenbuch Verlag, 1983.

Redick, John. "Nuclear Trends in Latin America." In *Governance in the Western Hemisphere*, ed. Viron P. Vaky, pp. 219–262. New York: Praeger, 1983.

Reinicke, Wolfgang H. "Cooperative Security and the Political Economy of Nonproliferation." In *Global Engagement: Cooperation and Security in the 21st Century*, ed. Janne E. Nolan, pp. 175–234. Washington, D.C.: The Brookings Institution, 1994.

————. "Arms Sales Abroad: European Community Export Controls Beyond 1992." *Brookings Review* 10 (Summer 1992): 22–25.

Richardson, J. David. *Sizing Up U.S. Export Disincentives*. Washington, D.C.: Institute for International Economics, 1993.

Risse-Kappen, Thomas. "Ideas Do Not Float Freely: Transnational Coalitions, Domestic Structures, and the End of the Cold War." *International Organization* 48 (Spring 1994): 185–214.

————. "Muddling Through Mined Territory: German Foreign Policy-Making and the Middle East." In *Germany and the Middle East: Patterns and Prospects*, ed. Shahram Chubin, pp. 177–194. New York: St. Martin's Press, 1992.

Rode, Reinhard. "Improving Nonproliferation Export Controls." In *Proliferation and Export Controls*, eds. Kathleen Bailey and Robert Rudney, pp. 101–105. Lanham, Md.: University Press of America, 1993.

————. *Sicherheit versus Geschäft: Die Osthandelspolitik der USA von Nixon bis Carter*. Frankfurt: Campus, 1986.

Rollo, Jim, and Alasdair Smith. "EC Trade With Eastern Europe." *Economic Policy*, no. 16 (April 1993), pp. 140–181.

Rose, Richard. "Government Against Sub-Governments: A European Perspective on Washington." In *Presidents and Prime Ministers*, eds. Richard Rose and Ezra N. Suleiman, pp. 284–347. Washington, D.C.: American Enterprise Institute for Public Policy Research, 1980.

Rosecrance, Richard. *The Rise of the Trading State: Commerce and Conquest in the Modern World*. New York: Basic Books, 1986.

Rosecrance, Richard, and Arthur A. Stein, eds. *The Domestic Bases of Grand Strategy*. Ithaca: Cornell University Press, 1993.

Rudolf, Peter. "Die Vereinigten Staaten und CoCom: Strukturen, Entwicklungen, Reformperspektiven." *Europa Archiv* 40 (June 6, 1990): 367–368.

Ruggie, John Gerard. "Third Try at World Order? America and Multilateralism after the Cold War." *Political Science Quarterly* 109 (Fall 1994): 553–570.

_____, ed. *Multilateralism Matters: The Theory and Praxis of an Institutional Form.* New York: Columbia University Press, 1993.

Samuels, Richard J. *The Business of the Japanese State: Energy Markets in Comparative and Historical Perspective.* Ithaca: Cornell University Press, 1987.

Sanjian, Gregory S. "Great Power Arms Transfers: Modeling the Decision-Making Processes of Hegemonic, Industrial, and Restrictive Exporters." *International Studies Quarterly* 35 (July 1991): 173–193.

Schiff, Benjamin N. *International Nuclear Technology Transfer: Dilemmas of Dissemination and Control.* London: Croom Helm, 1984.

Schlarp, Karl-Heinz. "Das Dilemma des westdeutschen Osthandels und die Entstehung des Ost-Ausschusses der Deutschen Wirtschaft 1950–1952." *Vierteljahrshefte für Zeitgeschichte* 41 (April 1993): 223–276.

Schmidt, Manfred. "West Germany: The Policy of the Middle Way." *Journal of Public Policy* 7 (April–June 1987): 135–177.

Schöllgen, Gregor. *Angst vor der Macht: Die Deutschen und ihre Aussenpolitik.* Berlin: Ullstein, 1993.

Schoppa, Leonard J. "Two-Level Games and Bargaining Outcomes: Why *Gaiatsu* Succeeds in Japan in Some Cases But Not Others." *International Organization* 47 (Summer 1993): 353–386.

Schwarz, Hans-Peter. "Adenauer und die Kernwaffen." *Vierteljahrshefte für Zeitgeschichte* 37 (October 1989): 567–593.

_____. *Die gezähmten Deutschen: Von der Machtbesessenheit zur Machtvergessenheit.* Stuttgart: Deutsche Verlags-Anstalt, 1985.

Seaborg, Glenn T. *Stemming the Tide: Arms Control in the Johnson Years.* Lexington, Mass.: Lexington Books, 1987.

Shah, Prakash. "The Chemical Weapons Convention: A Third World Perspective." *Disarmament* 16 (1): 88–99.

Shonfield, Andrew. *Modern Capitalism: The Changing Balance of Public and Private Power.* Oxford: Oxford University Press, 1965.

Shultz, George P. *Turmoil and Triumph: My Years as Secretary of State.* New York: Charles Scribner's Sons, 1993.

Sieg, Harald, Hans Fahning, and Karl Friedrich Kölling. *Außenwirtschaftsgesetz: Kommentar.* Berlin: Verlag Franz Vahlen, 1963.

Skocpol, Theda. "Bringing the State Back In." In *Bringing the State Back In*, eds. Peter Evans, Dietrich Rueschemeyer, and Theda Skocpol, pp. 3–37. Cambridge: Cambridge University Press, 1985.

Skowronek, Stephen. *Building a New American State: The Expansion of National Administrative Capacities 1887–1920.* Cambridge: Cambridge University Press, 1982.

Smaldone, Joseph P. "U.S. Commercial Arms Exports: Policy, Process and Patterns." In *Marketing Security Assistance: New Perspectives on Arms Sales*, eds. David J. Louscher and Michael D. Salomone, pp. 185–208. Lexington, Mass.: Lexington Books, 1987.

Snider, Lewis W. "Arms Exports for Oil Imports? The Test of a Nonlinear Model." *Journal of Conflict Resolution* 28 (December 1984): 665–700.

Solingen, Etel. "Macropolitical Consensus and Lateral Autonomy in Industrial Policy: The Nuclear Sector in Brazil and Argentina." *International Organization* 47 (Spring 1993): 263–298.

Sommer, Theo. "Bonn Changes Course." *Foreign Affairs* 45 (April 1967): 477–491.

Spaulding, Robert Mark Jr. "The German Trade Policy in Eastern Europe, 1890–1990: Preconditions for Applying International Trade Leverage." *International Organization* 45 (Summer 1991): 343–368.

Spector, Leonard S. *The New Nuclear Nations.* New York: Vintage Books, 1985.

———. *Nuclear Proliferation Today.* New York: Vintage Books, 1984.

Spiegel, Steven L. *The Other Arab-Israeli Conflict: Making America's Middle East Policy from Truman to Reagan.* Chicago: University of Chicago Press, 1985.

Stanley, Ruth. "Co-operation and Control: The New Approach to Nuclear Non-proliferation in Argentina and Brazil." *Arms Control* 13 (September 1992): 191–213.

Steinbach, Udo. "Germany and the Gulf." In *Germany and the Middle East: Patterns and Prospects*, ed. Shahram Chubin, pp. 210–225. New York: St. Martin's Press, 1992.

Steinberg, James B. *The Transformation of the European Defense Industry.* R-4141-ACQ. Santa Monica: RAND Corporation, 1992.

Steinmo, Sven, Kathleen Thelen, and Frank Longstreth, eds. *Structuring Politics: Historical Institutionalism in Comparative Analysis.* Cambridge: Cambridge University Press, 1992.

Stent, Angela E. *Technology Transfer to the Soviet Union: A Challenge for the Cohesiveness of the Western Alliance.* Arbeitspapiere zur Internationalen Politik no. 24. Bonn: Europa Union Verlag, 1983.

———. *From Embargo to Ostpolitik: The Political Economy of West German-Soviet Relations 1955–1980.* Cambridge: Cambridge University Press, 1980.

Stern, Paula. *Water's Edge: Domestic Politics and the Making of American Foreign Policy.* Westport, Conn.: Greenwood Press, 1979.

Stockholm International Peace Research Institute. *The Arms Trade with the Third World.* Stockholm: Almqvist & Wiksell, 1971.

Stratmann, Eckhard. "Made in Germany: Vom Weltmarkt zum Binnenmarkt." In *Grüne Wirtschaftspolitik: Machbare Utopien*, eds. Frank Beckenbach, Jo Müller, Reinhard Pfriem, and Eckhard Stratmann, pp. 327–349. Cologne: Kiepenheuer & Witsch, 1985.

Subrahmanyam, K. "Export Controls and the North-South Controversy." *Washington Quarterly* 16 (Spring 1993): 135–144.

Suleiman, Ezra N. "State Structures and Clientelism: The French State Versus the 'Notaires.'" *British Journal of Political Science* 17 (July 1987): 257–279.

Teeple, David Shea. "Atoms for Peace—or War?" *National Review*, 12 January 1957, pp. 35–37.

Temples, James R. "The Politics of Nuclear Power: A Subgovernment in Transition." *Political Science Quarterly* 95 (Summer 1980): 239–260.

Tetlock, Philip E. "Learning in U.S. and Soviet Foreign Policy: In Search of an Elusive Concept." In *Learning in U.S. and Soviet Foreign Policy*, eds. George W. Breslauer and Philip E. Tetlock, pp. 22–44. Boulder: Westview Press, 1991.

Tudyka, Kurt. "Gesellschaftliche Interessen und Auswärtige Beziehungen: Das Röhrenembargo." *Politische Vierteljahresschrift*, vol. 10, Sonderheft, no. 1 (1969): 205–223.

U.S. Arms Control and Disarmament Agency. *World Military Expenditures and Arms Transfers 1991–1992.* Washington, D.C.: Government Printing Office, 1994.

————. *World Military Expenditures and Arms Transfers 1993–1994.* Washington, D.C.: Government Printing Office, 1995.

U.S. Bureau of the Census. *Statistical Abstract of the United States: 1992.* Washington, D.C.: Government Printing Office, 1992.

U.S. Congress. Congressional Budget Office. *Budgetary Cost Savings to the Department of Defense Resulting From Foreign Military Sales.* Washington, D.C.: Government Printing Office, 1976

————. *Foreign Military Sales and U.S. Weapons Costs.* Washington, D.C.: Congressional Budget Office 1976.

U.S. Congress. House. Committee on Appropriations. *Foreign Assistance and Related Agencies Appropriations for 1979: Hearings Before a Subcommittee of the House Committee on Appropriations.* 95th Cong., 2d sess., 1978.

U.S. Congress. House. Committee on Banking, Currency and Housing. *Oversight Hearings on the Export-Import Bank.* 94th Cong., 2d sess., 1976.

U.S. Congress. House. Committee on Banking, Finance and Urban Affairs, *To Extend and Amend the Export-Import Bank Act of 1945.* 95th Cong., 1st sess., 1977.

U.S. Congress. House. Committee on Energy and Commerce. *Nuclear Energy Cooperation with China.* 98th Cong., 2d sess., 1984.

U.S. Congress. House. Committee on Foreign Affairs. *The Reauthorization of the Export Administration Act.* 102d Cong, 1st sess., 1991.

————. *Presidential Certification on the Delivery of AWACS to Saudi Arabia.* 99th Cong., 2d sess., 1986.

————. *Executive-Legislative Consultation on U.S. Arms Sales.* Congress and Foreign Policy Series, no. 7. Washington, D.C.: Government Printing Office, 1982.

————. *Export Controls on Oil and Gas Equipment: Hearings.* 97th Cong., 1981 and 1982.

————. *Saudi Arabia and the United States: The New Context in an Evolving "Special Relationship."* 97th Cong., 1st sess., 1981.

————. *Nuclear Exports: International Safety and Environmental Issues.* 96th Cong., 2d sess., 1980.

U.S. Congress. House. Committee on International Relations. *Nuclear Proliferation: Future U.S. Foreign Policy Implications.* 94th Cong., 1st sess., 1976.

U.S. Congress. House. Committee on Science, Space, and Technology. *Export Control Reform in High Technology.* 103d Cong., 1st sess., 1993.

U.S. Congress. House. *Report to Congress Pursuant to Section 601 of the Nuclear Non-Proliferation Act of 1978 for the Year Ending December 31, 1991.* Washington, D.C.: Government Printing Office, 1992.

U.S. Congress. Joint Economic Committee. *Arms Trade and Nonproliferation: Hearings.* 101st and 102d Cong., 1990 and 1991.

U.S. Congress. Office of Technology Assessment. *Global Arms Trade*. OTA-ISC-460. Washington, D.C.: U.S. Government Printing Office, 1991.

————. *Arming Our Allies: Cooperation and Competition in Defense Technology*. OTA-ISC-449. Washington, D.C.: Government Printing Office, 1990.

U.S. Congress. Senate. Committee on Banking, Housing, and Urban Affairs. *Proposed Trans-Siberian Natural Gas Pipeline*. 97th Cong., 1st sess., 1981.

U.S. Congress. Senate. Committee on Foreign Relations. *The Proposed AWACS/F-15 Enhancement Sale to Saudi Arabia*. 97th Cong., 1st sess., 1981.

————. *Multinational Corporations and United States Foreign Policy*. 93d Cong., 2d sess., 1974.

U.S. Congress. Senate. Committee on Governmental Affairs. *Nuclear Nonproliferation and U.S. National Security*. 100th Cong., 1st sess., 1987.

U.S. Defense Security Assistance Agency. *Foreign Military Sales, Foreign Military Construction Sales and Military Assistance Facts, As of September 30, 1990*. Washington, D.C.: DSAA, 1991.

U.S. Department of Commerce. *Export Administration Annual Report 1992*. Washington, D.C.: Government Printing Office, 1993.

————. *Export Administration Annual Report Fiscal Year 1991*. Washington, D.C.: Government Printing Office, 1992.

————. *Export Administration Annual Report FY 1989*. Washington, D.C.: Government Printing Office, 1990.

————. *Export Administration Annual Report FY 1984*. Washington, D.C.: Government Printing Office, 1985.

————. *United States Trade: Performance in 1985 and Outlook*. Washington, D.C.: Government Printing Office, 1986.

U.S. Energy Research and Development Administration. *Final Environmental Statement: U.S. Nuclear Power Export Activities*. Washington, D.C.: Government Printing Office, 1976.

U.S. Nuclear Regulatory Commission. *Annual Report 1989*.

————. *Annual Report 1980*.

Walker, William, and Måns Lönnroth. *Nuclear Power Struggles: Industrial Competition and Proliferation Control*. London: George Allen & Unwin, 1983.

Waltz, Kenneth N. *Theory of International Politics*. Reading, Mass.: Addison-Wesley, 1979.

Weaver, R. Kent, and Bert A. Rockman, eds. *Do Institutions Matter? Government Capabilities in the United States and Abroad*. Washington, D.C.: Brookings Institution, 1993.

Wellmann, Christian. "Gewerkschaftliche Alternativplanstrategie." In *Das Geschäft mit dem Tod: Fakten & Hintergründe der Rüstungsindustrie*, eds. Michael Brzoska et al., pp. 123–161. Frankfurt: Eichborn, 1982.

West Germany. Deutscher Bundestag. *Drucksache* 11/3995.

West Germany. Presse- und Informationsamt der Bundesregierung. *Vertrag über die Nichtverbreitung von Kernwaffen: Dokumentation zur deutschen Haltung und über den deutschen Beitrag*. Bonn: Presse- und Informationsamt der Bundesregierung, 1969.

Wilkens, Herbert, and Hans-Joachim Ziesing. "Die wirtschaftliche Bedeutung des Mittleren Ostens für die Bundesrepublik Deutschland." *Der Bürger im Staat* 31 (March 1981): 25–32.

Wilker, Lothar. "Bundestag und Außenpolitik." In *US-Kongreß und deutscher Bundestag: Bestandsaufnahmen im Vergleich*, eds. Uwe Thaysen, Roger H. Davidson, and Robert G. Livingston, pp. 383–399. Opladen: Westdeutscher Verlag, 1988.

_____. "Nuklearexport- und Nichtverbreitungspolitik—ein Prioritätenkonflikt für die Bundesrepublik?" In *Nuklearpolitik im Zielkonflikt: Verbreitung der Kernenergie zwischen nationalem Interesse und internationaler Kontrolle*, ed. Lothar Wilker, pp. 77–105. Cologne: Verlag Wissenschaft und Politik, 1980.

_____. "Das Brasilien-Geschäft—Ein 'diplomatischer Betriebsunfall'?" In *Verwaltete Aussenpolitik: Sicherheits- und entspannungspolitische Entscheidungsprozesse in Bonn*, eds. Helga Haftendorn, Wolf-Dieter Karl, Joachim Krause, and Lothar Wilker, pp. 191–208. Cologne: Verlag Wissenschaft und Politk, 1978.

Wörmann, Claudia. *Osthandel als Problem der Atlantischen Allianz: Erfahrungen aus dem Erdgas-Röhren-Geschäft mit der UdSSR*. Arbeitspapiere zur Internationalen Politik, no. 38. Bonn: Europa Union Verlag, 1986.

_____. *Der Osthandel der Bundesrepublik Deutschland: Politische Rahmenbedingungen und ökonomische Bedeutung*. Frankfurt: Campus Verlag, 1982.

Wulf, Herbert. "The Federal Republic of Germany." In *Arms Export Regulations*, ed. Ian Anthony, pp. 72–85. Oxford: Oxford University Press, 1991.

MAJOR NEWSPAPER AND MAGAZINE SOURCES

Arms Control Today
Atomwirtschaft-Atomtechnik
Aviation Week & Space Technology
Badische Zeitung
Businessweek
Congressional Quarterly Weekly Report
The Economist
Energiewirtschaftliche Tagesfragen
Europa-Archiv
Financial Times
Frankfurter Allgemeine Zeitung
Globe and Mail
Handelsblatt
Latin America Political Report
Neue Zürcher Zeitung
New York Times
Nuclear Engineering International
Nuclear News
Der Spiegel
Süddeutsche Zeitung

Wall Street Journal
Washington Post
Wehrtechnik
Wirtschaftswoche
Woche im Bundestag
Die Zeit

Index

About the Author

CLAUS HOFHANSEL teaches Comparative Politics and International Relations at Rhode Island College. Dr. Hofhansel has published a number of articles and book chapters on export controls, and his main research interests concern the domestic sources of foreign policy.

ISBN 0-275-95465-X

90000>

EAN

9 780275 954659

HARDCOVER BAR CODE